P9-DTF-480

IF YOU COULD LIVE

ANYWHERE

The Surprising Importance of Place in
a Work-from-Anywhere World

MELODY WARNICK

sourcebooks

Published by Sourcebooks
P.O. Box 4410, Naperville, Illinois 60567-4410
(630) 961-3900
sourcebooks.com

Library of Congress Cataloging-in-Publication Data

Names: Warnick, Melody, author.
Title: If you could live anywhere : the surprising importance of place in a
  work-from-anywhere world / Melody Warnick.
Description: Naperville, Illinois : Sourcebooks, [2022] | Includes
  bibliographical references and index. | Summary: "These days, plenty of
  people can work from anywhere. So, if you can work from anywhere, does
  it really matter where you work? As Melody Warnick has found from
  personal experience, in some ways it matters more than ever. If You
  Could Live Anywhere examines the powerful relationship between how we
  work and where we live. With a light voice and easy-to-understand tips,
  Warnick helps the reader develop a location strategy that puts them in
  the right place, which can make all the difference to their career
  success, entrepreneurial dreams, financial life, and ultimately, their
  freedom to craft a life that doesn't revolve around work at all"--
  Provided by publisher.
Identifiers: LCCN 2022010606 | (hardcover)
Subjects: LCSH: Employees--Relocation. | Quality of work life. | Quality of
  life. | Telecommuting--Social aspects.
Classification: LCC HF5549.5.R47 W37 2022 | DDC 658.3/8--dc23/eng/20220302

LC record available at https://lccn.loc.gov/2022010606

Printed and bound in Canada.
MBP 10 9 8 7 6 5 4 3 2 1

For Ella, who gets to choose her own places now,
and for Ruby, who has to learn to drive first

CONTENTS

— — — — —

THE ANYWHEREIST MANIFESTO

- - - - - -

1. When you work from anywhere, the right place can make you better at your work.
2. If you can work anywhere, you can live anywhere, too.
3. Where you live both matters a lot and doesn't matter at all.
4. Your values should show up in your place.
5. It's good to be wanted. It's even better to be needed.
6. When you're an Anywhereist, your town is your office.
7. We all do better when we all do better.
8. Investing in your place creates meaning in your life.
9. The right place reminds you of what matters most to you.

1

WHEN ANYWHEREISTS
RULE THE WORLD

The seven-year period that Amy and James Hebdon lived and worked in the Seattle area is longer than a lot of things. The Civil War, for instance. The number of years *Lost* was on the air. Just not long enough for the Hebdons to feel like they were ever more than temporary residents biding their time there.

It wasn't that they didn't like Seattle. They both adored the luxury apartment they rented in Kirkland, one of Seattle's upscale eastern suburbs. James was the rare breed of human who actually prefers Pacific Northwest–style dreary weather. But the city, they knew, could never give them the kind of life they imagined for themselves—one where kids and dogs caromed over a few rural acres, basement shelves displayed gleaming mason jars full of produce they canned themselves, and chickens scratched in the side yard.

Amy desperately wanted to buy a house, but by 2016, Seattle home prices had soared to astronomical levels. The house James's sister bought there cost $1 million. There was no version of the Seattle multiverse where Amy and James could afford anything like that. "I wanted to be able to have a place that was ours, where we could settle down and have a home," said Amy. "It's hard to ever feel quite settled if you have in the back of your mind that this isn't going to last."

Luckily, Amy and James had a secret weapon: they were location independent.

For nearly ten years, Amy had been a mostly remote worker, sometimes as a full-time W2 employee, sometimes as an independent contractor. But in 2017, she quit her job at a Seattle tech company to start her own digital marketing firm, and soon after, James joined her in the business. Within a few months, they were earning six figures in revenue. Their clients had no idea that they worked out of their house.

With the kinds of jobs they could do anywhere that offered a decent internet connection, they quickly realized they weren't limited just to working out of their Kirkland apartment. Why not a coffee shop or a coworking space? A national park campground? A South American beach? If they could work from anywhere, then the corollary was automatically true: they could *live* anywhere too. Like thousands of similarly location-independent humans, they began asking themselves this life-changing question: *If we can work anywhere, where should we live?*[1]

Amy and James are what I call Anywhereists, members of a fast-growing subset of people who aren't tied to a particular geography by what they do for a living. Corporate relocations, soul-crushing commutes to urban offices, living somewhere you're not really that fond of—when you're an Anywhereist, all those concerns slide off the table. Being free to work anywhere lets you make your own choices about where your life is going to play out.

Perhaps you're an Anywhereist too—or want to be.

Maybe, like Amy and James, you've started your own business in part to provide yourself some location flexibility.

Maybe you're a remote worker who puts in a nine to five with a company that doesn't demand your physical presence every day. Someone like Ryan Mita, a business-to-business (B2B) sales rep who used his COVID-19 remote status to move from New York City to Austin, Texas, just because he could.[2]

Maybe you're a solopreneur like Grace Taylor, an accountant who runs her business anywhere she happens to be (and caters to clients who are digital nomads like she is).[3]

Maybe, like an estimated 35 percent of the American workforce,[4] you're a freelancer who contracts for a range of clients. Someone like Jessica Araus, a teacher who became a freelance illustrator after she moved from Mexico to the Netherlands.[5]

Maybe you're semiretired like Ria Talken, who left Oakland for San Miguel de Allende, Mexico, which has 320 days of annual sunshine.[6] Or you're just flat-out done with paid work, perhaps because you hustled to retire early, and now you're looking to make all your place fantasies come true.

Whatever gets you to Anywhereism, here's the uniting factor: because your work exists where *you* are, you have a higher-than-average level of autonomy to decide where you want to live. Anywhereism isn't solely about the *where* of life either. Tied up in location independence is the freedom and flexibility to design *how* you want to live—what you value, what kinds of experiences you want to have, what success really means to you. (Hint: It probably isn't whatever gold star you get for putting in seventy-hour workweeks.)

Becoming an Anywhereist can be the antidote for the modern economy's epidemic levels of burnout, exhaustion, and stress, or in the words of writer Anne Helen Petersen, "the feeling that you've optimized yourself into a work robot."[7] Anywhereists work hard, but they also want to have a well-adjusted relationship with their time, energy, mental health, physical wellness, friends and family, leisure, and goals. To do all that, they often take control of their location first.

HOW TO BE AN ANYWHEREIST

Anywhereism isn't exactly new, but it's gained steam in the past two decades. Back in 2007, Tim Ferriss touted the idea of location independence in his massive bestseller *The 4-Hour Workweek*. Those cartoony palm trees on the cover beckoned millions of readers—entrepreneurs, freelancers, and anyone ground down by their nine to five—to fantasize about a sun-soaked life working on the beach while a margarita sweated in the sand nearby.

Entire companies soon climbed aboard the work-from-anywhere train. At web design and software company Basecamp, founders Jason Fried and David Heinemeier Hansson raved about their totally distributed team, with employees scattered from Copenhagen to Caldwell, Idaho. "Great talent is everywhere, and not everyone wants to move to San Francisco (or New York or Hollywood, or wherever you're headquartered)," they wrote in a 2013 guide called *Remote: Office Not Required*.

"Remote work is about setting your team free to be the best it can be, wherever that might be."[8]

The internet acted like a chemical spill, slowly dissolving the ties linking workplaces with physical spaces. Between 2009 and 2019, the number of location-independent workers grew by 140 percent.[9] Even at Fortune 500 companies like Xerox and Dell, nearly half of full-time employees were working remotely at least some of the time by 2016.[10] One survey found that, in 2019, 43 percent of U.S. companies allowed remote work.[11]

Naturally, not everyone was a fan. Asking a Google spokesperson whether the tech company permitted employees to telecommute, Nikil Saval, author of the 2014 book *Cubed: A Secret History of the Workplace*, received this clipped response: "No—and we discourage it."[12] Yahoo CEO Marissa Mayer famously revoked the rights of her 11,500 employees to work remotely in 2013, explaining that "some of the best decisions and insights come from hallway and cafeteria discussions, meeting new people, and impromptu team meetings."[13]

But the genie couldn't be put back in the bottle. Work-from-anywhere existed in the world, and millennials and Gen Z in particular wanted it so badly that they were willing to change jobs or give up vacation time to have it. For 77 percent of job seekers deciding between offer A and offer B, remote work is the perk that would tip the scales.[14]

Then came the COVID-19 pandemic, which no one has to tell you poured lighter fluid on the idea of Anywhereism. In March 2020, when office spaces around the world shut their doors in an attempt to slow the spread of the coronavirus, about 175 million Americans instantly shifted to doing their jobs remotely from couches and IKEA desks at home. According to a University of Oxford analysis, more than half of the American workforce held one of the 113 occupations that could reasonably be performed remotely, so work, like Celine Dion's heart, went on, even during a global pandemic.[15] As potted plants withered on cubicle shelves and tuna fish sandwiches moldered in office kitchens, employees clacked away at their laptops at home and finally figured out how to use Slack with their coworkers.

Was emergency remote work better than in-person work? Definitely not for everyone. Families struggled. Working moms in particular lost ground. Yet in spite of the domestic horrors of children moaning about online school and partners making unintentional, occasionally nude guest appearances on Zoom, some people discovered they preferred it. There was a sudden lush freedom in shedding time-sucking extras like commuting and navigating office politics. Some workers felt more productive. Others basked in the sense that they'd finally achieved a semblance of work-life balance because they could take their dog for a walk in the middle of the day. (Dogs were definitely the big winners in the COVID era.)

More than anything, many newly remote workers found that they really valued their location independence. With work and school gone virtual, nothing anchored them to a particular geography. The apartment elevators and germ-factory subway trains of the cities didn't feel safe, so people began stuffing themselves into camper vans for cross-country explorations of national parks, a COVID trend that bumped sales of RVs by 53 percent.[16] Or they booked one of the multitudes of hotels and vacation rentals advertising their suitability for remote work.[17]

Some employees didn't even mention they were going. One remote worker told me he hadn't noticed that a colleague was traveling for months because she'd used a virtual backdrop for her Zoom calls to hide the fact that she was at a different Airbnb every few days.

During the pandemic, an estimated one in ten Americans relocated.[18] Many of these moves were temporary, designed to combat the particular challenges of the pandemic era, like the impending insanity one starts to feel staring at the same four walls every day in a tiny city apartment.

On a broader scale, though, COVID prompted almost everyone to have a good, hard think about their location. What mattered most? A yard? A good school district? Being closer to family you hadn't seen for months? The pandemic was an inflection point that made an estimated 46 percent of Americans reassess where they lived.[19] Generally speaking, people wanted space, and lots of it, for cheap. Real estate markets nationwide went berserk in response. In once-affordable Sun Belt cities like Austin, Phoenix, Nashville, and Tampa, 2020 sales outpaced the national average by up to 25 percent.[20]

To move long distance during the COVID-19 pandemic was to gamble that your emergency-remote job would stay remote. The slightly more cautious were just waiting to get the thumbs-up that the switch to virtual work would last. A survey of Bay Area residents found that 34 percent said they were likely to move out of San Francisco within two years—but that figure increased to 46 percent when they were given the option to work remotely.[21] According to a 2021 Airbnb survey, a whopping 83 percent said that if they could work remotely, they were in favor of relocating. One in five already had.[22]

Once people try remote work, they tend to like it. In one 2019 survey, 99 percent of virtual workers said they hoped to stay remote, at least some of the time, until they retired.[23] With the pandemic, millions and millions of people who never saw themselves working from home fell in love with the perks—and proved that they could do their jobs outside the office long term. They didn't really see a reason to go back.

That forced companies from Twitter and Shopify to Nationwide and Fujitsu to pivot hard. According to one small 2020 survey, 82 percent of company leaders planned to make telecommuting a regular post-COVID perk, with nearly half saying they'll let employees stay totally virtual.[24] The cloud customer relationship management company Salesforce, for instance, announced they were killing the office altogether. "The 9-to-5 workday is dead," said president Brent Hyder, "and the employee experience is about more than ping-pong tables and snacks."[25] Empty offices prompted the City of London to announce a plan to convert some of the excess space into fifteen hundred new homes by 2030.[26] In America in 2021, office vacancy rates climbed to 16.4 percent, their highest levels in a decade.[27]

In the face of all this change, a number of companies, including Amazon and Apple, doubled down on the in-person office as the norm. But being able to work remotely, or at least to choose where and how you work, is arguably better for employees. As Laurel Farrer, the president of the Remote Work Association, explained, "People are saying, 'Wait a second, I don't have to drive two hours into the city anymore. And I don't have to wake up super early and drop my kids off at daycare. And it turns out I like seeing my kids during the day.' There are these little lifestyle changes, like, 'Oh, I'm healthier. It's easier to control what I'm doing. And I'm losing weight.' All of these personal changes" make work life more manageable and employees more content.[28]

There's no doubt that the pandemic provided a generation-defining kick in the pants for the Anywhereist movement. But even before the COVID era, almost half of Gen Z were free-lancers, and 73 percent of them insisted they worked this way by choice.[29] Early-career workers in their twenties and thirties had already declared their preference for autonomy, control, and fulfilling experiences over lucrative, high-powered careers.[30] The assumption is that as those workers get promoted into manage-ment roles, they'll steer their workplaces toward benefits like location independence.

Location independence may not literally mean *anywhere*. At many companies, tax rules or a hybrid remote work plan—some work done in person, some virtually—may limit your place choices to the state where your employer is headquartered or to a couple-hour radius around your office. If you're angling for Anywhereism as a full-time remote-work employee, it's wise to have this discussion early on with your boss (and possibly your accountant) to clarify what options are open to you.

Yet people want to be Anywhereists. And you don't have to talk your boss into letting you work from Montana to qualify. You don't have to be remote or online at all. In fact, you can be an Anywhereist simply by knowing that you could do your job in hundreds of different towns, and you get to choose which one.

Anywhereist Careers

The best Anywhereist jobs are truly location independent, meaning they can be done anywhere with an internet connection. Like these:

- Software developer
- Account manager
- Bookkeeper
- Business development manager
- Client services director
- Customer service representative
- Artist
- Entrepreneur
- Tutor
- Virtual assistant
- Writer
- Product manager
- Marketing manager
- Instructional designer
- Financial analyst
- Social media manager
- Web designer/developer
- Computer systems analyst
- Recruiter
- Interpreter/Translator

- ESL teacher
- Data entry clerk
- Sales manager
- Graphic designer
- Content director
- UX/UI designer
- Technical writer
- Loan processor
- Editor
- Life coach
- Career counselor
- Social media influencer
- E-commerce business owner
- Photographer
- Videographer
- Financial manager
- Research analyst
- Executive assistant
- Social worker
- Human resources specialist

WE ARE ALL ANYWHEREISTS

Janee Allen, for instance, relocated from California to North Carolina as a school reading specialist when she realized that virtually every school district around the country hired people to do what she did. She chose her favorite, got a job, and moved there.[31]

Doctors Katie and Matthew Lincoln graduated from medical school to a pick of possible locations. They ended up in small-town

Pennsylvania, not because they're laptop warriors Zooming in from the local coffee shop, but because like a lot of professionals— doctors, lawyers, accountants, nurses, teachers, and so on—their vocation is in demand globally, enabling them to find jobs almost anywhere. When their schooling ended, they hit a turning point that forced a location decision, and for that moment in time, they were Anywhereists.[32]

In that sense, we've all been or will be Anywhereists at some point. When we choose a college. When we graduate. When we take a new job. When we go back to grad school or change careers. When we start a business. When we retire or save enough to leave full-time work early. No matter what you do for a living or how portable it might be, at some point, you've had to figure out where you wanted the next season of your life to unfold. True Anywhereist stuff.

Some Anywhereists have such a love-hate relationship with location decisions that they keep themselves place fluid Kevin and Dani VanKookz, for instance, traded a $1,350-per-month apartment in Seattle for life traveling the United States in a Sprinter van. Their average month's expenses hover around $1,500.[33]

Other Anywhereists, like Darcy Maulsby, a writer and marketer in Lake City, Iowa, craft portable careers specifically so they have the freedom to work in a beloved community—in Darcy's case, her husband's rural hometown. It's a reverse engineering of the place-career connection: they know where they want to be, and they opt to do work that can keep them there.[34]

Not everyone is so sure. Recently, I watched my friends Matt and Megan wrestle with a work-based location decision. They were only momentary Anywhereists—they're both professors, and Megan was fielding job offers from universities around the country—but choosing the right city weighed just as heavily as choosing the right job. The couple had to sort through a confounding mess of apples-and-oranges factors like cost of living, kid-friendliness, schools, culture, and weather. How much simpler it would have been to pick the best job with the best salary than to decide where they want their children to grow up. (Spoiler: They finally chose Austin.)

You've probably been there at some point in your life. No matter what you do for a living or how far along you are in your career, you have at some point asked yourself, *Where should I live now?* It always feels momentous—a choice not just about your zip code but about your destiny and identity. The more freedom you have to take your work to a plethora of places, the more difficult the decision becomes.

FINDING THE RIGHT PLACE

In a personal finance group on Facebook recently, I saw a woman post, "Currently in [high cost of living area], just found out my husband is free to relocate anywhere in the U.S. with same pay!! Where are some low-cost-of-living, sunny places? Preferably liberal. We are in Seattle now."

The answers poured in, a stream 445 comments long. Durham, North Carolina. Charleston, South Carolina. Tacoma, Washington. Northern New Mexico. Memphis. Austin. Houston. Vegas. The front range of Colorado.[35]

Discussions like these are happening daily all over the internet. For those who are in a position to make a place decision, they inspire perhaps equal measures of wanderlust and panic. How is one meant to sort through 445 comments' worth of opinions about sunny, low-cost-of-living, politically liberal places? Do sunny, liberal, and low cost of living even matter in the end? What other factors could make us happier, wealthier, more successful, or more satisfied?

This book is meant to explore such questions, in part because I've explored them myself. I'm an Anywhereist and have been since the day I left my editing job in a converted nineteenth-century town house in Washington, DC, to do the same work from home by emailing marked-up PDFs to my boss over a crappy dial-up connection. When my family moved twenty-two hundred miles to St. George, Utah, the following year, I took the editing work with me, then ended up writing for the local city magazine. In the twenty years since, I've worked from all sorts of spaces: couches, kitchen tables, a Craigslist desk in a spare bedroom, a plastic chair next to a hospital bed, and most recently, an eight-foot-by-eight-foot office at the front of my house in Blacksburg, Virginia, where a prime view of dog walkers and UPS trucks provides semi-welcome distraction from whatever I'm writing at the moment.

Blacksburg is the town where I became obsessed with the connection between people and their places, primarily because I hated it when I moved here in 2012 due to my husband's job. (Full disclosure: My husband isn't an Anywhereist, so our moves, including the one to Virginia, have mostly been dictated by his career trajectory.) Anxious to feel more deeply at home in this bizarre new world, I embarked on a series of small behavior changes designed to plant my roots deeper—basic things like walking, shopping at the farmers market, and volunteering locally. My efforts worked, and I realized I was developing the "I love it here" sensation known in scientific literature as place attachment. I ended up writing a book called *This Is Where You Belong* as a sort of road map for developing place attachment, designed for readers who were as ambivalent about their towns as I'd been.[36]

The idea boiled down to this: You're probably not able to choose where you live. So how about you make the best of it. Bloom where you're planted.

In the intervening years, as I've continued to study place attachment and as I've talked to hundreds of movers and stayers, I've become fascinated with the people whose experiences are so different from mine—the people who *are* choosing where they live. So many of them are struggling to get it right. Everyone's making their location decisions practically blind, grasping at the straws of what we think might make us happy (sunny, low cost of living, preferably liberal) without any sort of well-reasoned process to walk them through it. That's difficult enough when you're moving for a job and deciding between a couple of local suburbs. What about the people who can work anywhere and therefore live any-where? How do they do it?

One of my core beliefs is that any city can become the right place for us when we decide we want it to be. But that doesn't eliminate the need to get smart and intentional about our location decisions in the first place. I want to help you make the best loca-tion decision you can so that once you're in your new place, you can fully hydrate with the well-being elixir that is place attachment.

Location independence, I've discovered, is also a game changer for places themselves, opening up small towns and mega cities alike to swaths of new residents who might never have considered moving there before. That's reworking the economic calculus for these communities, which are now vying to offer resources that can make your life better professionally, financially, and emotionally. In *If You Could Live Anywhere*, I'll share inspiring stories of how places are welcoming and nurturing Anywhereists and other locals, from Kansas to Ireland, Alabama to Bali.

Location independence has the potential to fundamentally alter the global economy. It can also change everything for *you*, just like it did for Amy and James Hebdon.

By 2020, the Hebdons had worked up a spreadsheet to compare candidate communities on factors like median income, average home price, tax burden, crime rates, and weather. (Amy liked it warmer, James liked it cooler; they compromised on a USDA gardening zone of 6 or higher.) Originally, Amy and James planned to piggyback exploratory road trips off work conferences, but when 2020 canceled them all, they hit Google hard, then made a short list of states—Kentucky, Kansas, Mississippi, Tennessee—to visit. Amy said it's like using a dating app. You can do a ton of online research, but at some point, you just have to meet in person.

Their location decision was terrifying. Because they were self-employed, any parameters they set were theirs alone. They could literally go anywhere, and there are around ten thousand municipalities on planet earth.[37] That's a paralyzing number of options. But as they made their in-person visits, something about Tennessee just felt right. They were drawn to Clarksville, a city of 132,000 on the Kentucky border, and ended up buying a house there that would give them triple the space they had in Seattle for less than half the monthly cost. Within two weeks of their move-in day in November 2020, they bought a dog. The chickens took a lot longer—it turns out they needed a city permit—but eventually the poultry arrived too. Just like Amy always wanted.

There were moments during the process when James and Amy had to shake off cold feet. What if this wasn't the right town? Or the right house? Should they keep looking? Since moving to Clarksville, though, Amy says they haven't looked back. Yes, their house has some issues. (Who builds a drawer that can fit only a single roll of aluminum foil??) But now that they're out of Seattle, they realize how much they'd been missing. They're hoping that the low cost of living in Tennessee will help them stay there, living the kind of life they want, for a long time to come.

2

YOU NEED A LOCATION
STRATEGY

Lisa Comingore and her wife, Michelle, arrived in Tallahassee, Florida, more out of luck than anything else. Lisa got into law school there, and they just stayed on. For eighteen years, they made their home in Florida, Lisa as a lawyer, Michelle as a state employee, and they loved it.[1]

Then somewhere along the way, amid two bouts of breast cancer, three hurricanes, and a recession job loss that Lisa couldn't bounce back from, Tallahassee lost its luster. When Hurricane Michael lobbed a tree onto their house, that was it. "It just was like one thing after another," Lisa said. "Quite frankly, we were just done."

Above the chaos and disenchantment, there was Indiana, shining like a beacon of post-Florida sanity. Indiana was where both Lisa and Michelle had grown up and where their aging parents still lived. Good friends were peppered around the state. For the two women, it was like suddenly realizing that your platonic best friend is actually Ms. Right. "It just seemed like a good move,"

Lisa said. They both arranged to work remotely and boomeranged home in June 2019.

Only Indiana hasn't been what they expected. After so many years in a state that doesn't bother with deep freezes, the midwestern winter felt like wrath-of-God-level cold. Maybe she was projecting, but on Lisa's rare ventures out to the grocery store, everybody seemed miserable. COVID hit, and they couldn't see friends or family. All the reasons they moved to Indiana in the first place were falling apart.

What now? Should they go back to Tallahassee? Was it really that bad? Michelle in particular misses the deep roots she put down in the Florida Panhandle city. But as foundling Anywhereists, they're also drawn to the idea of limitless place possibilities and feel an obligation to consider them. Tampa is now on the leaderboard, along with north Georgia, with its miles of hiking trails. "It's almost like, because we can live anywhere, it's too many choices," Lisa said.

Yet some people she knows are absolutely breezy about relocation. Recently, a friend posted on Facebook that he and his family were moving from Indiana to Naples, Florida. When Lisa asked how they decided to go, he said, "Oh, you know us. We like to move across the country every five years."

Why is relocation so fraught for some Anywhereists and such a no-brainer for others? That's because there are three kinds of Anywhereists, each with their own approach to place, mobility, and location decision-making.

First are **the Wanderers**. These are the digital nomads, the vanlifers, the frequent movers, the people who dream of trading a three-bedroom house for a backpack—in other words, people who, left to their own devices, prefer to keep their relationship to place a little loose. Once they have the freedom to work from anywhere, they typically turn "anywhere" into "everywhere." Motto: *There's a big world out there, and I want to see it.*

Second are **the Seekers**, people who take seriously—perhaps too seriously—their right to make a choice about where to live. They do the research, check out towns, maybe move to a new town, find that it's not working, and try again. The process of finding the best place can bog them down, and they like to keep their options open until the end. Motto: *The right place is out there, and I'm going to find it.*

Third are **the Settlers**. Give this word its nineteenth-century spin, and you think of pioneers establishing a foothold in the western prairie. That's what Settlers do. They've made a place decision—sometimes to move to somewhere entirely new, sometimes to stay in a familiar place or to boomerang back to a long-ago hometown. Now they're putting down roots, with everything that means: maybe buying real estate, building a business, meeting the neighbors, or volunteering locally. Motto: *This is the place.*

In some ways, the three kinds of Anywhereists are more like three stages of an evolving relationship with where we live. First, we're a little place promiscuous. Then we're hunting for The One. Finally, we settle into a committed life. It's a lot like, say, dating in your thirties. And like dating in your thirties, there's not always a tidy, linear progression Occasionally, Wanderers decide to settle. Seekers give up and become Wanderers. Settlers can unsettle too. As I explained in *This Is Where You Belong,* there is no right town for everyone, just the right town for you right now. As our lives change, a town that was a great fit once upon a time may no longer feel so right anymore. We slide from Settler to Seeker and back again as we reexamine our place decisions.

That's what happened to Lisa and Michelle, who were dumb-founded by their friend's cheerful Wanderer approach to moving every five years. Settlers at heart, they've unwillingly turned into Seekers who just can't figure out the best place to be. Is it near family? Where they have friends? Where snow won't trap them inside for several months of the year? Where they can hike when-ever they want?

"I don't know," Lisa said when I spoke to her and Michelle in the dead of winter. Their still-unmade decision loomed over their heads like a cartoon question mark. Lisa looked at me half expec-tantly, as if I could solve this problem for her. Maybe I could tell her where to live.

"I don't know either," I told her.

"I wish you did."

They'd been lingering in place-decision purgatory for months, aware that they were not loving Indiana but not quite sure whether a new state—or a return to their old state—would ultimately offer something better.

So they agonized, discussed, made spreadsheets, analyzed budgets, and planned extended visits elsewhere. "I feel like we're on a merry-go-round of trying to figure out where we want to be," Lisa sighed.

DECISIONS ARE HARD

When you're an Anywhereist, confronting a thousand options for where to live, the process you develop for giving each location due consideration can feel disconcertingly iconoclastic. One city you reject out of hand because...well, you're not quite sure why. Was it an article you read? A friend who hated her work trip there? The cities you're drawn to can feel just as mysterious. Why here and not there? Who knows?

In his 2004 book *The Paradox of Choice*, Barry Schwartz wrote that rather than giving us a sense of bounty, an endless array of options invokes feelings of overload, anxiety, and analysis paralysis.[2] Imagine being in a shoe store where you have three thousand options for new sneakers. What seems like a boon quickly turns into a bummer as you obsess over arch support, sole treads, and price points. You thought you knew what you wanted when you walked in. Now you can barely remember what you were looking for. Are the factors you're weighing at all important, or have you simply been swept up in the moment? Every shoe requires its own yes or no, subjecting you to an exhausting number of micro decisions.

Worse, even after you've pulled the trigger, studies show that you tend to be less satisfied with your choice when you had so many options to choose from in the first place. There's a niggling voice in the back of your mind that says, "What if that other shoe was better?" Or even, "What if there was a 3,001st option I didn't consider?"

Patrick McGinnis, author of *Fear of Missing Out*, calls FOBO, or fear of better options, the "insidious twin" of FOMO. McGinnis, who coined both terms, thinks FOBO is worse.[3] You refuse to commit to anything—from a dinner order to a Netflix show to a new town—because you worry that something better might be out there. Counterintuitively, leaving your options so open tends to pile on stress and keep you feeling stuck.

Naturally, FOBO and its ilk are afflictions of affluence, the result of living in a world with a glut of possibilities. But with an estimated thirty-five thousand decisions to make every day, it's no wonder that so many of us feel tapped out with decision fatigue. When we have to spend so much time fretting over the little choices that contour our days, we may struggle to find the mental or emotional energy to make the more consequential ones.

Even when you're deciding among a limited pool of place candidates, the process is exhausting. Every three or four years, Leah Love and her husband, who's in the navy, receive a list of job openings in cities around the world—a dozen or so options for their next permanent change of station (or PCS in military parlance). In 2021, Leah tapped the hive mind of a military spouse Facebook group for advice, since in the small world of the navy, "it's pretty likely that if you haven't lived there, you know someone who has," she told me. But the crush of different opinions added weight to their already hefty lists of pros and cons. Ultimately, they moved to Rhode Island, but not without some serious emotional labor.[4]

For Anywhereists faced with even more choices, deciding where to live next is utterly exhausting. "I don't think I fully appreciated just how taxing it'd be for me to find a place," Amy Hebdon recalled, "to say, 'Okay, I could live anywhere, but I'm going to live here.'" Even after their move to Clarksville, she and James suffered moments of panic where they wondered if they'd made a cataclysmic mistake.[5]

Part of the difficulty is that no one has really laid out how to go about choosing where to live. There's no known process. It's all a bunch of Anywhereists figuring it out as they go along.

What you need is a location strategy.

THE STARBUCKS EFFECT

Location is everything. That old saw of a real estate motto is as true for Anywhereists as it is for big businesses. It's just that corporations are typically far more strategic than Anywhereists about developing a standardized approach to where they locate.

Take Starbucks. What began in 1971 as a café down the street from Pike Place Market in Seattle has grown into the world's largest coffeehouse chain, a behemoth that operates over thirty thousand locations in more than seventy countries. How do they know where to put all those retail storefronts? They've devised a location strategy that tells them where a Starbucks is most likely to succeed, based on their analysis of factors like the following:

- **Neighborhood income:** Apparently $60,000 in median household income is the bottom rung for a new store.
- **Age:** Starbucks is happy to take an eighty-year-old's money, but its ideal customer is in the eighteen-to-forty demographic. The company ensures that the area has a lot of people in that marketing sweet spot.
- **Visibility:** Starbucks' goal: twenty-five thousand passing cars on the adjacent street per day, the better to spur impromptu latte purchases. A store built on the side of the street with more morning commuters is preferable, since customers are more likely to pick up a coffee on the way to work than coming home.
- **Proximity to businesses:** No Starbucks is an island. The coffee giant wants to place its stores near other successful retailers that drive traffic to the area. And because people

like to pop out for coffee during work breaks, locations near office parks, universities, or industrial areas do better.[6]

For a company like Starbucks, location strategy begins with knowing the target market, in this case consumers willing to pay a little more for premium coffee, and figuring out how to find them on the ground. In big cities, you'll sometimes stumble across a Starbucks every couple of blocks. It feels a little spooky—are they going for total world domination?—but creating that sense of familiarity and freezing out competition are parts of the location strategy too.

For the coffee company, site selection is an art form they're so skilled at that merely the presence of a Starbucks exerts a "Starbucks effect" on neighborhood real estate prices. In their 2015 book *Zillow Talk*, property-finder app Zillow CEO Spencer Rascoff and Zillow chief economist Stan Humphries assert that living within a quarter mile of a Starbucks can almost double your property values over time. In seventeen years, homes near Starbucks saw increases of 96 percent, compared to 65 percent for homes farther away.[7]

Cult-favorite grocery store Trader Joe's boasts a similar phenomenon. One study found that homes near a Trader Joe's sold for nearly four times the price of homes near an Aldi, the discount grocer.[8] That may spur the feverish desire many Americans have for their own nearby Trader Joe's; locals have been known to start Change.org petitions or Facebook groups like "Bring Trader Joe's to Northern Kentucky." But David Livingston, an expert in supermarket location research, said that filling out the "Request a TJ's in my city" form on Trader Joe's website is unlikely to help. "They are not going to open a store based on a petition, because everyone wants a Trader Joe's," he told Trader Joe's fantasists in Pennsylvania's *Morning Call* newspaper. "But only people who are educated and have high disposable incomes will actually support one."[9]

I'm not recommending that you borrow the location strategy of a coffee retailer or a fancy grocer as the best guide for your relocation decisions. Instead, you can develop your own personal location strategy centered around the geographic factors that will help *you* succeed. To do so, you'll need to get clear on what a good life looks like for you and how a well-chosen location can help you achieve your vision.

CRAFTING YOUR LOCATION STRATEGY

So how do you decide where you're most likely to thrive? The process can be as clinical or emotional or well organized or stressed out or hopeful as whoever's doing the deciding.

Some Anywhereists build spreadsheets.

Some dive down spiraling rabbit holes of internet research.

Some interview everyone they've ever known who's lived in a particular city.

Some make meticulous site visits.

Some close their eyes, spin a globe, and point.

Some pray.

Some wish they could just stay put.

In studies, most Anywhereists cop to being relatively practical as they choose a new place to move. They care about the things you'd think they should: quality schools, good hospitals, affordable homes.[10] Yet as I interviewed over a hundred people for this book, regularly asking them what drew them to the place they're currently living, the answers were surprisingly esoteric. "My family lives nearby" makes sense. But what about "I like the weather"? Or "There are great local hiking trails"? Or "I enjoy the arts scene here"? Or "The taxes are low"? What about "I just wanted to check it out"?

To want an inexpensive spot of land to raise chickens, like Amy Hebdon did, feels reasonable. But how much weight do the chickens get among other factors? Do chickens trump weather or expenses? Should chickens outrank good schools for a couple who doesn't have kids but might in the future?

Maybe you're considering the basic elements and amenities that constitute a community, but you don't always know how to rank those competing interests. Something tells you that you should care more about public transportation than poultry, yet psychologically, chickens keep roosting at the top of the decision-making ladder.

Making it more fraught is that you're not Starbucks. You don't get to plunk down multiple storefronts all over the world. Only about 6 percent of Americans own a second home; the rest of us have to make do with one.[11] That alone can make the decision feel portentous.

Even though they'd been gearing up for literally years to become Anywhereists and move away from Seattle, once Amy and James Hebdon were confronted with the expansiveness of their decision, fear set in. "The lack of constraints can make it really, really hard and give you a lot of anxiety when it comes to making a choice," Amy said.

That can lead to ineffective approaches to decision-making, like impulsiveness, when you close your eyes and point just to get it over with, or deflection, when you avoid the decision for as long as you can to keep from getting overwhelmed.

How do you come up with your own location strategy? In the rest of this chapter, we're going to work through some exercises together that will help you decide what matters most to you in a place. Easier said than done. No one can tell you what to think, not even me. You'll have to do some soul searching to figure out what kind of community would offer the best fit right now for you (and possibly your partner, kids, or anyone else who'll be making the move with you).

First, figure out if you should move at all. The first exercise below can help with that. Then move on to exercises 2, 3, 4, and 5 to think through more of the details. You can download a free workbook at melodywarnick.com to give you a place to collect your data.

Exercise 1: Should You Move?

Just because you're an Anywhereist doesn't mean that you have to leave the place you're living. You can live wherever you want— including your current city!

Still, the temptation may be there, like a mosquito buzz in the background. You should probably think hard about whether moving is the right thing for you and your loved ones. Here are some questions to help you work through it:

1. Do you have a compelling reason to move right now? Do you have a compelling reason to stay put?

2. How often do you find yourself thinking about moving?

3. Do you have another destination in mind?

4. Can you see yourself living in your current place in five years? What about in twenty?

5. Does it feel like a good fit with who you are as a person? With who you hope to be?

6. What are your dominant emotions here? Joy? Anger? Calm? Stress? Inspiration? Do you think that would change elsewhere? What about your environment draws those feelings out?

7. How have you changed since moving here? Do you feel like you're better than you used to be?

8. What makes you happy here? How long is the list of things you enjoy?

9. What are the top five things you complain about here? Are any of them deal breakers for you?

10. Do you feel certain that your biggest annoyances about living here won't also be present in a new place?

11. Are you running away from things you don't like or running toward something you're excited about?

12. Are you financially able to manage living in this place?

13. Who in this community would you miss if you left next week?

14. Does your current place provide what you need or want at this point in your life?

15. Will you be able to achieve your personal goals and ambitions living here?

16. How do the members of your family feel about moving? Will they be supportive? If not, are the potential benefits worth their temporary unhappiness?

17. How do you think your life would be different elsewhere? Is there a way you could achieve some of those changes without a long-distance move? Would moving to a new house locally rather than to a new location be sufficient?

18. What do you risk by moving? (Loss of relationships or social capital, for instance.) What do you risk by not moving? (Perhaps the chance for proximity to family or financial savings.)

19. What regrets can you imagine having if you do move? If you don't?

20. If you make a pros and cons lists for staying vs. moving, which is longer?

This isn't a Buzzfeed quiz, so there's no way to punch in your answers and get an instant response telling you to move or stay. But the process of thinking about these questions hopefully evoked feelings and ideas that can help you understand whether you have more to gain by relocating or by doubling down in your current community.

If you decide you're not up for moving right now, brilliant. Put this book down, and go on with your life, content in the knowledge that you've made an intentional, informed decision to stay put. For now.

Still confused? That's okay. Work through the next exercises, and see if you gain more clarity.

Exercise 2: What's Your Geographic History?

Chances are good you've already lived in a few places. Those experiences can give you some good clues as to what you historically have liked or disliked.

1. **Start by making a chronological list of all the places you've lived.** You can do this in on paper, in an online document, or in the free workbook at melodywarnick.com.

2. **For each place you remember living, write down the first words that come to mind about that location.** When you think about that community, do you feel warm? Secure? Panicked? Depressed? Nostalgic? Longing? Deliriously happy?

    Naturally, whatever comes to mind will be tangled with the experiences, good and bad, you had while you lived there. Thinking about the town you lived in when your parents got divorced may stir up some darkness for you, not because the location was awful but because that moment in your life was. Don't worry about separating those different threads. Right now, simply capture the feelings that come to mind when you think about a place.

3. **Dig deeper into what really worked for you in these locations.** Maybe you loved the feeling of romantic possibility you felt as a twenty-year-old exchange student in Paris or the sense of simplicity you experienced in small-town Iowa.

4. **Think about what didn't work for you.** Loved Paris, hated the sharp-eyed Parisians judging your clothes. Think about what was less helpful for you in the places you've lived in the past.

5. **Construct a love/hate list of common factors that emerge.** Perhaps you'll notice that your best experiences have always been in large cities or that your happiest place memories revolve around frequent gatherings with family. What can you extrapolate to integrate into your location strategy going forward?

Exercise 3: What Are Your Place Values?

Most of the consequential decisions we make in our lives become easier when we apply our values to them. In her book *Don't Overthink It*, Anne Bogel describes doing this with the weighty decision of where to send her child for high school. At first, she struggled between school A and school B. Then she remembered that one of her key values was neighborliness; her family had chosen their home precisely because the neighborhood was small, friendly, and walkable. That made the choice clear. They opted for the school that was closest to home.[12]

Similarly, identifying and applying our values as we decide where to live can make a location strategy clearer while giving us the satisfaction that we're making a decision based on ideals that are central to who we are.

From the following list, choose the five values that matter most to you in your location strategy. Or, if you prefer, rank all the values in order of their importance in your life. You can even add your own words if any come to mind.

Abundance	*Civic engagement*
Achievement	*Collaboration*
Adventure	*Commitment*
Ambition	*Community*
Autonomy	*Contribution*
Balance	*Cooperation*
Beauty	*Creativity*
Belonging	*Culture*
Calmness	*Diversity*
Charity	*Environment*

Excellence	*Open-mindedness*
Fairness	*Originality*
Faith	*Peace*
Family	*Power*
Flexibility	*Preparedness*
Friendship	*Purpose*
Fun	*Recognition*
Generosity	*Relationships*
Growth	*Security*
Happiness	*Self-control*
Health	*Service*
Independence	*Simplicity*
Individuality	*Spirituality*
Joy	*Stability*
Kindness	*Success*
Leadership	*Teamwork*
Learning	*Tradition*
Love	*Vision*
Making a difference	*Well-being*
Motivation	*Work*

Exercise 4: What Does Your Good Place Look Like?

In the wonderfully philosophical sitcom *The Good Place*, Earth's recently deceased residents inhabit an off-brand version of heaven featuring all-you-can-eat frozen yogurt and parties with lots of puppies. Spoiler: Turns out, the good place was anything but. But the thought experiment is still useful!

If you were the architect of your own personal good place,

what would it look like? Sound like? Smell like? How big would it be? What food would be on permanent offer? What kind of people would live there with you? What would you do for fun? What elements would make this the perfect place for you? You can use your learnings from Exercise 2 to guide some of your thinking about what kinds of communities really sizzle your bacon.

No, this magical unicorn of a city doesn't exist. But by imagining in detail a place designed to cater to all your fondest wishes, you may get a feel for what qualities to look for in the real cities up for consideration.

Exercise 5: What Are Your Deal Breakers?

Now that you've imagined your best life, start strategizing about how to create it. Do you absolutely have to have inexpensive housing? Well-ranked elementary schools? Fabulous weather? If you can't have everything, which factors stay, and which factors go?

If you're at the beginning of your location strategy process, you can use the list below to ask yourself broad questions about which elements are crucial and which are just nice to have. How important is X to me? Do I care about Y at all? Rank these elements in order of importance.

To get a bit more into the weeds if you're struggling with a location decision, create your own rank-order system by grading each item on a scale from 1 to 10 based on how important you think it is to your future location, with 1 meaning you really couldn't care less about it and 10 meaning it's absolutely vital to your well-being in a place.

There's no right or wrong way to feel about these elements (though we'll delve later in the book into why some might affect your place satisfaction more than others). For now, just allow yourself to experience your gut reactions and what they tell you about what you want.

THE BASICS

- **Infrastructure:** Are local roads, highways, bridges, sewer, water, and electric lines in good repair? Does the community fund public goods sufficiently? Are services affordable?
- **Internet access:** Is there fiber or broadband? How fast are internet speeds in town, both for uploads and downloads? How accessible is high-speed internet? What does it cost?
- **Safety:** How common are different kinds of crimes, from burglaries to assaults? Is the local police force effective?
- **Medical care:** How close is a healthcare facility for emergency treatment? For specialized care? Are there enough high-quality or specially trained doctors, dentists, and mental health therapists in the area to meet your needs?

COST OF LIVING

- **Overall cost of living:** How expensive is the city? Compared to where you live now? Compared to the nation (or the world) as a whole?
- **Housing affordability:** Could you afford the average rent here? Could you afford to buy a home? How available is affordable housing?

- **Housing stock:** What do homes look like? Can you afford the amenities you value, like a backyard or a basement?
- **Taxes:** What state and local taxes will you pay?
- **Other expenses:** Could you afford other things you care about, like restaurant meals or entertainment? Are there new expenses you haven't accounted for, like air conditioning or heating oil?

ENVIRONMENT

- **Climate:** What's the climate like here? How extreme are seasonal changes? How is the climate expected to change in the next ten or twenty years? What are the average temperatures throughout the year and the extreme highs and lows? How much precipitation is typical? Do you have any allergies that would make it difficult to live here?
- **Natural disasters:** What disasters is this area prone to? How common are they? What would dealing with them require (like paying for flood insurance or prepping to evacuate in wildfire season)? Is climate change expected to affect these events in the near future?
- **Beauty:** What is the local landscape like? Do the aesthetics of the area, including the built environment, appeal to you and meet your needs? How close is a beach or mountains? Are there trees and flowers in natural and built areas?
- **Outdoor amenities:** How easy is recreational access to the outdoors, like trails, rivers, parks, or lakes? Are these resources properly cared for? Well used?
- **Sustainability:** Are there easy ways to recycle? Is there

access to alternative energy sources, like solar, wind power, or electric car charging stations?

- **Air and water quality:** How clean is the air? Are there ongoing sources of pollution? Is the water drinkable?

PEOPLE

- **Size:** How many people live here? How dense is the local population?
- **Proximity of family and existing friends:** How close would the important people in your life be: parents, grandparents, siblings, adult children, best friends, old college roommates?
- **Demographics:** How old is the average resident? Are more of them married or single? How many have children? How many are senior citizens?
- **Diversity:** How diverse is the community in terms of race, culture, ethnicity, socioeconomic status, gender identity, sexuality, politics, religion? Will you be in the majority or the minority? How open is the community to people like you? To people who are not like you?
- **Politics:** How did this community vote in the last election? Do residents fall to one extreme side of the political spectrum, or are opinions diverse? Do civic leaders like the mayor run with a political affiliation? Is the city council politically diverse?
- **Friendship:** What are the entry points for newcomers (clubs, community events)? Where do people congregate? How easily do you imagine making your first friend?

- **Relationships:** If you're single, what is the dating pool like? Are there potential mates? Sensible ways to meet people?
- **Personality:** What are community members like? What appears to matter to them? Do you imagine having things in common?

TRANSPORTATION

- **Public transportation:** Is there easy, affordable access to reliable public transportation like buses or a metro system? Can you live a car-lite life?
- **Traffic:** Does the community regularly experience traffic backups? Will you need to drive often on a freeway or on major thoroughfares to get to services you need?
- **Walkability:** Can you walk or bike to services you need?
- **Accessibility:** How easy is the community to navigate for someone who has a disability or is in a wheelchair?
- **Proximity to a major airport:** How close is the nearest international airport? Is it a hub? How expensive is it to travel from there?

WORK AND EDUCATION

- **Education:** What are local schools like? How are they ranked? What kinds of programming are available to help children with special needs?
- **Extracurriculars:** Are there activity options for children and adults, like classes, camps, and community sports leagues?

- **Local business community:** Are there opportunities for in-person networking or career development? Is the local economy vibrant and growing? Does it welcome newcomers?
- **Colleagues:** Are there people who do what you do in the community already? Are there coworking spaces?
- **Job markets:** Are there options for in-person work in your field nearby? Could your children find after-school or summer jobs when they're old enough?
- **University:** Is there a university nearby? Does it offer opportunities for continuing education? Are there public lectures and concerts on campus?
- **Certifications:** Would you need a new certification or license to work in another place (as a teacher or a lawyer, for instance)?
- **Library:** Is the public library well funded, well stocked, and well used?
- **Child care:** What kind of child care is available here? What does it cost? Is it easily available, or are there waiting lists?

FUN

- **Wellness:** How much space and money does this community dedicate to leisure activities that you enjoy? Are there places to exercise in the way you prefer?
- **Food:** Will you have access to the kinds of food and experiences you most enjoy? Is there a vibrant restaurant culture? Is there access to ingredients you frequently use? Is

there an active farmers market? Is food grown locally?
Would it be easy for you to grow your own food? Will you
have access to your favorite grocery store?

- **Culture:** Will it be easy and affordable to go to movies,
concerts, art exhibits, plays, or live performances?

- **Shopping:** Can you buy what you need, want, or enjoy in
your town?

- **Proximity to a regional metro area:** How close is the
nearest large city? What amenities does it offer?

- **Engagement opportunities:** How easy is it to volunteer
locally, run for civic office, or otherwise get engaged?

- **Spirituality:** Is a faith community of your religious tradi-
tion available?

- **Joy:** Can you do the things that bring you joy here? Will
it be harder or easier than in the place you currently live?

THE LIFE PLAN

Coming up with a location strategy is disconcertingly like coming
up with a whole life plan. Because it's never just about picking
a city. It's about figuring out who you are and what you want. If
you've worked through the exercises in this chapter, you've done
some serious emotional labor to examine your feelings, experiences, identity, values, goals, and desires, and the result of that
may be a clearer sense about both the best-fit geography and the
best-fit life.

In chapter 13, we'll talk more about how to translate those
epiphanies into boots-on-the-ground decision-making, including
how to negotiate disagreements with your partner. But here's one

more consideration. As someone who can work from anywhere, you'll be taking your career with you wherever you go. Your location strategy is a life plan. It's also a career path. How to integrate the two is worth thinking hard about.

3

YOUR TOWN IS YOUR OFFICE

There's a little town in Oregon called Remote. Well, "town" might be a stretch. Remote is an unincorporated hamlet in southwest Oregon, home to a smattering of residents for whom the combined store/gas station/post office on Route 42 is the center of civilization.

Yet for a while in 2020, Remote, Oregon, became the unintentional "job capital of America," according to Brian Feldman, who wrote about a strange phenomenon in his tech newsletter BNet. Feldman noticed that when job sites like LinkedIn or Monster reposted online listings for remote jobs, the designation "remote" would automatically be geotagged with an actual location: Remote, Oregon.[1]

It was, of course, just a technical error on the part of the digital scrapers—"unless thousands of companies are all operating out of one of the three buildings in the small town nobody drives through anymore because of the highway," Feldman wrote. But for a delightful moment, it made it look as if getting hired as, say, a full-stack engineer at Netflix would require you to pack your bags and move to this tiny blip of a place along the Coquille River, which, like Remote itself, isn't as big as it sounds.

I like to imagine thousands of people dutifully relocating to Oregon to start their new remote-work jobs. It's not a choice. The work is there, so you just go.

Instead, those hapless remote workers have to figure out two things: (1) the best place to live and (2) the best place to work. You're not just choosing a town that's a nice place to live. You're choosing a town that's essentially going to double as your office.

THE PARADOX OF PLACE

Not everyone agrees that it matters where you work if you can work from anywhere. As writer Daniel H. Pink suggests, "When being anywhere at all is possible, being anywhere in particular is irrelevant."[2]

Fifty years ago, you absolutely had to be local to a university to get a college degree. Now, a vast array of remote options make it possible to get your MBA from a university three thousand miles away without ever setting foot on campus. Likewise, full-time employment once required you to be a cubicle dweller. Showing up in person was mandatory. Now you can just Zoom in from Boseman or Brisbane, with a backdrop that hides the fact that you're nowhere nearby. Miles have dropped away, erased by a good internet connection. Entire workplaces have gone digital. Physical offices have been converted into apartments. Locations have started to blend into a blurry nothing special. So who cares where you do your work? Nowhere? Everywhere? It's all the same.

That's the line taken by author Stephanie Storey, whose 2015 debut novel, *Oil and Marble*, a thriller about Leonardo da Vinci and Michelangelo, came out to rave reviews. That same year, Stephanie sold the Los Angeles condo she shared with her husband, actor Mike Gandolfi, and committed to the life of a Wanderer.

It was a departure for the couple, who for years had lived near Hollywood to facilitate Mike's career as a sitcom writer and actor and Stephanie's as a freelance producer of talk shows such as Arsenio Hall's. But they'd found over the years that California figured less and less in their TV work, which was now just as likely to take them to cities like Vancouver, Atlanta, and New York. "You never know where your next production is going to shoot," Stephanie said. She planned to travel cross-country on a self-funded book tour before heading to Europe to research the next novel anyway, so she thought, "Why pay for a book tour *and* a mortgage?" Abandoning a fixed home address freed her and Mike to work wherever their jobs happened to take them.

Over the next five years, that was a lot of places. Stephanie and Mike mostly lived out of suitcases in Airbnbs or Marriott hotels (it helped to stay brand loyal so they always knew how to work the TV remote). Occasionally, they rented an apartment for several months, as Stephanie did in Washington, DC, while she handled contract work for a nonprofit there. As Wandering novelists and actors, they logged serious road time. Visiting the mechanic to fix their Ford C-Max's cracked windshield again and again was the nomad equivalent of doing home repairs.

COVID offered a surprisingly welcome respite from the constant travel, reminding them why they used to live in a single place. Daily conversations at Stephanie's parents' house in Arkansas began to revolve around where to settle down postpandemic.

Whether they choose Boulder (too small), Austin (too hot), or Los Angeles (earthquakes and an increasingly long fire season that rains ash from the sky like snow), Stephanie knows they're in for a mixed bag. Staying semiplaceless ensures they never have to compromise.

Plus, Stephanie and Mike are keen to stay mobile. High on their location strategy list is having a nearby international airport so they can continue to pursue far-flung jobs as needed. They're choosing a modified work-here-or-anywhere Wanderer life.[3]

Many of the 36.2 million Americans expected to be working remotely by 2025 (a figure that's up 87 percent since before the pandemic) are place agnostic now too, convinced that the whole point of being able to work anywhere is that it doesn't really matter where you live, at least not for your job.[4]

But is that true? Is there any sort of qualitative difference between doing your online marketing from Chicago or from Chiang Mai? Between calling a client from Nantes or small-town Nebraska? Does it make all the difference or none at all? Can it be both?

That's the paradox of place: In the world of modern work, places seem to matter to our success either a ton or not at all. Usually some of both at the same time. But there is evidence that place matters more to your work life than you think.

HOW YOUR TOWN HELPS YOU INNOVATE

A few years ago, a Harvard-based group of economists asked the question: Who becomes an inventor in America?

Scientific innovation is one of the key drivers of U.S. economic growth, and the researchers wanted to pinpoint any environmental factors that might make someone more likely to innovate. By analyzing U.S. patent records filed between 1996 and 2014, the economists—Alexander M. Bell, Raj Chetty, Xavier Jaravel, Neviana Petkova, and John Van Reenen—built a database that tracked 1.2 million inventors from birth to adulthood. They identified their race, class, gender, and, importantly, their location.

Depressingly, demographics were a significant predictor of outcomes. White kids grew up to be inventors at three times the rate of Black kids. Four times as many men as women innovated. If your parents were in the top 1 percent for income, you had ten times the chance of becoming a successful inventor as someone who grew up with a family income below the median. None of that was particularly surprising.

But there was one part of the study where the results were a little more interesting: *where* you grew up mattered. A lot.

If you were a kid growing up in a place with a lot of inventors nearby, being exposed to their ideas and the sheer possibility of innovation, you were much more likely to become an inventor yourself.

Place even determined the kind of invention you'd probably come up with. Growing up in Silicon Valley, software capital of the country, increased the odds that you'd hold a patent related to computers. If you grew up in Minneapolis, home to a lot of medical device manufacturers, chances were that your patent was, you guessed it, for a medical device.[5]

Raj Chetty and his colleagues had already studied how the neighborhoods where kids are raised impact their income mobility, finding, for instance, that growing up in Michigan or Nevada makes you less likely to outpace your parents' incomes than growing up in California or Texas.[6] Since studies have shown that neighborhood income segregation leads to achievement gaps at school, that connection seems fairly clear.[7]

This new finding about innovation was different—what the Harvard economists called an "outcome of exposure."[8] It's proof that the places we're from form us. They affect what we think about, what we're interested in, what we see as possible for ourselves—down to something as nitty-gritty as sending you on the track toward inventing a medical device rather than a new computer technology. Communities shape our opportunities.

Where you grow up matters to the kind of work you end up doing, and so does where you live now. There's a kind of alchemy that occurs when ambition meets a place equipped to properly nurture it.

Consider the way Renaissance Florence embodied a community that prized and developed talent in its residents. It's no coincidence that great artists and thinkers like Leonardo da Vinci and Michelangelo emerged from the winding streets of the same Italian city. The place helped them along. Whether da Vinci would have reached his full *Mona Lisa* potential in Lichtenstein or Milan, we can't know for sure. But his success even now (his *Salvator Mundi* is the priciest painting ever sold at auction) seems directly linked to the environment in which he worked.[9] That tells you a little something about the impact of the place in which you, as an Anywhereist, do *your* work.

"If even someone with the same natural ability as Leonardo couldn't beat the force of environment, do you suppose you can?" wrote Paul Graham, the founder of start-up accelerator Y Combinator, on his eponymous blog. "You might think that if you had enough strength of mind to do great things, you'd be able to transcend your environment. Where you live should make at most a couple percent difference. But if you look at the historical evidence, it seems to matter more than that."[10]

Your own personal historical evidence might show it to matter more as well, perhaps in unexpected ways. For me, launching my short-lived copy editing career in a world-class city like Washington, DC, may have made me more ambitious. On the other hand, its grandness made my real goals harder to achieve. When I lived there in my early twenties, so did 4.8 million other people. I knew I wanted to write, but slots at the local parenting magazine were cutthroat competitive. Only when I relocated to more bucolic southern Utah did less competition render me braver. I started writing for a local magazine, nothing prestigious or even well paid, but it got me started when a start was what I needed.

Your own career path has likely been shaped by the places you've lived in similarly mysterious ways. Without perhaps realizing it, your ideas about your work—what you do, how you approach it, how much time you spend on it, how intensely you care about it—bear the stamp of where you lived in those career-building years. So while it's true to say that, in a purely logistical sense, the *where* of your career doesn't matter for a work-from-anywhere employee, freelancer, or entrepreneur, in behavioral, emotional, psychological, and financial ways, it really does.

If you're smart about the place you live as an Anywhereist and how you engage there, your location can help you succeed. Make more money. Be more creative. Create valuable connections. Form a community. Achieve better work-life balance. Find more personal contentment. Make a meaningful impact. Build the kind of career you really want, and do your best work.

YOUR TOWN IS YOUR OFFICE

A few years ago, Lori Goler, Janelle Gale, and Brynn Harrington of Facebook's human resources division began to work with Wharton Business School Professor Adam Grant to figure out what motivated the tech company's employees. Was it salaries that average $120,000 a year? The lunchroom featuring free pizza and a frozen yogurt bar? What made them stay happy and engaged at work?[11]

Sifting through survey answers from Facebook's thousands of global employees, they realized that workers had three main motivators at their jobs. Let's call them profession, people, and purpose.

Profession means liking the actual work you do. Employees want their jobs to provide chances to learn, grow, and reinforce their strengths.

People means that employees want to feel respected and valued at work by other employees and higher-ups. They want to feel connected with bosses who act like mentors and with colleagues who become friends. They want to belong to a larger community.

Purpose means that employees want to feel like they're making some sort of meaningful impact. They want whatever work they do to align with their values and their personal missions, to know that it contributes something positive to the world.

The Facebook research mirrored some things Gallup had already discovered about millennials, who broke the mold for how we think about what employees want from their jobs. First, Gallup researchers found, millennials want a steady paycheck; they're more highly educated and carry more student loan debt than previous generations. Yet they also want to be passionate about their work. They want to feel that their job nurtures them as a person, helping them build on their existing strengths and skills with ongoing mentorship and coaching. And they find their deepest satisfaction in feeling like what they do makes some kind of positive contribution to the world.[12] Profession. People. Purpose.

In the Facebook study, interestingly, wanting fulfillment with profession, people, and purpose wasn't limited to millennials or Gen Z. Grant, Goler, Gale, and Harrington didn't find significant differences among age groups at all. The youngest workers were a little more intense about their professions because they were in the launch phase. As people aged, purpose started to take precedence. "But overall," they wrote in the *Harvard Business Review*, "the differences between age groups were tiny. And that's not just true at Facebook. In a nationally representative study of Americans across generations, millennials, Baby Boomers, and Gen Xers had the same core work values—and tended to rank them in the same order of importance."[13]

These three motivators of profession, people, and purpose mattered whether employees excelled at work or tanked their performance reviews. Whether they were in the New York office or in Kuala Lumpur. Whether they were marketers or software engineers. From person to person, emphasis on one element or the other shifted slightly, but overall, workers' goals were remarkably consistent. As the authors concluded, "We're all hoping to find a what, a who, and a why."

Specifically, we're hoping to find our what, who, and why *at work*—and not many people have. In 2020, the portion of workers in the United States who were engaged at their jobs—enthusiastic about and committed to their work and workplace—hovered around 36 percent. About 15 percent were flat-out disengaged; they were phoning it in, if not actively trying to sabotage their workplaces à la April on *Parks and Recreation*. At any given moment, about half of Americans are thinking about switching jobs or changing career paths altogether.[14]

Maybe part of the reason so many of us are dissatisfied at work is that we're expecting too much of our workplaces. We're looking for happiness or wholeness by way of profession, people, and purpose, and an office just can't bear up under the weight to provide it all.

A community, on the other hand, may be able to.

For an Anywhereist, the place you live does double duty. It's your home and your office, all at once. Without the time suck of a daily commute, without eight-plus consecutive hours spent in your office, you likely have more time to just *be* where you live. And instead of spending the majority of your waking hours among coworkers, you're probably sharing a little more face time with local friends and neighbors. Being an Anywhereist collapses where you live and where you work into one life-affirming location.

So what if we stop looking to work to give us 100 percent of the profession-people-purpose experiences we need to feel good about our lives, and we start looking for profession-people-purpose experiences in the cities we live in? What if we shifted our thinking so that motivation and emotional fulfillment come at least in part from engaging experiences with our place communities, not just our workplaces? What if we started to treat our towns a little bit more like our offices?

You do that by setting up shop in the place you live, as Brett and Kate McKay of the website Art of Manliness put it. Just as a craftsman's workshop is kitted out with the equipment they need to do their best work, "when it comes to crafting an extraordinary life," they wrote, "your 'shop' is the place you choose to live. And just as for the traditional craftsman, this place must have the right tools, environment, and fit to unlock your full potential."[15]

I'm not suggesting you install a cubicle along Main Street or hang your motivational kitten posters above your favorite table in the local indie coffee shop. I'm saying that you should start looking to your town as a resource to bolster your professional life. Your place can boost your desire to succeed, give you opportunities to learn and grow, channel your strengths, connect you with locals who become de facto coworkers and mentors, make you more content, and encourage you to start something new like a business or a project to give back. And by the way, it can also help you save and make more money.

By adding measures of profession-people-purpose success into your personal location strategy, you can reach the twin goals of a better career and a better life. So in the rest of the book, I'll share examples of how places are helping their Anywhereists find greater measures of the following:

- Recognition
- Wealth
- Entrepreneurship
- Connection

- Creativity
- Adventure
- Learning
- Purpose
- Happiness

If you're a Seeker choosing where to live, you'll get a sense of how to integrate these qualities into your personal location strategy so that your town helps you fulfill your profession-people-purpose needs.

If you're a Wanderer who's not ready to commit to anyplace in particular, you'll gain some ideas on how to access whatever your temporary community has to offer and extend your ability to stay on the road.

If you're a Settler who's already committed to a place, you'll start to see more of the ways your community can help you get ahead, and you'll know how to get more engaged, make your town better, and offer a leg up for others.

There will be plenty of real-life examples of how Anywhereists choose their towns and how they're impacted by them, location strategy sessions with practical pointers, and place studies that highlight a single community that's doing it right.

I believe that when you're an Anywhereist, you should be getting more out of your community than anyone else, precisely because you can choose it. *If You Could Live Anywhere* will show you how.

4

ALL THE TOWNS WANT YOU

Location Strategy Value: Recognition

On a June morning in 2020, Mackenzie Cottles smiled over Zoom as she told a couple from New York City how much there is to love about living in the Shoals, Alabama. "We always kind of say that we were Music City before Music City," she said.

Aretha Franklin and the Rolling Stones made albums at Fame Recording Studio here, not far from where Jason Isbell and Sheryl Crow headlined the inaugural ShoalsFest in 2019. You'll hear music at the local arts festival, the Native American celebration, and the Renaissance festival—maybe everywhere but the annual Helen Keller Festival at the homestead in Tuscumbia where Annie Sullivan taught six-year-old Helen how to sign. For the Shoals' 150,000 residents, scattered among four towns along the Tennessee River, there's typically a lot to celebrate.

The couple from New York didn't need convincing. As Mackenzie recounted later, this particular pair had been stuck through the pandemic in a postage stamp–sized apartment, staring at their laptops from opposite ends of the dining room table.

The desperation to leave mounted, and because their jobs had gone remote, they could. Somewhere along the line, they learned about Remote Shoals, a program that was offering up to $10,000 to any remote worker willing to move to this stretch of Alabama that most non-Alabamans had never heard of.

For the pilot year of the program, launched by the Shoals Economic Development Authority in June 2019, ten tech workers moved there. Then a global pandemic struck. Halfway through 2020, they'd already had about 450 applicants for twenty-five slots.[1]

Needless to say, this is not how economic development is traditionally done.

THE BIG FISH

For decades, if you were an economic developer working for a region like the Shoals, your one goal was to reel in a big fish, a major company that would hire local workers and bring in tax revenue. New jobs were the key to economic growth. If you could convince a CEO to build a new factory or relocate a headquarters, thus boosting the county's property tax rolls and local job numbers, you were winning. To do that, economic development authorities handed out financial incentives like gumballs. Free land! No taxes for ten years! Cash for jobs!

To exchange incentives for the promise of jobs, development, investment, and growth is a gamble, and it doesn't always work out. In 2017, the Chinese company FoxConn was given $4.5 billion in incentives to build a display-panel manufacturing plant on three thousand acres of farmland in Mount Pleasant, Wisconsin. The factory was expected to bring thirteen thousand jobs to a rural area south of Milwaukee. Donald Trump described it as "one of the great deals ever." Yet within a few months, even the interns were let go for lack of work.[2]

Cities like to catch a big fish anyway. When Amazon announced its search for a location to build a second headquarters outside Seattle, every economic developer in the country broke out in a cold sweat. What ensued was a bizarre version of *The Bachelor*, with suitors from cities around the country lining up to offer their charms, including tax breaks and real estate deals. Around 230 communities threw their hats into the HQ2 ring in 2017.[3]

This time, the cities that came out on top for Amazon weren't necessarily the ones that could offer location, location, location or even huge incentives (St. Louis's package totaled $7 billion).[4] They were the ones who could offer talent, talent, talent.

That's the industry shorthand for skilled, educated workers, and they're a hot commodity these days for both businesses and communities. To win Amazon's HQ2 beauty pageant, Arlington, Virginia, offered a $573 million incentive package, including a $22,000 cash grant for each job that paid over $150,000. But they also presented a plan to get Amazon the twenty-five thousand workers they would need, down to creating a K–college STEM education pipeline that would pump employees into Amazon's loving arms for generations to come.[5]

It's always a chicken-and-egg situation. A town can attract a big fish with the assumption that people will move where there are good jobs available. Or it can attract skilled workers first—the talent—and use them to prove to interested companies that, hey, your future employees are already here.

Usually, it's a mix of both. But more and more cities and towns have become talent attraction and retention machines, vying to convince educated residents to move there, work there, and stay there, hopefully forever. Sarah Kerner, economic development director for Springfield, Missouri, told me that "talent attraction and retention" has been the homily she's preached to community leaders for years. "It used to be reversed. The company is here, and the people will come to the company, like, 'Okay, I guess I have to live here.' It's totally flipped now."[6]

SWEET HOME ALABAMA

How do cities attract talent? Lately, with cash. In 2018, the paradigm of talent attraction shifted dramatically when the city of Tulsa, Oklahoma, announced a program called Tulsa Remote. The idea was this: if you were a full-time remote worker willing to move to Tulsa, you'd be given $10,000.

A fancy website clarified the value proposition: "Hi, remote workers! We'll pay you to work from Tulsa. You're going to love it here." In the background of the homepage, videos scrolled a wish list of demiurban Anywhereist fantasies: twentysomethings clunking away at laptops in a loft space, ethnically diverse beautiful people enjoying drinks at a rooftop bar.

There were other perks for Tulsa Remote participants too, like a desk at a coworking space and discounted downtown apartments. Program participants would get access to members-only events and Slack channels that would help them connect with their new community and one another.[7]

No one had ever given financial incentives straight to workers willing to move, yet it made sense that instead of handing out corporate welfare checks to big companies like Amazon, cities funneled some money straight to the people. Every new resident who moved to Tulsa represented a huge payoff in economic activity: one more person to buy real estate, pay taxes locally, shop at the local supermarket, and tweet about how much they adored their adopted community. And every new highly skilled worker in the area was additional proof to big-fish tech companies that Tulsa was somewhere their employees might want to live.

The media loved it. Anywhereists loved it. In the first two years of the program, almost five hundred people moved to Oklahoma as part of Tulsa Remote.[8]

Around the country, other civic leaders took notice, including, 550 miles away in Alabama, the Shoals Economic Development Authority. Though the Shoals didn't on its face have much in common with Tulsa and its four hundred thousand residents, the authority decided to give Tulsa's crazy new model for attracting remote workers a whirl. In 2019, the organization launched Remote Shoals, a program that in its pilot year would pay $10,000 in cash to each Anywhereist who moved to the area.[9]

At first, the Shoals targeted only tech workers, whom they paid in installments on a sliding scale based on the recipient's income. (The more you make, the more they give you, based on the idea that you're more valuable to the community.) By the second year, the program was expanded to anyone who makes at least $52,000 a year as a remote worker. Applicants have included single twentysomethings, married fiftysomethings, families with kids, a school administrator, a Veterans Affairs official, and a sports podcaster for NBC who, "since he's not going to games anymore," said Mackenzie, "then he's like, you know, 'I can live wherever.'" They're fleeing cities as far-flung as Seattle, Orlando, and Portland, Maine, for the Shoals.

The cool $10,000 gets Anywhereists to open the door to this down-home corner of Alabama, but the payout shouldn't be the only reason Anywhereists come. "We want to make sure that we're what they need and that they're kind of what we need," said Mackenzie, who grew up in the area and is a natural cheerleader for it. "We don't want someone who wants nightlife if we can't provide that. We don't want to sell our community as something it's not."

In their Zoom interview, Mackenzie asked the couple from New York what their perfect community was, a standard litmus-test question for applicants to Remote Shoals. "We're looking for somewhere that has space, pace, and community," they replied.

Mackenzie beamed. "That's exactly what we have!" she gushed.

There's space because you can move to the Shoals and buy yourself a few acres that ensure you rarely see another soul. Pace because you can get from one side of town to another in twenty minutes. Community because of people like a local business owner who moved to the area twelve years ago. She hated it at first, Mackenzie explained, but over time, she came to appreciate how few barriers to entry there were and that getting involved was as simple as seeing something cool and saying, "Can I help?" Now she contributes to some of Mackenzie's programming and tells her customers, "I would never want to live anywhere else."

Initial reluctance giving way to full-throated hallelujah chorus is often the process here. Mackenzie knows that when people hear the word "Alabama," an image rises in their mind of what kind of place this is. Unless they've lived here, they're almost certainly wrong about it. She wants to have the chance to correct Anywhereists' preconceived notions.[10]

MOVING FOR DOLLARS

Tulsa and the Shoals aren't the only cities dangling financial carrots to people looking to relocate. In the past decade, many of the perks that communities have traditionally proffered only to corporations are now going straight to Anywhereists, in a buyer's market where someone devising a location strategy can tap into cash payouts, free land, tax breaks, student loan debt repayment, or housing incentives for moving to a new town. Here are a few examples:

- **Northwest Arkansas:** The part of the state that includes Walmart headquarters in Bentonville gave remote workers who moved to the area a $10,000 cash incentive, plus a new bike "to help you take advantage of the...322 miles of world-class mountain biking trails that has made outdoor enthusiasts flock to the area." The six-month, $1 million program was funded by the Walton Family Foundation.[11]
- **Topeka, Kansas:** The Choose Topeka initiative offered remote workers who moved to Topeka and stayed a year up to $5,000 to reimburse renting expenses or $10,000 if they bought a home.[12]
- **Butler County, Ohio:** Transplants could get a reverse scholarship to pay down student debt at a rate of $300 a month, up to $10,000 total, for moving to one of Butler County's small towns north of Cincinnati.[13]
- **Newton, Iowa:** This suburb of Des Moines, with about fifteen thousand residents, offered newcomers a $10,000

cash bonus for buying a new single-family home, plus a welcome package with over $2,500 in gifts from local businesses.[14]

- **Hawaii:** During the pandemic, a group of business leaders and local nonprofits, in partnership with state government, promised free airfare, discounted hotels and coworking spaces, and opportunities for community involvement to any remote worker willing to relocate to the islands for at least a month—though the Movers and Shakas program clarified that "we hope you choose to stay longer."[15]

- **Albinen, Switzerland:** A village of only 240 residents high in the Alps offered up to 25,000 francs—close to $25,000—for each adult who relocates there and buys property locally, plus an extra 10,000 francs per child. The catch: If you leave before ten years, you have to repay the money.[16]

- **Savannah, Georgia:** The city on the Gulf Coast had already been paying technology companies who relocated there up to $2,000 per employee to cover relocation fees. In 2020, they gave the money directly to qualified tech workers. "All we really did was disconnect the need for the company to move here," explained Jennifer Bonnett, the vice president of innovation and entrepreneurship for the Savannah Economic Development Authority.[17]

- **Vermont:** With the governor of Vermont on board, the state's Agency of Commerce and Community Development developed a grant program that offered remote workers willing to move to Vermont up to $10,000 in reimbursements for things like moving expenses, membership fees for a coworking space, and internet access. (The program ended in 2020 when the initial $500,000 allotted to it dried up.)[18]

And that's just the tip of the iceberg. Similar initiatives are popping up in such quick succession—everywhere from Morgantown, West Virginia, to Augusta, Maine—that a website, MakeMyMove.com, keeps tabs on the current offers. It's fantasy fodder, both amazing and slightly nuts, for Anywhereists willing to be wooed by a random community.

Not everyone loves it. Current residents in places with remote worker attraction programs tend to grumble about how their community is spending gobs of money to attract newcomers while longtime locals are struggling. Why not mail a check to current residents who've already proved their loyalty?

A few critics suggest that the practice of offering incentives to lure newcomers to your place brings to mind the old Groucho Marx remark about "I don't want to belong to any club that would have me as a member." After West Lafayette, Indiana, debuted its $5,000 remote worker offer, urbanist Aaron Renn polled Twitter: "How much would the state of Indiana have to pay to get you to move there?" More than half marked "never moving there," no matter how good the bait was.[19]

Speaking about Vermont's Remote Worker grant program, the state auditor groused, "I actually heard from a lot of people that some of the publicity was very negative, people laughing at us. If Vermont is so good, why are you paying people to come there?"[20]

The answer is, for much of the same reason that places ply

businesses with incentives or that companies give new recruits a signing bonus or extra vacation days: because everyone's competing for talent, and *Anywhereists are the talent.* As Winona Dimeo-Ediger, editor in chief of Livability.com, told me, talent attraction and retention is "a whole industry that most people don't know exists and functions at all. They don't know it's in their city. They don't know that maybe they were affected or touched by it in any way. And therefore they don't know how to leverage it or access those programs either. And that's a huge problem."[21]

Knowing that, as an Anywhereist, you're a hot commodity right now gives you some power in the war for talent. Communities want you something fierce, and they're fighting to get your attention.

As place values go, maybe wanting to be fought over isn't the most noble in the world. But it's good to be wanted, in a town or in a job. Part of what researchers found at Facebook was that employees felt more satisfied with their careers when they were recognized and appreciated for their contributions. In a workplace, recognition might translate into a raise or a public shout-out for your killer PowerPoint. But according to a 2015 survey, only 21 percent of respondents felt like they were getting paid what they deserved. Three out of four felt like the best employees weren't being given proper recognition.[22]

Remember, your town is your office. So having a city proffer a check for moving there is like getting a well-deserved raise or having a recruiter ping you after looking at your LinkedIn page— reassuring and flattering. It lets you know how eager the community is to have you there. Even without a financial incentive, simply feeling welcomed by a new place increases your chances of developing place attachment, that sense of rootedness that makes you want to stay. You're happier in your city when you know you're wanted there.

THE WAR FOR TALENT

So far, Dallas, Texas, hasn't ponied up any cash to new residents willing to relocate there. They haven't had to. In the past ten years, the metro area has added 1.3 million new residents, making it the fastest-growing place in the country.[23]

This is not a city that's suffering for lack of economic growth. More than 150 companies have relocated their headquarters to the region in the last decade, enticed by low taxes, bargain-basement real estate prices, and an accessible international airport.[24] Dallas has gotten so good at reeling in big fish that they created a new problem for themselves: too many job openings, not enough people to fill them. Even the fastest-growing metro in the country can't keep pace with the demand for talent.

Pre-COVID, fields like management, finance, architecture, engineering, constructing, "and really anything that touches a computer" had an unemployment rate of less than 1 percent in Dallas, according to Jessica Heer, the senior vice president for regional marketing and talent attraction for the Dallas Chamber of Commerce. To fill their vacancies, businesses poached employees from one another. It wasn't a sustainable solution. Eventually, Heer began telling CEOs to "stop stealing from your neighbor and steal from your neighboring state." A marketing campaign called Say Yes to Dallas became the city's pickup line for twenty- and thirtysomethings in tech-centric cities like Chicago, Nashville, and New York City. "We want you here," they were told.[25]

In Dallas, the chamber didn't need remote workers to bring their own jobs as much as they needed them to apply for the ones on offer in the city. And since the chamber's research showed that a new job, or the promise of one, was still the top motivation behind a decision to move, the Say Yes to Dallas website played up the city's booming job market. "Our key messaging is, 'There's a lifetime of opportunity,'" Heer told me. "Whether you're starting your career or you're moving to wrap up your career, there are options in our region. Young people like options. They want to have forty jeans options as opposed to two."

It's hard to measure the outcomes of campaigns like this, because people create their location strategies based on a million small details, not just one website. But since its launch, Say Yes to Dallas has had seven hundred thousand page views. The eyeballs are enough of a win in a crowded marketplace—and the end game for some of the cities offering cash incentives. Even if you scoffed at Tulsa Remote, you may have gleaned a few Tulsa fun facts while you read about it: that if you move there, you can throw a Frisbee around their $465 million downtown park, march in their pride parade, or race DIY rafts down the Arkansas River (it's a thing).

Incentive money alone shouldn't be the sole factor to inspire a move. But if thinking about the money or seeing a well-placed marketing campaign motivates a research process that lands Tulsa on your short list, then for the city, that was money well spent. "I think it certainly pays off a lot better than paying millions upon millions of dollars in tax incentives for big companies," Richard Florida, the author of Who's Your City?, told NPR. "The small-scale incentive to a human being is better."[26]

WHERE EVERYONE'S GOING

On the other hand, Richard Florida suggests that if a city is good enough, affordable enough, and armed with enough quality-of-life amenities, it doesn't need $10,000 incentives. Newcomers will track it down and move there on their own.[27] The first rule of economic development may be talent attraction, but the second rule is quality of life. To attract Seekers, you have to create the kind of place people want to live.

Livability is one of the media companies tracking what that might look like. For its annual list of the Top 100 Best Cities to Live in the United States, Livability surveys one thousand millennials (currently the most geographically mobile age group) and crunches data around broad categories they know Seekers look at to make location decisions, like education and transportation. In 2020, editor in chief Winona Dimeo-Ediger and her staff were just about to release the new results after months of work when COVID hit and cities started snapping shut like oysters. Worried that the list would strike a tone-deaf note at the moment of the unfolding pandemic, they postponed the release and redid the survey to figure out if 2020's "flee the plague" vibe had shifted things for millennials.

The short answer: Not really. In the midst of the pandemic, "people's relocation priorities didn't change," said Dimeo-Ediger. "It's just that more people were able to act on the things they cared about."[28]

What they cared about more than anything else was affordability. For 70 percent of respondents, a town's cost of living ranked in their top three decision-making factors.[29] Expensive cities or ones without affordable housing got crossed off the list.

For most millennials, climate, traffic, culture like good food and museums, outdoor recreation, and proximity to family had weight too. So did the pure hassle of moving; more than a quarter cited it as a reason to stay put.[30]

As an Anywhereist, mostly you're making decisions on factors that affect your day-to-day life. Do you want to sit in traffic or fork over more than 30 percent of your monthly income to rent? No. Do you want to have good weather and options for Mexican food on Friday night? Yes.

Anywhereists prioritize simply having a nice life for a price they can afford. So during the pandemic, they started abandoning spendy, crowded superstar cities for the big geographic winners of the COVID era: suburban counties, 91 percent of which saw growth; vacation spots like Cape Cod and Lake Tahoe; small cities like Sarasota, Florida, and Charleston, South Carolina; and small towns.[31]

The people fleeing cities—82 percent of urban centers saw more move-outs than move-ins, with New York City, Seattle, San Francisco, and Boston shedding the most residents—didn't necessarily go far. Most pandemic movers stayed somewhere in their same metro area.[32] But without a downtown office forming the center of gravity of one's existence, living farther out became not only okay but desirable.

Small-town economic developers in particular were pumping their fists and whispering, "It's our time to shine." Rural communities like McPherson County, Nebraska, and Holmes County, Ohio, had already seen surprising growth from spikes in remote workers.[33] Suddenly, small-town consultants Becky McCray and Deb Brown were fielding an endless stream of questions about how to attract them. "There is no longer any question whether we can decouple work from place and choose where to live separate from where to work," Becky said—a boon for underdog locations.[34]

There's even an inspired turn of phrase to describe places that prosper without proximity to big-fish employers: "Zoom towns." Zoom towns are small, sometimes out-of-the-way communities with a good internet connection and an interesting local culture that are great options for Anywhereists who just need an internet connection to work.

All these small communities need is a way to broadcast to the world that they exist, that they're open for business, and that they're ready for their star turn as an Anywhereist-friendly Zoom town. Without the budget for a massive marketing campaign like Say Yes to Dallas, little out-of-the-way communities have to find more creative ways to hang the welcome banner.

Enter programs like Remote Shoals.

THE JUST-RIGHT CITY

Joe and Ana Kuykendall had been living in the Orlando, Florida, area for five years when Joe first heard about the Remote Shoals program. He and his wife both worked remotely for the same software development company, and they'd been talking about leaving Florida for at least a year. "The price of living was just getting outrageous," Joe said. "Even these cute little bungalows, we were completely priced out of those."[35]

One day, Joe googled an article about remote worker-recruitment programs and read about Remote Shoals. Something clicked. The Shoals appeared to check a lot of their boxes, like

affordability and walkability. "The incentive opened the door," Joe
said. "It gave us the idea that, 'Hey, this could work.'"

After an interview with Mackenzie and her team, Joe and
Ana drove out for a visit in June 2020 with their seven-year-old
son. Before the weekend was over, they'd made an offer on a 1905
three-bedroom home in Florence, Alabama. Three months later,
they moved in, another win for Remote Shoals' talent attraction
(see page 54) game.

As Marcus Andersson, cofounder of the Stockholm-based
place marketing firm Future Place Leadership, explained, in the
world of talent attraction and retention, marketing programs like
Say Yes to Dallas and Remote Shoals are just the tip of the iceberg.[36] A place's next steps are talent reception, or programs that
welcome newcomers (think Tulsa Remote's meetups and Slack
channel); talent integration, which gives newcomers a social and
professional network (like through a young professionals' mixer);
and talent reputation, like place branding and local ambassador
programs.[37]

Some places are better at these steps than others. When Tim
Carty worked in economic development for Iowa City and Cedar
Rapids, Iowa, he put a button on their website that said "Recruit
me." If you clicked it, you'd soon get an email from Tim or a
colleague offering to connect you to local employers or housing, provide information about schools and neighborhoods—
whatever it took to convince you to move to the area. That's
talent attraction.[38]

Once you got there, you'd be linked via the Wingman program
(yes, he has since realized it's a sexist name, and he's sorry) to
someone who could show you around and help you develop an

emotional connection to your new town.[39] If you were a twentysomething dude who liked craft beer and hiking, Tim Carty
would try to match you up with another twentysomething with
a brewery in their basement and a map of all the local trails. "We
wanted to make sure that we were connecting people who had
similar interests and people that were in the same stage of life,"
Tim explained. That's talent reception.

There was even a bit of talent integration, since your wingman
committed to a one-two-three list of activities: hanging out with
you in person once, inviting you to two community or networking events, and introducing you to three other friends they think
you'll like. "It was impactful stuff," Tim said. And just what a new-
comer Anywhereist might need to feel recognized and valued in
a new community. The "Recruit me" button is an expression of a
community's intention: *We want you here.* That small bit of energy
spent to recruit you feels good.

Of course, just because an economic developer wants you
doesn't mean everyone's hanging the welcome banners. In Dallas,
Jessica Heer admitted, most locals understand why it's a coup to
lure an AT&T or a Comerica, but they don't get why Dallas wants
you when it's already exploding in population. Heer's friends made
comments like, "Why would you have more people move here?
You're bringing people who are going to put a strain on our public
infrastructure and put more cars on the road and things like that."[40]

Even in smaller cities, people sometimes express dismay at
talent attraction efforts. Winona Dimeo-Ediger recalled an emotional conversation she had with a friend living in Santa Fe, New
Mexico, who felt her small city of eighty-four thousand had been
overrun by Texans and Californians. "She came to me and said,

'Winona, I have to say, I feel like the work you're doing in marketing places and telling people to move...is hurting my city.' It was
kind of intense."[41]

The challenge, Winona said, is "that for every Santa Fe, there
is a small city that needs to grow and is begging for new residents.
Truly its survival is staked on connecting with people who are
meant to be there and who are looking for their perfect place to
live." So the trick becomes aligning the people in the big cities who
are saying "This isn't working for me anymore" with the smaller
cities that are saying "We have to grow. Please come here."

For Joe and Ana Kuykendall, finding the Shoals felt like the
right match with a place that wanted them. They're still collecting their installments of the $10,000 from Remote Shoals, which
they've primarily used to pay for their moving expenses. Even
without the cash infusion, moving to Alabama has been a financial net positive by lowering the Kuykendalls' monthly expenses
by about $1,000. Their $1,500-a-month mortgage is cheaper than
their $2,000 Florida rent was. Property taxes in Florida were
around $4,000 a year; in the Shoals, they're $600. Even their auto
insurance is half of what it used to be before the move.

Because they need less money, they're able to spend more
time doing the stuff they love, like hiking (you can get to a trail
in fifteen minutes, they say) and eating out. The University of
North Alabama is at the border of their neighborhood, and
sometimes they can hear Leo, the college mascot lion, roaring
from his enclosure on campus. It's a strange soundtrack for their
work calls, requiring Ana to sometimes pause and say, "I'm sorry.
That was a lion."

They're definitely not in Florida anymore. But it's clear that the Shoals wants them more than Florida did. If they sit on their front porch, their neighbors will stop to chat. (Unspoken Alabama rules dictate that if you sit on your front porch, you're fair game for socializing.) They run into people they know when they go out. They have a regular barber, plus a coffee guy who knows their names and their order. "You definitely feel known, which was a big thing for us," Joe said.

Even though they work remotely, they don't want to be isolated. "We still want to get to know our neighbors. We want to get to know people. We want to be a part of a community that we can actually invest in. And we felt like we got that here."[42]

There's a just-right city out there for most people. Maybe not a singular soul mate—it's hard to believe in that for marriage, let alone locations—but there's a place in the world with just the right qualities you're looking for. And you, in turn, are the right person for a particular city. Now you just have to find each other.

Location Strategy Session: Recognition

Workers want to feel valued and incentivized on the job. So do residents. Luckily, communities all over the world are working hard to make Anywhereists feel wanted, with a warm welcome or cash money. Here's what to do to get the recognition you deserve.

1. **Research:** A $10,000 incentive (and maybe even a bike!) from a town that wants you to move there is a great starting point. Check out the offers online (try MakeMyMove.com). Just don't make that your

endpoint. Look closely at the elements and amenities the town has to offer. Does this spot fit with your place values? And everything else you're looking for? Otherwise, the cash isn't worth it.

2. **Click to get recruited:** Tim Carty and Winona Dimeo-Ediger have teamed up on a business called RoleCall that helps places install "Recruit Me" buttons on websites and at the end of those gorgeous place-marketing videos. If someplace captures your curiosity, click the button (or otherwise reach out).

3. **Ask for what you want:** Businesses do it, so why not you? If you're contemplating moving to a town, contact the local economic development authority or the chamber of commerce for advice and see what happens. Is the response personalized? Did an actual human get back to you? (The odds of that happening are better in a smaller town than a big city, FYI.)

4. **Find your own wingman:** If no wingman or other ambassador program exists in a community on your list, ask the chamber of commerce or convention and visitors bureau to connect you with a resident who's moved there in the past two years. They can give you the real dirt on questions like, "What was your biggest financial surprise moving here?" and "How does this town treat people of color?"

5. **Let yourself be marketed to:** Most cities are tooting their own horns with websites geared toward potential newcomers or visitors. Yes, it's marketing, but it's

also usually a wealth of information about what there
is to love in a place.

6. **Look beyond the superstar cities:** There's a lot to
    love about big cities. All the culture. The people. The
    coffee shops and Urban Outfitters. If a huge city is
    what you want, you probably know it. But if you can
    live anywhere, give small towns, rural areas, midsized
    cities, resort communities, and (gasp!) even the sub-
    urbs another look.

Place Study: Topeka, Kansas

Population: 126,397

- **Big problem:** A few years ago, data showed that 40 percent
  of people who worked in Shawnee County commuted in from
  places as far away as Kansas City, sixty miles east. As part of a
  strategy to get more people to commit to not just working but
  living locally, Choose Topeka launched a $10,000 incentive
  program to help remote workers buy a house. (People who
  get a full-time job in town get $15,000. Hooray, Settlers.) By
  the end of January 2021, 350 remote workers had expressed
  interest, and 15 had moved in.

- **Why you want to live here:** State capital vibes, public art
  everywhere (those murals won't Instagram themselves), and
  different festivals for country, blues, and classical music. Plus
  the cheesy taters at Lonnie Q's BBQ are a whole thing.

- **Who's applying:** People who love that Kansas is in the middle.
  Sometimes applicants have ties to other midwestern states;
  sometimes they just like a slightly more measured pace to life.
  "We've heard stories time and time again from people—whether

they're from Chicago or Atlanta or San Francisco—where they still don't know anyone and they've lived there for six years or more," said Barbara Stapleton, vice president of business retention and talent initiatives for Greater Topeka Partnership. "They're ready to be able to find more connection within a community. And they like that they can still be an hour from an airport and that there's still plenty of opportunities as it relates to arts and culture and restaurants."[43]

- **Where to live:** On the Choose Topeka website, they break it down into "upscale, elegant neighborhoods" and "charming, affordable neighborhoods." In the latter category's ridiculously adorable Westboro neighborhood, you can find a bungalow with gleaming hardwoods for less than $250,000.

- **If you're thinking about it:** The best candidates for Choose Topeka are folks who are "generally looking for a new adventure," said Bob Ross, Greater Topeka Partnership's marketing director.[44] They're ready to throw themselves at something new.

- **Fake tagline:** "A great place to run out of gas." After Choose Topeka launched in 2019, Stephen Colbert cracked that the incentives would help them build an intentional community "because right now, Topeka's current residents are all drivers who ran out of gas on their way to anywhere else." In response, GO Topeka, the economic development agency behind Choose Topeka, made a hilarious video of a woman with an empty gas can—the proverbial stuck driver—stepping inside a Topeka bar, then chucking the gas can into the corner when she's welcomed with a beer and open arms. Whatever accident brought her there, she was ready to stay.[45] Check and mate.

5

EVERYTHING'S CHEAPER
IN PANAMA

Location Strategy Value: Wealth

When the economy collapsed in 2009, nearly nine million Americans lost their jobs.[1] Susanna Perkins, fifty-six, was one of them.[2]

She was left unemployed when the attorney she'd been working for closed up shop. In a case of worst timing ever, her husband, Mark, had quit his electrical engineering job a few years earlier to get a master's degree and pivot into teaching middle school science. But the recession hit within a few months of his graduation, and the nearby Florida school districts laid off more than three thousand teachers. Mark couldn't even pick up shifts as a sub. At age sixty, he started working as a bicycle courier on the streets of downtown Orlando.

With essentially no retirement savings between them—they'd raided Mark's IRA to pay for graduate school, then cashed it in entirely to cover living expenses after the economic collapse—their financial situation was dire. "At this point, I wasn't going to find a job," Susanna recalled, "and we had to do something. We were hemorrhaging what little savings we had."

Living abroad had been a recurring fantasy of Susanna's. Even before their finances imploded, the Perkinses talked about spending time overseas in retirement, partly to immerse themselves in a foreign culture, partly to save money. Now it had turned into something else: the most obvious and immediate way to stop their economic free fall.

So they moved to Central America. Las Tablas, Panama, specifically. It's a town of ten thousand along Ecuador's southern coastline, where the beach beckoned from ten minutes away and mangos fell from shade trees into the street.

There, the Perkinses found a fully furnished three-bedroom house for $400 a month in rent. Just $3 of propane powered their gas stove for three months. They paid less for high-speed internet than they did back in Florida. Groceries were cheaper too, as long as you avoided spendy imported American goods like bottled salad dressing. In an average month, they spent $1,700, about a third of what they'd been spending in Florida.

The Perkinses' relocation may have been more dramatic than most. But wanting to prioritize affordability in your location strategy is a common Anywhereist tactic. According to Livability's data, lower cost of living is the number one thing that attracts new residents thinking about where to move.[3]

There's also a push factor to cost of living. Overinflated prices drive Anywhereists out of cities that they otherwise like, which explains why in the last nine months of 2020, a net 38,800 residents left San Francisco, ranked repeatedly as the most expensive city in the nation, by some estimates more than twice as pricey as the national average.[4]

If your job is in San Francisco, maybe you have no choice but to live in a place where the median household income is $112,376, the average property value is $1.2 million, and rent for a one-bedroom apartment in 2019 was $3,550.[5] That math becomes a lot harder to justify when you can work anywhere. As the pandemic progressed, a third of people who moved did so to escape financial pressures where they lived.[6]

Even for those of us living in less outlandishly priced neighborhoods, it's hard not to fantasize about the money-saving potential of life in a less expensive place. On the occasions when I allow myself to get sucked into Realtor.com, it's to look at home listings for cities I know are cheaper than mine—Indianapolis, say, or Cleveland.

In truth, I wouldn't even have to go that far. Here in Blacksburg, where the local university draws a steady stream of new residents and geography limits growth, the median home price is $330,000. (I know, I know, San Franciscans are playing the world's tiniest violin.) Thirty miles down US-460, the median home price is just $166,000. I could move to the tiny hamlet of Narrows and cut my mortgage by at least 50 percent. Yet here I remain for a multitude of reasons, not least of which is that the main dining establishment in Narrows is a gas-station Burger King.

Money is rarely if ever the only factor in an Anywhereist location strategy. But for the majority of Anywhereists, it's in the top three, a prerequisite to every other factor you're weighing—and it should be. Because if you do enough arithmetic with a cost-of-living calculator, you realize that a different place could seriously change your financial picture.

You could reduce your rent or mortgage payment. Put more money into savings. Work less. Eat out more often. Retire early. Live like kings. Have the kind of life you've always dreamed about.

Or maybe just stop freaking out about money all the time.

There's even a name for this approach to rearranging your financial life through the power of place: geographic arbitrage.

HOW TO BUY HAPPINESS OR A CLOSE FACSIMILE

Geographic arbitrage, simply put, is taking advantage of the differences in cost of living among locations to save money and/or raise your quality of life.

When a Californian sells a two-bedroom house for $750,000 and snaps up something much grander in Idaho for less money—a common occurrence these days—that's geographic arbitrage.

When a young couple trades Manhattan for affordable upstate New York, that's geographic arbitrage.

When a digital nomad thrives on $10,000 a year because they live in Thailand, they have geographic arbitrage to thank.

Historically, local salaries reflect the local cost of living. So if you move from high-cost Boston to lower-cost Tucson for a new job, you can expect your income to take a hit too. You'd be spending noticeably less on rent in Tucson, but you'd be making less too. Net gain: zero.

Anywhereists escape this cycle. Because many Anywhereists salaries aren't location based, they make the same income whether they're living in Boston or Tucson (or Bali or Tallinn), allowing them to amplify the effects of geographic arbitrage wherever the cost of living is lowest. Moving from Honolulu, the fourth most expensive city in the United States, according to Move.org's rankings of the seventy-five most populous metros, to St. Louis, the fourth least expensive, could reduce your monthly outlay by around 49 percent.[7] In actual dollars, that turns $5,000 a month in living expenses into $2,550. With the savings, you get to upgrade your lifestyle, pad your (early) retirement accounts, shift to part-time work, or buy a few thousand frozen burritos. (You do you.)

Often the farther you're willing to go geographically, the farther your money goes as well. Tim Leffel, a travel writer and author of *A Better Life for Half the Price*, told me that many Anywhereists—retirees, remote workers, online entrepreneurs—leave home "because they're not able to have the kind of standard of living they want on the money they're going to have coming in. If they go live somewhere like Chiang Mai or Mexico or Portugal, they can live a pretty fulfilling life on a lot less money."[8]

Tim's a practitioner of geographic arbitrage himself, having relocated with his family from Nashville to Guanajuato, in the Sierra Madre mountains of central Mexico. He bought a four-bedroom house there for $86,000. Property taxes are $120 a year. Tickets to the symphony are $6. Visiting family in Florida, where lunch for two costs $40, he confessed to sticker shock. "We didn't get hardly anything! Like, nobody ordered drinks!"

There are ethical issues to think about here. Is it ugly to take advantage of global economic inequities to live your best life? To resettle in a foreign country precisely so you can afford household help or fancy dinners out?

In the United States, geographic arbitrage can fuel gentrification in once-inexpensive neighborhoods, ultimately driving up costs and forcing locals out because they can no longer afford rent or rising property taxes. En masse, it exacerbates for others the financial problems you're trying to solve for yourself.

But taken one budget and one relocation at a time, geographic arbitrage can be the fastest path to economic stability and everything that comes with it. The reality is, a lot of us struggle with money. Debt loads are higher than they've been for years, and forgoing every Starbucks latte and avocado toast till the end of time won't have the sizable impact on your finances that moving to a lower cost-of-living (LCOL) city could. And there are benefits beyond money when you reduce your cost of living:

- **You can buy time:** If you're a freelance Anywhereist, relocating to an LCOL city can free you from having to work so many hours to cover basic expenses. If it's a New York to Vietnam–level sea change, you may be able to switch to part-time work. Or perhaps your family is eager to have one parent stay at home while raising kids. Moving to an LCOL area might allow you to make that switch.

- **You can buy options:** If you can put more money in savings from a cost-of-living decrease, you can pay off debt, stash more cash in the bank, or fund what writer Paulette Perhach calls a "F*ck-Off Fund." With enough money tucked away, you can leave the bad job, the toxic boyfriend, the abusive landlord, knowing your savings will tide you over until something better comes along.[9]

- **You can buy freedom:** Members of the FIRE movement—Financial Independence, Retire Early—save aggressively so they can quit working altogether in their thirties, forties, or fifties. Geographic arbitrage is often a tool they use to keep out of the workforce. (More on that later in this chapter.)

- **You can buy actual things:** If owning a home is still part of your American dream, that milestone can be dramatically more attainable in certain cities. The savings differential, or simply an overall price index decrease, may make other objects of desire more affordable, like a nicer car or all-organic groceries. Whatever goals you've had for yourself, whatever items make you feel like you're living your best life, may be more in reach in an LCOL area.

- **You can buy happiness:** Okay, not really. But freeing up money with a move to an LCOL place lets you invest more in the stuff that boosts your well-being. A whopping 76 percent of people worldwide prefer experiences to owning things, and having more money left at the end of the month lets you more easily afford an African safari or season tickets to the local triple-A baseball team.[10] Or just more therapy.

By keeping your overhead low, you put yourself in the best position to live the life you want to live, not just the life that's handed to you.

Money, of course, represents different things to different people. Maybe what you'd like to do with your cash is experience one of the most expensive cities in the world, like Hong Kong or Zurich. Only you can decide how important cost of living should be in your overall location strategy.

One thing is clear: it's not enough to love a city. You have to be able to afford it.

THE MAGIC OF GEOGRAPHIC ARBITRAGE

I will not tell you to eliminate your daily coffee run. Enough other people have done that, and the success of geographic arbitrage does not typically hinge on small economies alone. According to one study, your daily cup will cost about $5.33 in Denmark but only $1.31 in Bulgaria.[11] You could relocate from Denmark to Bulgaria, buy a coffee every day, and still net only an extra $1,467 a year.

But according to the Bureau of Labor Statistics, in 2019, housing sucked up almost a third of the average American family's annual spending.[12] As line items go, things like transportation, food, insurance, even a daily coffee habit, don't come close.

Housing is expensive—and getting steadily more so on a dollar-for-dollar basis. From May 2020 to May 2021, real estate prices in the United States soared more than 15 percent nationwide, the biggest climb in fifteen years.[13] And with house prices far outpacing incomes, home ownership is increasingly out of reach for middle-class Americans.

Most researchers measure housing affordability as an equation: the median local house price divided by the gross median household income in a market.[14] A total under 3.0 counts as affordable. So, for example, if the median household income in your area is $100,000, and the median home price is $295,000, congrats! Housing is considered affordable in your market (though it might not always feel that way).

But hardly any city in the world meets that 3.0 affordability standard. According to a 2021 study of ninety-two major housing markets in eight countries, not a single city in Australia, Canada, Hong Kong, Ireland, New Zealand, Singapore, or the United Kingdom qualified as affordable. The United States squeaked past the threshold in just four cities: Pittsburgh, Pennsylvania; Rochester, New York; Buffalo, New York; and St. Louis, Missouri.[15]

Meanwhile, over in Australia, housing prices in all five of the urban cities in the study were so out of whack with local incomes that they were described as "severely unaffordable," meaning they scored a 5.1 or higher on the affordability ratio.[16] Picture average incomes of $100,000 and average home prices of $550,000. In Sydney, Australia, where housing prices have risen 70 percent since 2012, the thirtysomethings anxiously trying to buy their own places are, according to Josephine Tovey writing in the *Guardian*, "the ones huddled, sharing auction horror stories and lamenting why we didn't get in sooner, or wondering aloud whether we should all just move to Bulli [an hour away] and lump the long commute (though the median house price there has grown by almost 60% in five years, so...maybe not?)."[17]

It's not your imagination that things are getting worse. In the past two decades, housing prices globally have risen three times faster than median household income.[18] For young people trying to enter the housing market for the first time, the standard financial-industry advice not to spend more than 30 percent of your gross monthly income on housing-related expenses sounds like a taunt. In what world is that even possible?

Hence in 2016, 38.1 million American households were "cost burdened," an economic term that means "house poor."[19] Maybe there's some parallel *House Hunters* universe like the one Twitter mocks ("HUSBAND: I'm a hat critic for a blog. WIFE: I found a cigar box containing 2 gold coins. HUSBAND: Our budget is $1.4 million").[20] In actuality, one in four Americans spends more than 50 percent of their monthly income on housing, having normalized being uncomfortably in over their heads.[21]

Where they'll probably stay. Unless they move.

Anywhereists don't have to resign themselves to a "severely unaffordable" housing market because that's where their job is. They can choose.

Consider this example. In the most expensive housing market in the United States, the San Jose metro area, the median home price is $1.4 million. That's a monthly mortgage payment around $7,639. Yikes.

Meanwhile, in Decatur, Illinois, the nation's least expensive market in 2020, you can buy yourself a home for a median $109,900. Your new mortgage payment? $520 a month.

Even that's not always affordable to Decatur residents, a quarter of whom live below the poverty line.[22] But if you're the kind of remote worker or retiree Anywhereist whose income doesn't depend on local market rates, you can thrive. Think of that housing affordability equation. The median Decatur home price divided by the median San Jose household income of $125,000 equals an affordability ratio of 0.879.

They don't have a category for "seriously affordable," but maybe they should. It's available only to Anywhereists.

THE CALIFORNIA CONDITION

In 2020, software developer Jeremy Sandberg convinced his bosses at a Seattle area tech company to let him work remotely. He and his wife, Janie, a stay-at-home mom to their three kids, immediately launched their own location strategy session. They were looking for the trifecta of inexpensive, close to family, and sunnier than where they'd lived for the past ten years, and they found it in the city of Henderson, Nevada.[23]

The best part: selling their sixteen-hundred-square-foot

house in Bellevue, Washington, for $765,000, then turning around and paying $455,000 for their thirty-eight-hundred-square-foot Henderson home. "Getting a house of this square footage in Washington, we would have spent like $1.5 million," Janie said. Not only is the house enormous, with a guest room her husband commandeered as an office, but it's freed up money they hope to use to start a business or create passive income streams. "Was Henderson the one perfect choice? No, because there's never one perfect choice," said Janie. "But it has been a really, really good move for us and our family."

Because we're wonky, irrational creatures, we tend to treat the first price we see for an object or experience as a reference point, a phenomenon known in behavioral economics as price anchoring. If the first sandwich you spot on the menu is $10, you'll decide that the $15 sandwich is too expensive.

That's how we think about real estate too. You form an internal sense of what's appropriate to spend based on home prices you've seen in your local market. As home prices go up, so does your sense of what's okay to pay.

When you move, your price anchoring goes a little crazy. *In my old town*, you think, *a $300,000 house was expensive! Here, that's cheap!* Or vice versa. When my family moved from Austin to Blacksburg, we were so averse to paying Blacksburg's then-higher real estate prices that we rented for six years. Now, after eight years of living here, my price anchoring has reset. Local prices are *the* prices, the only ones that make sense to my brain.

So if you're moving from an HCOL area to an LCOL area, the variance between old prices and new prices might make you feel the way Tim Leffel, the travel writer who lives in Mexico, does after he goes from the lofty lunch menu prices in Florida to the produce section of the local market in Guanajuato. "Sometimes it's comical," he said, "like oranges will be five pounds for $1." In other words, you feel rich.

We could rename that phenomenon the California Condition. Over the past fifteen years, Californians fleeing ridiculously high housing prices in their state have had the unfortunate effect of driving up prices in attractive LCOL areas like Boise, Austin, and Phoenix. They're so amazed by what comparatively feels like penny-ante prices—and they may have a big payout from their California home burning a hole in their pocket—that they spend what to locals in these towns feel like exorbitant amounts. Over time, housing affordability declines as a result.[24]

It's a complex problem. But in the long term, if enough Anywhereists flee expensive cities, demand for housing there goes down, flattening prices. Geographic arbitrage could end up recalibrating affordability for everyone in a too-hot market like San Francisco, including for the people who are stuck there. And when you're creative about which LCOL market you move to (as opposed to, say, moving to Boise), you may provide a much-needed boost to the local economy.

For Melanie Allen, practicing geographic arbitrage has been the key to gearing up to retire early. She was living in Los Angeles when she first heard about FIRE, and though she loved California, she realized "there was no way I could achieve financial independence if I stayed."

An HCOL place was holding her back from the life she really wanted: less work, more travel and adventure. So she sold her Los Angeles home for nearly double what she paid for it, moved to

Savannah, Georgia, and used the cash to put a hefty down payment on a home there, with enough left over to pay off her car and student loan debt. A year later, she moved again to an even lower-cost town in rural Pennsylvania. There, she was able to pay for a house outright.

With no mortgage in Pennsylvania and rental income coming in from her Savannah house, she saves a hefty chunk of her income, making FIRE closer than ever for Melanie. (She blogs about her journey at PartnersinFire.com.) "Living in this low-cost-of-living town has allowed me to build my cash reserves back up, invest more, and keep my monthly expenses low," she said. "I don't think I'd be close to ready to quit if I still lived in Georgia, and I know I wouldn't be prepared at all if I had stayed in Los Angeles. Moving has given me so many more options than I could have ever dreamed of."[25]

Cheap Countries Where You Might Want to Live

A cheap place is not always a desirable place. But according to *International Living*'s 2021 Annual Global Retirement Index, these ten countries hit the sweet spot of affordable price ranges and high quality of living.[26]

1. Costa Rica ($1,400–$2,000 a month)
2. Panama ($1,765–$2,890 a month)
3. Mexico ($1,600–$2,500 a month)
4. Colombia ($1,030–$2,720 a month)
5. Portugal ($1,600–$2,500 a month)
6. Ecuador ($1,600–$2,400 a month)
7. Malaysia ($1,500–$2,000 a month)
8. France ($2,100–$2,500 a month)

9.   Malta ($2,000–$2,500 a month)

10.   Vietnam ($900–$1,470 a month)

AVOIDING THE TAX MAN

There's geographic arbitrage that helps you pay off a mortgage or a student loan. Then there's geographic arbitrage that helps you hide your money in an offshore tax haven. That's the kind that hundreds of people gathered near a beach in Playa del Carmen, Mexico, in May 2021 to learn about at Nomad Capitalist Live, billed as "the world's #1 offshore conference."[27]

With a speaker lineup that included Robert Kiyosaki, the author of *Rich Dad, Poor Dad*, and Mikheil Saakashvili, the former president of Georgia, the conference catered to those who are already very rich or desperately want to be, with high-level sessions on tax havens, foreign real estate, expat mortgages, and second passports. Their guru? A thirtysomething named Andrew Henderson, the founder of Nomad Capitalist, who coaches people to overcome their pesky country loyalty and instead go where they're treated best.

When Andrew was getting ready to launch his first company, he read an article that got the wheels spinning. It ranked the United States, where Andrew was from, as fortieth on a list of countries with the world's safest banks.

Huh. That meant there were thirty-nine other countries in the world where the banks were safer. Why was he so committed to banking in the United States?

For that matter, why do anything in the United States if other countries promised cheaper taxes, better healthcare systems, and, by the way, more beautiful beaches? Why be loyal to the country you're from if other countries treat you better?

Spurred by these less-than-patriotic thoughts, Andrew began practicing an extreme form of geographic arbitrage called flag theory, which he writes extensively about at his website NomadCapitalist.com.[28] People like Andrew base different parts of their lives in different countries to maximize their money, as if they're planting flags all over the map. Specifically, there are five flags he believes you should think about:

- **Citizenship:** You might get a second passport from a country that doesn't tax income earned by nonresidents.
- **Banking:** You could open an offshore bank account in a country that doesn't tax capital gains.
- **Play:** You can save money by vacationing and shopping in places with low or no sales tax.
- **Living:** You buy or rent a home in an LCOL area or a place that allows you to claim a second country of residence, like Panama or the Philippines.
- **Business:** If you own a business, you'd base it somewhere with lower taxes and asset protection or a country with business-friendly hiring policies.[29]

If all this conjures up images of James Bond–like jet setting, bags of gold bricks at the ready, well, most of Nomad Capitalist's clients are simply entrepreneurs and digital nomads who'd rather be smart about their finances than be tied to one particular place. Some become what is known as "perpetual travelers," or PTs (it's sometimes said to stand for "prior taxpayers"), hoping that if they never spend too long in any one place, they won't have to pay taxes anywhere. (Bonus: They'll probably never serve jury duty either.)

Countries don't all tax residents in the same way. Some only tax income you earned in their territory. Some tax you based on where you live, no matter where your income came from. Some, like Bermuda and the United Arab Emirates, have no personal taxes at all: no capital gains tax, no estate tax, nothing.[30] (Countries often make up for that with a stamp tax or really high sales tax.)

Then there's the United States, one of only two countries—the other is Eritrea—where taxes are based on your citizenship.[31] As Grace Taylor, an accountant whose clients are primarily Wanderers, either expats or digital nomads (she's a digital nomad herself), explained, "Let's say you settle down in Spain, and you live there for the rest of your life. You never set foot in the United States again. Potentially, you're still filing U.S. tax returns for the rest of your life."[32] Unless you renounce your U.S. citizenship, which some of Andrew's Nomad Capitalist clients do.

If you're an American digital nomad or expat who lives outside the United States for at least 330 days a year, you may, however, qualify for the foreign earned income exclusion that exempts a bit more than $100,000 of your income from American taxes.[33] "It can turn out to be a pretty advantageous answer for some of these digital nomads," Grace told me, "because they don't spend long enough in any foreign country to be a tax resident there, but they do spend long enough outside the U.S. to avail themselves of this particular exclusion." In other words, it's complicated—and reason you might hire an accountant like Grace rather than just plug numbers into TurboTax.

Flag theory notwithstanding, most Anywhereists aren't trying to get out of paying taxes altogether. Even if the foreign earned income exclusion went away tomorrow, Grace thinks her nomad clients would continue to be nomadic, drawn by the freedom, not the financial savings.[34]

But there's nothing wrong with optimizing your taxes where you live, even if you stay forever in your country of origin. In America, state governments rely on the idea that you will. In 2021, nine states—Alaska, Florida, Nevada, New Hampshire, South Dakota, Tennessee, Texas, Washington, and Wyoming—don't impose any personal state income tax at all, and most dangle that fact as a talent attraction gambit. That's likely one reason so many people said yes to Dallas—the marketing campaign's website reminded workers they'd save thousands in taxes by relocating to Texas.

State tax breaks goose mobility. According to a 2017 study by Enrico Moretti, an economist at UC Berkeley, and Daniel Wilson, vice president of microeconomic research at the Federal Reserve Bank of San Francisco, when New York cut its personal income tax rate for top earners from 7.5 percent to 6.85 percent in 2006, it attracted an extra three star scientists a year—the highly educated, well compensated elite in the top 5 percent for filing patents. That's not a bonanza, but as Moretti and Wilson pointed out, the effect can be exponential over time, increasing local innovation and attracting other scientists.[35]

Indeed, population is growing in no-income-tax states 109 percent faster than in the highest-tax states, like Oregon and Wisconsin. So are GDP and jobs, according to the American

Legislative Exchange Council, which suggests that living in a low-tax state makes you more likely to become self-employed, start a business, or hire other workers.[36]

As your bank account grows, so do the benefits of fleeing a high-tax state for a low-tax one. A 2019 *New York Times* article described a stampede of tech workers taking their IPO riches from California to Texas or Florida for the tax advantages. Facebook cofounder Eduardo Saverin gave up his U.S. citizenship and moved to Singapore.[37] Flag theory at work.

You probably don't have start-up millions to shelter. But according to SmartAsset.com's income tax calculator, if you're a single person making $100,000 in Honolulu, Hawaii, you can expect to pay $7,228 a year more in state taxes than if you were living in Hanover, New Hampshire.[38] That's not nothing.

Taxes are complicated, and if they figure largely in your location decision-making, you'd be wise to consult an accountant to double-check your math before you make a major move. If you're telecommuting, you may be taxed based on where your company is located, not where you are. You may pay titanic property taxes to make up for lower state income taxes. Or you may have to sift through multiple tax brackets to figure out what you'll owe. (California has nine.)[39]

Also, maybe my politics are showing, but take a hot minute to reflect on what taxes do for the place you live. No one loves to pay taxes, but when cities compete to attract and retain by boasting "We're the cheapest!", they're in a race to the bottom—and as Seth Godin said, "Every great brand (even those with low prices) is known for something other than how cheap they are."[40]

Tax money is what keeps your city running, so if you're a

Seeker, weigh what public money pays for to make a place attractive. Are the schools well ranked? Is the library stocked with the books you want to read? Are there useful public amenities like rec centers and swimming pools? Are the roads well maintained? Are there beautiful public parks or gardens? Does the city government seem well staffed and efficient? Is the police department responsive? If you can appreciate what you get for your money locally, you'll feel less resentment when you have to write the check.

Just think of it as a good investment in a town you love.

SPEND LESS, MAKE MORE

If you want to increase your net worth, you have two levers for doing it: earn more or spend less. A lot of practitioners of geographic arbitrage focus on the "spend less" part, moving to places where they can save money on housing, taxes, and general cost of living, making their income stretch further. Even businesses do it. A 2020 survey by the venture capital firm Initialized found that more than a third of the companies it funds intended to become fully remote (compared to one-fifth before the pandemic).[41] For them, delocating altogether by abandoning physical headquarters—essentially becoming corporate Wanderers—reduces overhead, creates more cash flow, and improves employee quality of life.

In 2017, the all-distributed software company Zapier made headlines for offering its eighty-five employees a $10,000 "delocation package" bonus to cover moving expenses for anyone who wanted to leave San Francisco. Zapier cofounder Wade Foster explained the thinking behind the geographic nudge in a company blog post. While the Bay Area was the tech-worker big leagues, its crippling cost of living kept employees in place-attachment limbo, feeling like they could never actually put down roots. "Despite loving the area, the realities are many of us need to look elsewhere to create the life we want for our families."[42]

Zapier made the boss move of giving all its employees, no matter their location, the Bay Area pay rate. Most employees were already making upward of $90,000 a year—a smidge below the median income in San Francisco, but almost double the median in a city like Indianapolis. This was a nod to the power of geographic arbitrage, Zapier's way of saying, "Take the money and run."

Not all companies with a distributed workforce are so generous. Some use a cost-of-living differentiator in their salary calculations to justify paying less to employees in LCOL areas. At tech company Buffer, a level 2 engineer in Barcelona makes only 85 percent of what they'd make with the same job title in Brooklyn.[43] Those kinds of salary adjustments render at least some of the potential of geographic arbitrage moot.

On the other hand, your geographic mobility may also make you nimbler when it comes to earning. Sharon Tseung, for instance, knew after a solo trip to Europe that she wanted to try her hand at nomadism, but she needed to figure out how to make it work financially. So she pored over YouTube videos about how digital nomads built businesses or worked remotely and gleaned tips from books like *Rich Dad, Poor Dad* and *The 4-Hour Workweek*.

A few key concepts hit her between the eyes: Money can buy you the freedom to design your life. Don't work for money; make money work for you. Build assets, not liabilities. If you don't want to work forever, build passive income streams.

Sharon, who'd always been preternaturally wise about finances (she bought a rental property at age twenty-two), got serious about developing micro businesses that she could manage abroad with little effort. On Etsy, Sharon started selling Photoshop and Microsoft Word templates that she designed herself. She joined Merch by Amazon, selling designs for print-on-demand apparel. Ads on her blog *DigitalNomadQuest* brought in a fairly steady stream of cash. "It was a total transition from actively working to passive income," Sharon said.

Once she was on the road, she logged expenses obsessively—her first year as a digital nomad cost her around $17,000—but her true religion was hustling to drive her passive income numbers higher. Two years later, when she returned to her hometown in the Bay Area, she had a higher net worth than when she left.[44]

For John Forberger, a B2B tech public relations freelancer, moving to Canada during the pandemic—which was possible because his partner is Canadian—allowed him to take advantage of a favorable exchange rate as he worked for U.S.-based clients. "People are really looking for that American dollar. We're basically living up here with 28 percent off everything."[45]

In other places, it might be easier to start a side hustle or launch a business. Maybe it's just more inspiring.

As life in Panama eased the Perkinses' financial pain, Susanna finally had the emotional bandwidth to contemplate pivoting her career. She'd been freelancing as a writer, designer, and website builder, but "before we went to Panama, I was so stressed about money that I was practically incapacitated," she said. "Finding the next project required a level of creative thought that was just almost impossible for me at that time."

She curled up with her laptop in a hammock and brainstormed

a website called WordPress Building Blocks, where she would teach readers how to build their own WordPress sites. Eight years later, the site is still her main source of income. If she hadn't moved to Panama, she doesn't think she would have ever launched it.

She wouldn't have created FutureExpats.com either, her website about retiring overseas. In 2012, Susanna posted a roundup of various quality-of-life rankings for cities worldwide. Most of the places in the top spots, from Vienna to Vancouver, British Columbia, were outrageously expensive.

But Susanna believes that if you're adventurous, an LCOL town can offer Anywhereists a great life. Though she and Mark have moved back to Florida to care for her husband's aging parents, they plan to return overseas in the future. For now, they're watching their kids become geographic arbitrage experts. During the pandemic, one of their sons, a software engineer, traded Seattle for the Caribbean island of Antigua. "He's seen firsthand the exodus that started from some of the expensive techie cities like San Francisco, Seattle, Boston, New York," Susanna said. "Why not go somewhere else? Where for $2,000 a month, you could have a three-thousand-square-foot house?"[46]

- -

Location Strategy Session: Wealth

Whatever their income, Anywhereists can make their location choice pay off by taking advantage of geographic arbitrage. Relocating to a place with less expensive housing, lower taxes, and an overall lower cost of living makes your income go further, reduces financial stress, and may even motivate you to explore new lines of work. Here are a few more ways to turn your place into a wealth-generation tool.

1. **Look beyond the biggest line items:** Housing and taxes consume the biggest chunk of the average budget, and they're typically what we think about when we think about geographic arbitrage. But don't ignore the other expenses that fluctuate from place to place—everything from child care to food to fuel. (Ever been gobsmacked on a road trip by how much less gas costs across state lines?) Make a budget to track your current expenses, and estimate how high or low they'll be in a new city.

2. **Eliminate a vehicle:** Ninety-five percent of Americans own a car, but if you opt for a walkable or bikeable city or one with reliable public transportation, you could save upward of $10,000 annually.[47] Simply cutting back on driving will save you money.

3. **Calculate the cost of moving:** According to the American Moving and Storage Association, the average long-distance move costs around $5,000; expect to pay more if you're moving overseas.[48] You can lower expenses by DIYing things like packing, driving your own U-Haul, or selling your furniture beforehand so there's less bulk to move. If the whole point is to save money with a move to an LCOL area, make sure you do the math for the actual relocation.

4. **Practice house hacking:** People who are serious

about FIRE often do something called house hacking by buying a multifamily duplex or apartment building, living in one unit, then renting out the others.[49] In an affordable city, that could cover your mortgage and hopefully bring in extra cash. Next-level house hacking? Get a roommate.

5. **Gauge fun money:** Living well means being able to afford to do activities you value, whether it's skiing, seeing a play, or eating at a five-star restaurant. You'll likely get the biggest break on entertainment and leisure activities overseas, but smart practices will save you money no matter where you live. Consider volunteering as an usher so you get into the play for free or eating lunch out, not dinner (it's nearly always cheaper).

6. **Beware surprise expenses:** If you intend to save money by moving to an old house in an LCOL area, you may be horrified to realize the house needs a new roof. And propane tanks are really expensive. And you run the heater more because the weather's colder. You can't possibly predict all the financial ripple effects of a move, so pad your savings account as a way to expect the unexpected.

7. **Follow geographic arbitrage influencers:** Some Anywhereists are transparent online about their spending in LCOL places and how it's affected their lives. One of my favorites is Our Rich Journey, a family that achieved FIRE and moved from San Francisco to Portugal (www.youtube.com/c/OurRichJourney).

Place Study: Wichita Falls, Texas

Population: 104,279

- **Peak cheapness:** According to the Best Places cost of living calculator, if 100 equals a totally average American cost of living, Wichita Falls rates 74.5. That makes it the fifth cheapest place in the country in 2021.[50] Housing is particularly inexpensive; if you're coming from San Francisco, expect to pay 93 percent less. Because it's Texas, no state income tax either!

- **Bang for your buck:** Think of Wichita Falls like a pre-*Fixer Upper* Waco—so much undiscovered potential. Buy a reno-ready bungalow with excellent bones for under $70,000, a third-acre lot in a new subdivision for $25,000, or a brick three-bedroom home in the neighborhood of $150,000. Renters rejoice too. Lots of historic buildings in the steadily revitalizing downtown have been turned into hip apartments. At the Austin School Lofts, an eighty-nine-year-old former elementary school, it costs $1,055 a month to rent a two-bedroom apartment with original classroom details preserved.

- **Who moves here:** Young families. California refugees. Retirees. Single women. Former military members with fond memories of their time in Wichita Falls. Or just people who did a Zillow search and saw that you can buy a house here for under $100,000. The common denominator: They're all looking for a lower cost of living.

- **What's here:** As home to Sheppard Air Force Base and Midwestern State University, a waterpark and an art museum, Wichita Falls is a great place to raise kids. The local high schools have a 99 percent graduation rate.

- **Just right:** A couple of hours from Dallas, Denton, and

Oklahoma City, Wichita Falls isn't a suburb or an exurb. It's a stand-alone town with its own thriving community. Realtor Debbie Dobbins, a transplant from California, calls Wichita Falls a "three bears community" because "it's not too big, it's not too small, it's just right." It's so affordable for her to live there that she's basically debt-free, and that allows her to run a business and donate to community causes.[51] The low cost of living makes it a great spot for single women too; they can afford to buy a house without the extra income from a partner.

- **Why it's so cheap:** Wichita Falls started life as an oil boom-town that eventually busted; later, its geographic isolation kept it small. So there's not the same shortage of housing inventory as there is in bigger cities. That may be changing with the arrival of investors eyeing a good deal and Californians willing to pay cash. Even so, people who move to Wichita Falls usually want its slower lifestyle. "We don't have traffic, so you can get from one end of the town to the other in fifteen minutes," said Debbie. "And it just feels friendlier than being in a big city."

DON'T MOVE TO SILICON VALLEY

Location Strategy Value: Entrepreneurship

Janee Allen figured you'd probably have to be close to a millionaire to start your own bakery in California.[1]

Janee Allen was not a millionaire.

She was a trained pastry chef who worked two jobs just to stay above the poverty line in Santa Cruz, California, where she lived with her husband, Knowles, a photographer. By day, Janee was an elementary school reading intervention specialist, by night a counselor in a group home. In the cracks between, she somehow found time to nurture her wild yeast starter as tenderly as a mother caring for a baby. Her coworkers sighed with pleasure at the sourdough loaves she baked.

In her fantasies, Janee imagined herself opening her own bread bakery, yet in Santa Cruz, she could never afford to make baking her livelihood. Money was a daily catastrophe. When their landlord raised the rent on their apartment from $1,400 to $1,600, she and Knowles had to move. Where would that extra $200 come from?

One day in 2015, Janee had an epiphany. *We can work pretty much anywhere. Why are we here?*

Janee wasn't a traditional Anywhereist with a laptop job, but she recognized that there are elementary schools all across the country, and she figured (correctly) that it wouldn't be too much effort to find a similar job in a new place. That summer, she and Knowles set out on a thirty-day cross-country camping trip to road test other parts of the country.

The couple fell in love with North Carolina, specifically Graham, a small town off I-40 halfway between Greensboro and Chapel Hill. Taxes were low. Housing prices felt silly after their experience in California (thanks, price anchoring!). They bought a thirteen-hundred-square-foot brick house on a forested acre that cost them less than $100,000. It was the most space they'd ever had in their adult lives.

The low cost of living in North Carolina gave them some financial breathing room, and Janee resurfaced the idea of starting her own bakery. She was going to call it Sour Bakery.

To test the waters, she delivered some bread samples to a meeting of local entrepreneurs. Afterward, the coordinator of the nearby North Park Farmers Market asked her if she'd open a stand there. The words running through Janee's head were *This is ridiculous.* "Yes" somehow came out of her mouth. She was dumbfounded by how immediately and intensely everyone in Graham wanted her to succeed. "Those foodies and entrepreneurs wanted Sour Bakery to be a part of Graham's growing economy," she told me.

Janee created a Kickstarter campaign to get the $5,000 she needed to rent a commercial kitchen space and buy initial supplies, and soon she was selling sourdough baked goods not only at the farmers market but to local restaurants and markets.

Her carbs are the killers of diets. They are the stuff of pastry dreams, golden brown, with flaky layers that shed all over your clothes. On Saturday mornings at the farmers market, she typically sells out her supply. Her regulars scoop up scones, pastry bars, and brioche rolls with glee.

Sour Bakery has done so well that at long last, Janee has quit her job at the elementary school and gone to baking full-time, the dream she'd had since culinary school that just wasn't possible in California. Likely none of her success would have happened if she hadn't moved to Graham, North Carolina.

THE ENTREPRENEUR WITHIN

There are a lot of Janee Allens out there. At least twenty-four million Americans imagine themselves someday becoming their own boss, according to a 2019 survey, though only about fifteen million Americans have actually taken the leap.[2] Entrepreneurship is easier to fantasize about than to figure out. Nearly 30 percent of brand-new businesses fail in their first two years.[3]

Even successful entrepreneurship doesn't always look like you'd expect, with fewer start-ups and retail storefronts, perhaps, than solo businesses or gig economy work. Simply being one of the one in three Americans who operates a side hustle makes you an entrepreneur.[4]

In a nutshell, entrepreneurs identify a market opportunity for a new product or service and act on it to make money. And Anywhereists are more likely than almost anyone to follow this unpaved path. Why?

First, they want the freedom. To work from anywhere as a remote employee relies on the good graces of your employer; they can retract the decision at will or put restrictions on where exactly you can live—for instance, only within the state where the company is based. If you want to be in charge of choosing your place and your work on a daily basis, you may have to become your own boss.

Second, if you're a Settler who is committed to living in a certain community, like your hometown, you may need to take up entrepreneurship to make it work. Limited local job opportunities in some rural communities and small towns can force the locals who really want to stay there to invent their own opportunities.

Third, there's a Venn diagram overlap in the personality types of people who become entrepreneurs and those who become Wanderers and Seekers. They're risk-takers, open to new adventures and ideas, inclined to forge their own paths. Whatever inner force compels a person to sell their house and strike out for Indonesia may be the same one that makes them launch their own Japanese translation company or house-sitting service.

Whether or not you're interested in running your own business, there are few Anywhereists who wouldn't benefit from a more entrepreneurial mindset, keen on problem solving, ideating, and flinging open the door when opportunity knocks. Even billion-dollar corporations have started incentivizing entrepreneurial activity from within to get employees to start thinking more like entrepreneurs. L'Oréal operates an internal incubator. Activision, the publisher of games like *World of Warcraft*, runs a competition each year in which teams of employees are given a

$5,000 budget to solve a real company challenge.[5] One study by Boston Consulting Group found that companies that innovate like this get four times the market share as their competitors do.[6] In modern corporate culture, entrepreneurially minded businesses and people are the ones that thrive.

Entrepreneurial places are more likely to thrive too. Research has shown that communities with high levels of entrepreneurial activity tend to see more local GDP growth, more wealth, and more job creation—a potential cascade of resources to invest in quality of life locally.[7] There's also the investment in local human potential. As Janee Allen discovered in Graham, living in an entre-preneurial ecosystem, among residents who are just as anxious as you are to get your business off the ground, pushes you to take risks and turn all your wildest ideas into moneymakers. These places create fertile ground for opportunity, and whether or not you ever intend to abandon the world of W2s, that merits a spot on your location strategy list.

THE AMBITIOUS CITY

"Great cities attract ambitious people," wrote Y Combinator cofounder Paul Graham. "You can sense it when you walk around one. In a hundred subtle ways, the city sends you a message: you could do more; you should try harder."[8]

Your town is your office, and in the same way that enthusiastic teammates or a particularly driven colleague can heighten your engagement with your work, an entrepreneurial community can spread its sense of motivation to residents. The vibe of collective striving propels you forward, in no small part because you want to make your place better.

In Bucksport, Maine, for instance, residents were figuring out economic next steps for the former paper mill town on the banks of the Penobscot River. As part of a revitalization effort, the town was building a waterfront walkway, but once you'd taken a walk, there was no place on Main Street to settle back and have a glass of wine. This was a gap to fill—always a good impetus for entrepreneurship—and Colleen and Michael Gross noticed because the grapes they grew in their own Bucksport backyard were starting to make a decent wine.[9]

Hitting economic rock bottom as a community had spurred a risk-taking mentality for residents like the Grosses. What was there to lose? With a vision of running a European-style tapas and wine bar, Colleen and Michael leased the 1824 Heywood House in downtown Bucksport—and were instantly inundated with support. Their neighbors were ecstatic. "Everybody had a positive feeling about the potential for this little town," said Colleen. "And so they were thrilled that there was something sort of tangible and concrete that was being done."

Lickety-split, the town helped them apply for a business license. The bank offered a fantastic business loan. The economic development office showered them with resources on business management, while the chamber of commerce promoted the restaurant, Verona Wine and Design. "The momentum was unbelievable," Colleen said.

Even the owner of another restaurant in town, MacLeod's, peppered them with advice. When I mentioned to Colleen how surprising I thought it was that a small business owner would help a potential competitor, she said, "George's philosophy was the more, the better." A rising tide lifts all boats.

Opening the doors to a new business, which the Grosses did in June 2016, is no small feat. Keeping them open is another matter entirely. Nationwide, the rate of new employer business actualization—a measure of whether you hire employees within two years of opening—is less than 10 percent. Indeed, at Verona Wine and Design, Michael and Colleen mostly managed the foundling restaurant on their own, working around Colleen's job as an occupational therapy assistant with the local school district and Michael's as the shop teacher at the high school.

But shortly things got busier, and they hired help. Now they employ up to seven people in the summer high season, and Colleen's quit her job to manage the restaurant full-time. COVID was hard, with just a couple of parties at a time allowed inside. But Verona Wine and Design is still hanging on, a testament to all the Bucksport residents who wanted the Grosses to succeed for their sake and the town's and who made them believe the leap was possible.

Some cities seem to naturally cultivate a community-wide sense of entrepreneurial possibility, even when the ambition comes from outside the town. Ludington, Michigan, for instance, is a land of cherry orchards and small farms, a place that bred an entrepreneurial pioneer spirit into locals. It's an energy that Chris and Jenna Simpler have felt as they settle into the area as innkeepers.[10]

Looking for a bed-and-breakfast property where "a guest could walk out the front door and walk right into downtown, past the shops, the restaurants, bars, right to the lake or the beach," the Simplers' location strategy wish list was as long as your arm. They were amazed when the old Cartier Mansion in Ludington, a town of eighty-one hundred on the shores of Lake Michigan, ticked 98 percent of their boxes.

At the time, they were living in New York, so they started reaching out to community members, "who accepted us as if we are from the area," said Chris. "There's no 'you're an outsider. Who are you coming into our town bringing your big city ideas?'" The Ludington Bed and Breakfast Association, made up of seven small inns, functioned like a single organism. The town was ambitious together, making it possible for two Anywhereists to arrive and be absorbed by a shared ethos of success.

For your location strategy, ask yourself: What kind of place would make you believe in your own capabilities? What kind of place would push you toward more ambitious goals? What kind of place would urge you to realize a dream you've been pondering for months or years? And then would offer you the resources to make big things happen for yourself?

SIROLLI AND THE HIPPOS

In the end, it's not enough for entrepreneurialism and opportunity to be a vague feeling in the air. As an Anywhereist, you want to live in a place that actually helps you do your job better, whether you're growing your business, looking to launch a new one, or just trying to get ahead as a remote worker. True entrepreneurial ecosystems have solid resources to get you where you want to be.

When Rani Navarro Force started dreaming of opening a gluten-free bakery in tiny Wathena, Kansas, one of the first people she called was Teresa McAnerney of the nonprofit Northeast Kansas Enterprise Facilitation (NKEF). "What do I need to do to start a business here in Kansas?" she asked.[11]

Rani had already found a space for rent in a former coffee

shop in Wathena, population two thousand, and she knew she had the goods to sell there. A coworker sampling one of her gluten-free blueberry muffins had raved, "It tastes just like a regular muffin, but it's, like, way better!" Her breads, cupcakes, and cinnamon rolls came from recipes Rani developed when her teenage daughter, Stephanie, was crippled by a severe gluten allergy, and everyone agreed they were delicious.

As to whether it made sense to open a niche business in a town where foot traffic was as slow as the tractors trundling down the main drag, Teresa McAnerney put Rani's mind at ease. An energetic blond and a natural-born networker, Teresa seemed to know every entrepreneur in a five-county region, and she worked her connections doggedly to knock past obstacles with finances, infrastructure, markets, policy, culture, or talent. If she didn't know the answer, she knew who would. All Rani had to do was ask.[12]

The asking was important. NKEF bases its economic gardening approach on the Sirolli method, pioneered by a graying Italian man named Ernesto Sirolli. At age twenty-one, Sirolli moved from Italy to Africa to work for an NGO. For his first project, he and his colleagues aimed to teach Zambians living near the Zambezi River how to grow tomatoes and zucchini. Such a fertile valley! Why didn't they have any agriculture? No worries. The Italians would fix that!

Congratulating themselves for arriving in the nick of time to save the Zambians from starvation, Sirolli and his colleagues planted beautiful tomatoes that grew as lushly as if they were under an Italian sun. It was a triumph!

Then one night, two hundred hippos emerged from the river

and ate absolutely everything. As Sirolli described it in a TED Talk, the anguished Italians exclaimed, "My God, the hippos!"

"Yes, that's why we have no agriculture here," replied the Zambians.

"Why didn't you tell us?"

"You never asked."

Shaken by this experience, Sirolli decided that to drive a community's success, he needed to ask first rather than foist his goals on others. From then on, he began to work like a professional matchmaker, connecting the good ideas bubbling up in a community to whatever outside knowledge and resources were needed to make them happen. "You become a servant of the local passion, the servant of local people who have a dream to become a better person," he explained.[13]

In a fishing village in Western Australia, Sirolli helped link a Maori man smoking fish in a garage to a restaurant in Perth willing to buy it. When word got around, five more fishermen came to him. Sirolli advised them to ship their fresh-caught tuna to Japan, where it sold for $15 a kilo instead of the 60 cents they were getting at the local cannery. Within a year, Sirolli was helping with twenty-seven different projects. He called his method "enterprise facilitation," and it has since been used in more than three hundred communities worldwide to start forty thousand businesses.[14]

The key to the method is that no one works alone. To be successful, Sirolli said, entrepreneurs have to create a great product, market it, and manage their company's finances. That's at least one to-do too many. It's almost impossible to execute all three jobs well, at least by yourself. Facilitators like Teresa McAnerney function as bridges between local entrepreneurs and the help they need—talent, technology, advice, money, encouragement—to thrive.

In the five largely rural northeastern Kansas counties where Teresa works, she's faithful to the Sirolli method of serving the local passion, meaning she'll never approach you first. But the second you mention that you might be interested in starting a business, it's go time. She'll pepper you with questions: What are your hopes for your business? What do you want to achieve? What kind of help do you need? She'll teach you how write a business plan. She'll hand out your business cards at McDonald's. Levels of self-employment are slightly higher in rural areas than suburbs and cities, as business ownership becomes a way of Anywhereist life. Teresa will do all she can to make sure your business survives here.

She'll likely also invite you to a monthly meeting of NKEF's Board of Knowledge, a brain trust of about seventy-five area entrepreneurs and small business owners who dispense advice from the banquet room of a local restaurant. When Marie Antoinette Bakery, the gluten-free cafe in Wathena, wasn't cash flowing the way she wanted it to, Rani Navarro Force asked the Board of Knowledge for ideas. "Diversify income streams!" they told her. In small towns with limited foot traffic, "we always ask our clients, 'What can you sell out the back door?'" Teresa said.

NKEF members helped Rani devise a plan for selling her baked goods wholesale and connected her with a food scientist at Kansas State University who could test her recipes for nutritional value and shelf life. With a business loan NKEF helped arrange, Rani was able to find a facility to manufacture and package them. Now Marie Antoinette's gluten-free products are being sold in 175 midwestern grocery stores.

None of these services costs clients anything. Teresa gets paid by contributions from the five counties that form the NKEF. Everyone else, including the members of the Board of Knowledge, is a volunteer, often former recipients of NKEF assistance themselves. "We just want to help people," said Teresa. "It really is altruistic."

Of course, not purely altruistic. In the same way that Remote Shoals isn't solely about enriching remote workers, NKEF has an ulterior motive for building the region's entrepreneurial ecosystem: the potential for more jobs, higher tax revenues, and simple financial survival for places whose residents might otherwise hunt down their Anywhereist dreams anywhere else. They want your business to succeed not just because it's fulfilling for you, but because your success has a wider economic value for all your neighbors.

But there's also value in the civic economy that entrepreneurs create, one that makes life better for residents community-wide. In one study from the Netherlands, local business owners were more likely to intervene in neighborhood problems; researchers suspected that spending more time locally gave them more opportunities to act on behalf of their place but also that they had a greater belief in their own abilities to solve problems.[15] Meanwhile, a study out of Baylor University indicated that highly educated people—the kind of talent every city wants to attract and retain—are more likely to stay in their community when there's an abundance of local retailers, who are seen as integral to quality of life.[16]

In eighteen years, NKEF has helped over fifteen hundred clients. Over 266 businesses have started as a result. Recently, the Board of Knowledge helped Rani find a building so the bakery could expand its production line. For a while, Rani thought about moving the business to a larger city with better supply chains. But she's attached to rural Kansas now and grateful for all the help she's received there. So she stayed.

HIGH-POTENTIAL GEOGRAPHIES

Entrepreneurship, even for solo practitioners like me, revolves around relationships. As Olav Sorenson, a sociologist with the Yale School of Management, wrote, "Seeing others, particularly those who one knows and perceives as similar to oneself, engaged in entrepreneurship encourages people to become entrepreneurs themselves."[17] Mere proximity to entrepreneurs in your town makes you believe you can do what they're doing, helps you identify business opportunities, and legitimizes the path as a career choice. When your neighbors are entrepreneurs, it increases the odds that you'll try it too.

Being among the right people in the right place has traditionally helped entrepreneurs find funding as well. In the United States, 78 percent of venture capital goes to entrepreneurs in just three states—California, Massachusetts, and New York.[18] I once heard a venture capitalist from Manhattan explain that when she finds a business she's interested in, she'll invest only if the founders are willing to relocate the company to New York, so she can provide coaching, connections, and supply-chain guidance within her own local network.

At venture capital firm Sequoia, whose headquarters are in Menlo Park, California, a mile from Stanford University, the location rule is even stricter: if they can't ride a bicycle to the business, they won't invest.[19] (One of their first investments in

1977 was a little company called Apple, so it appears to be working for them.)

That "here only" approach may be changing. These days, some investment firms aim to fund businesses precisely *because* they're outside the major hubs of San Francisco, Los Angeles, Boston, and New York. Steve Case, the founder of AOL, named his seed fund "Rise of the Rest" because he's targeting what he calls "high-potential geographies," mostly midsize cities with up-and-coming entrepreneurial ecosystems like Salt Lake City, Richmond, Birmingham, and Lexington.[20] (Bonus for Anywhereists looking to live there: As writer Patrick Sisson points out, midsize cities offer "a more approachable, neighborhood-oriented version of the urban lifestyle that sent many to the larger cities in the first place.")[21]

There are also places offering business investment as a talent attraction strategy. A local competition in Cape Girardeau, Missouri, for instance, awards entrepreneurs $50,000 to relocate and grow their businesses there for at least a year.[22] A program called Start-Up Chile is even more ambitious. With funding from the Chilean government, in its first year, it gave about USD $25,000 to twenty-two startups from fourteen different countries, along with free office space, mentoring, and visas for founders willing to live there and work on their projects for six months. Their goal: To turn Chile into one of the world's foremost entrepreneurial ecosystems.[23]

In the post-COVID world, the links between geography and investment money may be loosening up. "Everyone's investing everywhere, and people are taking meetings with anybody anywhere," said Anywhereist Rina Patel, the founder and CEO of SHE, an online social and emotional wellness community for female-identifying teens. Rina's a Wanderer who cherishes her place autonomy so highly that she was the only member of her MBA graduating class who declined an office job, for fear it would hamstring her ability to choose where to live. "Maybe that's a very millennial thing," she laughs. Launching her own start-up allows her to stay geographically mobile—and to take off to Miami when she hears lots of young entrepreneurs are living there these days.[24]

Recently, on a call with potential investors, Rina was advised, "If an investor tells you you have to move to a city for them to invest in you, run the other way. That should not be a prerequisite of investment in your company at all." You can get money for a big idea and remain an Anywhereist. On the other hand, many smaller-scale sources of financing are still local, offered by banks, credit unions, and nonprofits that are more likely to say yes when they know you. Even crowdfunding, which Janee Allen did for Sour Bakery, calls on local funders.

For most entrepreneurs, though, the most common source of start-up capital is your own savings. The right place can help with that too.

When Arianna O'Dell quit her New York City job on a whim, she (semi-legally) subleased her apartment for $400 monthly profit and used the extra cash to move to Barcelona, Spain. When imminent poverty threatened, she started her own marketing and design agency, becoming one of the 30 percent of entrepreneurs who create a business out of necessity and not choice. Later, she added an e-commerce store and a songwriting business to her entrepreneurial portfolio.

If your life in New York City costs $5,000 a month, your comparable expenses in Santiago de Compostela, Spain, will likely run you $1,786, about a 60 percent savings. For Arianna, geographic arbitrage essentially allowed her to be her own venture capitalist, self-funding her business and her life with the money she saved—about $6,000 in five months.[25]

The willingness of people in your place to invest—fiscally and emotionally—creates a sense of possibility that's useful for Anywhereists no matter what kind of work you do. And it allows you to live where you want. As Garrett Moon wrote in *Entrepreneur* magazine, "in the modern era of entrepreneurship, location shouldn't stop anyone from starting a company. In fact, it could actually become a great asset."[26]

WE ALL DO BETTER WHEN WE ALL DO BETTER

Local economies are complex bits of machinery. It's impossible to pinpoint a single element that makes the difference between a vibrant town of bustling storefronts and a place littered with run-down strip malls.

But we know that, in general, entrepreneurial communities generate more of the economic activity that raises local GDP, and they're more likely to innovate solutions to their own economic and community problems and to bounce back from cycles of boom and bust. "Against the backdrop of a weak global economy, we regularly see a strong local economy in cities such as Boulder that have a high entrepreneurial density," wrote entrepreneurial ecosystem expert Brad Feld in his book *Startup Communities*.[27]

During the pandemic, some of the most resilient communities

were the ones that had an apparatus designed to support local
ambition and entrepreneurship. In Dubuque, Iowa, for instance,
Jordan DeGree regularly coached small-town entrepreneurs at
his Innovation Lab, a downtown accelerator and coworking space
where he met with small-town entrepreneurs. The shutdown in
spring 2020 threatened Jordan's business model just like it threatened everyone else's.[28]

His bold idea: What about getting community organizations
to fund free coaching for all the small business owners trying to
survive this? A utilities board kicked in money, as did a bank and
a community foundation. Innovation Labs pivoted to Survival
Coaching, virtual one-on-one sessions with entrepreneurs like
yoga teacher Molly Schreiber, who was frantic about the mind-
fulness program she ran at more than thirty elementary schools,
all now closed for the pandemic. "I'm going to lose my contract,"
she told Jordan. "We have to lay off employees. I don't know if I'm
going to be able to keep running my business."

Jordan said, "Okay, that's a good place to start."

Within a few sessions, he'd helped her figure out how to move
her services online. The new virtual model took off. Less than
a year later, Molly's program had exploded to 215 schools. She'd
hired five new employees and had increased her overall revenue
by 300 percent.

Of the more than one hundred businesses that Jordan and
his two teammates coached in the first year of the pandemic, 85
percent reported positive business growth. That means the small
midwestern towns where these entrepreneurs live probably did
better too, and Jordan thinks that's a victory for Anywhereism.
"If we become this homogenized one-size-fits-all country,"

Jordan told me, "you lose the ability to really give people that opportunity to choose the where, the what, and the how that's right for them."

When entrepreneurs thrive, so do Anywhereists. You may not ever run the kind of business that requires a Survival Coaching session or, like Janee Allen, open a brick-and-mortar bakery that decides your fate as a Settler. But being in a community with an apparatus of support, mentorship, and financial investment for entrepreneurs means you could if you want to—a satisfying thought. And a local culture of ambition and opportunity may make you more successful in whatever Anywhereist work you do, not to mention happier in an increasingly vibrant place. We all do better when we all do better.

Location Strategy Session: Entrepreneurship

Anywhereists don't have to run their own businesses to benefit from a place's strong entrepreneurial ecosystem, which can help you be bold, take risks, and bring good ideas to fruition in your work and your life. Here's how to find and support the entrepreneurs in your community— and maybe become one.

1.   **Look up your chamber of commerce:** In most com- munities, the chamber of commerce is the epicenter of resources for small business owners. Show up for networking events, sign up for a boot camp, maybe even join a committee. More chambers actively aim to serve remote workers now too.

2. **Sign up for coaching:** Having someone local look at your business can help you connect to the creativity and innovation that Jordan DeGree says are key to collective success. If you can't find a free program, you might hire a successful entrepreneur in your community to consult with you.

3. **Invest locally:** When I typed the name of my town into Kickstarter's search bar, eighty-one projects popped up for funding. A local artist wanted help printing a comic book. An entrepreneur was opening a wine bar. Another had plans for a tie-dye T-shirt shop. Throw some money at the entrepreneurial dreams of people living in your place.

4. **Participate in a start-up week:** Entrepreneurially minded communities host events like business plan competitions that are open to the public (and often rely on audience participation and voting).

5. **Join 1 Million Cups—or bring it to your community:** 1 Million Cups is a free program started by the Kauffman Foundation with chapters in 150 communities nationwide, from Aberdeen, South Dakota, to Yuba City, California. Entrepreneurs and community members gather over coffee and provide group brainstorming and feedback to a different entrepreneur each time. Find them at 1MillionCups.com.

6. **Read the local business publication:** Bigger communities like Kansas City and Cleveland offer magazines, online or in print, to document the goings-on of the local business community. If a city has one (or

even a dedicated business section in the local newspaper), it's a good indicator it's building an entrepreneurial ecosystem.

7. **Learn how to start a business:** What would it take
to start the side hustle you've been dreaming about?
Your town's website should tell you what you need
to do. Bonus if you can apply for a business license
online.

Place Study: Camden, Maine

Population: 4,850

- **Proximity to the ocean:** 0 miles, although the harbor officially sits on Penobscot Bay.
- **Famous for:** Being a summer home to wealthy elites, like
author David McCullough and filmmaker J. J. Abrams.
- **Why it's a great place to build a business:** Because living rural
requires Anywhereist ingenuity. When Alissa Hessler fell in love
with the man who would become her husband, he had just
signed the mortgage papers for a home in midcoast Maine.
A native Californian, Alissa's idea of Maine was "Lobsters and
cold." Love won anyway, and she quit her job doing global
product launches for a tech company to move there. To make
money, Alissa and Jacob launched a graphic design firm, built
websites, took photos, wrote copy, and developed marketing
plans for local businesses. They also started teaching destination photography workshops. "I was taking those skills that I'd
had from all those different careers that I'd had in the city and
creating something for myself," she said—something she never
would have done if she'd stayed in a city.[29]

- **Why rural barriers to entry are lower:** There are more holes to fill and less competition. Lower overhead helps too. Alissa advises people to research what's missing locally—a coffee shop? a bookstore? a tutoring center?—and supply it. One couple who opened a brewery in another small town in Maine asked their neighbors what they wanted, then created it (live music, an outdoor pizza oven, wintertime knitting circles). "When [rural residents] see young people move in, and those people are willing to talk to people and start something, they're really supportive," said Hessler. Now, "the whole town feels like they're invested in this business."

- **Fantasy vs. reality:** Since moving to Maine, the Hesslers have started a hobby farm. It's not as glamorous as it sounds, what with scrubbing poop and chopping wood. "I would say that I work much harder here than I did in the city. But it's all work that feels much more fulfilling."

- **Weird money thing:** In rural areas, people like to barter services. In exchange for marketing and design work, Alissa's gotten acupuncture, frozen chickens, and Thai food from her favorite Asian restaurant in Camden.

- **Small-town side project:** To chronicle the stories of other city folk who go rural, Alissa launched UrbanExodus.com, a website that became a book, then a podcast. From talking to so many rural Anywhereists, she knows they're looking for self-reliance, access to nature, a higher quality of life, and an ability to buy more with their money. "If you can buy a studio apartment in Queens, you can buy a five-bedroom house with acreage in a rural area," Alissa said. "If you can do what you're doing and you don't have to live in the city, why are you?"

7

THE COLLEAGUE IN THE
NEIGHBORHOOD

Location Strategy Value: Connection

Kate Schwarzler had been visiting Independence, Oregon (population ten thousand), for years before she had an epiphany: "I love it here. Here's my chance to build a life that I want in a place that I want to live in."[1]

Independence was where Kate's parents lived, and over holidays and long summer weekends, she'd watched its piecemeal economic revitalization come together in slow-motion snippets: a restored downtown building one visit, a new bakery the next.

She wondered how her work as a landscape architect would fit in there. In Denver, where she lived, if one job wound down, you just found another in the city. Independence was more like the tiny lumber town where Kate had grown up, so utterly dependent on a single industry that when logging fell apart, so did Halsey, population nine hundred. The message Kate got in Independence was, "If you want a good job, you better bring it with you."

So Kate did. First she started her own landscape architecture consulting business, CREO Solutions. That was going well, but she missed working in an office with colleagues. Hidden around Independence, she suspected, were Anywhereists just like her— remote workers, freelancers, entrepreneurs, and consultants who also yearned for a built-in work community.

A beautiful old opera house in downtown Independence had sat vacant for ten years. On a whim, Kate called the landlord and told him she wanted to start a coworking space there. The landlord agreed and offered to do some renovations to get the building up to snuff. By April 2016, Kate had opened the doors to Indy Commons.

Much has been written about the rise and bitter fall of coworking spaces, the most famous being WeWork, which was started by a couple of entrepreneurs who had the idea to rent out empty office space in their Brooklyn building. By 2015, WeWork operated fifty-four coworking spaces around the globe, with thirty thousand clients fraternizing across the foosball tables and other coworking spaces, including luxurious all-female the Wing, crowding in on market share.[2]

For WeWork, things went sour in 2020 when, amid reports of mismanagement and hazy finances, the company's $47 billion valuation plummeted 70 percent within a month. Eccentric cofounder and CEO Adam Neumann stepped down. Ultimately, plans for an IPO were shelved altogether.[3]

On the other hand, places like WeWork aren't just renting office space. They're selling the idea of a mutually enriching work community, and the concept retains rabid fans. Among WeWork members, 54 percent said that WeWork had helped accelerate the growth of their company.[4] In another survey, 90 percent of people who used any coworking space at all were pleased with their decision.[5]

Though the very idea of the office has taken a beating during the pandemic (sample headline: "Death of the Office" in April 2020's *Economist*), credit where credit is due, it does one thing really well: brings humans together in the same space.[6]

We tend to like that. Some workers pine for it. In one October 2020 study of seven hundred full-time employees who had switched to working remotely in the pandemic, the top thing people said they missed was social connections with colleagues, followed closely by human contact in general. Also on the wish list: face-to-face meetings, lunch with coworkers, collaborating in person, casual run-ins with others, and learning from others. About a third of remote workers even wanted access to a little more watercooler chat.[7]

Tech talent is arguably the best equipped to keep their jobs remote forever. According to one survey, almost half of tech workers moved during the pandemic, a sign that they were distancing themselves from the concept of daily work in an office. Yet postpandemic, three out of four clamored to return to work in an office (though more than two-thirds preferred a hybrid model that didn't require showing up five days a week).[8]

Studies have shown that being physically among coworkers makes collaboration and relationship building easier, leads to better communication, gives you broader knowledge about your job, and makes you more innovative.[9] The more serendipitously colleagues interact, the better the outcomes.[10]

But at least part of the appeal is that we're inherently social creatures. Or at least other people are. Not so much me, I assumed. As an introverted solopreneur, I'd always worked alone.

Then early in the pandemic, I tried out a virtual coworking space called Caveday for an assignment. For each session, I logged into a Zoom room with one hundred or so strangers. Together, we'd grind through three hour-long work sprints punctuated by short stretching breaks.

At least once a session, we'd be shunted into digital breakout rooms with two or three other "cave dwellers" with whom we'd talk about what we planned to work on and what we hoped to ignore, like email or existential dread. Occasionally, we discussed a prompt provided by the session's host: "What band did you listen to when you were thirteen?" "What's your best trick for being productive?"

Frankly, I'd never really seen the appeal of coworkers. In a brief, early-twenties stint of working in an office before I went freelance, I dreaded the daily interludes when an older colleague would fill me in on every last morsel of workplace gossip, including the drinking problems of the company's owner. *Just leave me alone and let me get back to work!* I wanted to say and never did. I quit instead.

So Caveday surprised me. Working alongside other people—just a gallery of tiny faces in Zoom—I found myself unexpectedly energized. And accountable. Distraction would hit, and I'd stare at these focused strangers for inspiration and redirection. I had no idea, really, what other people were doing, but it was clear that everyone was working hard, their lips pursed in concentration, their eyes squinted in the glow of the computer screen. One guy wrote inscrutable math equations on a whiteboard, *A Beautiful Mind* style.

The boost of productivity I got from knowing everyone in my immediate (virtual) vicinity was working surprised me, even though social scientists have known for a long time that people tend to work harder if they sense they have an audience. After I filed the article about Caveday, I became a member. (Most of this book was written in the Cave.)

I'm not advocating for Zoom and other tech tools to replace in-person interactions. I'm saying that interactions of all kinds matter and probably even more within your chosen geography.

When you can work from anywhere, you get to choose where you live. But you also get to choose exactly where you do your daily work. The couch? A home office? It's worth considering what exactly that should look like. What kind of work environments make you feel energetic? Productive? Connected? Do you like working alone, or would you rather invite a few more humans into your life?

As an Anywhereist, your town is your office, so that makes your "coworkers" the people in your community. Potentially, they're also your future office mates. You might want to find room for them as part of your location strategy.

THE CLUSTER

We do well when we're around people doing the same kind of work we are. Call it the personal economy version of cluster theory.

In economic development, cluster theory is the idea that industries grow and excel when they congregate together. Writing in the *Harvard Business Review* twenty years ago, Harvard Business School professor Michael Porter explained that the "economic map of the world is dominated by what I call clusters: critical masses—in one place—of unusual competitive success in particular fields."[11]

Furniture manufacturers in North Carolina. Mutual fund companies in Boston. High-end shoemakers in northern Italy. Even when you can order anything you want with the click of a button, "the enduring competitive advantages in a global economy lie increasingly in local things—knowledge, relationships, motivation—that distant rivals cannot match."[12]

It's like the Shoals trying to attract tech workers so tech companies start to settle there. Once one tech company comes, others often follow. Similar businesses in the same place can collaborate, draw on a larger and better-trained talent pool, and find economies of scale by sharing supply chains. For an Anywhereist, cluster theory works like this: you may benefit from locating somewhere where other people are like you. Either they do what you do for a living, or they do what you do for fun.

That was the idea for Ryan Mita, who does B2B sales for a children's book company. He lived in Brooklyn when the pandemic hit and watched as friends and coworkers fled the city. One designer from his publishing company moved home to Florida. A marketing person relocated to Nashville. "I think almost everybody from the team now lives outside New York," he told me.[13]

So when his lease ended in October 2020, Ryan moved to Austin, Texas, for two cluster theory–motivated reasons. First, he had a few friends there whose social networks he could leverage. Second, he knew Austin was home base for several big educational technology companies, and he was looking to pivot into that field. Zoom helped connect him to friends of friends who lived locally, and he hit up existing contacts to find access to the companies he was interested in.

Socially, Austin was harder than Ryan expected. Sometimes his New York brain was flummoxed by the Southern friendliness of Austinites, like the cashier making small talk in the grocery store. Was she hitting on him? Was he supposed to ask her out? Anywhereists face the added complication of having to construct new social and business networks simultaneously without the easy entry point of new colleagues. "The main way most of us are connected to our local, geographical communities is through work," Sean Blanda, a location-independent editorial director for a tech company, told the *Guardian*. "When you remove that, you have to work harder to feel connected."[14]

Socializing *is* literally work. One study included it as one of four categories of labor typically performed by digital nomads. (The others were articulation work like planning, scheduling, and organizing; deep work like writing, editing, or coding; and collaboration work like communicating with clients or cocreators—arguably another kind of social work.)[15]

Whether or not the day's labors require you to collaborate or network may change the kind of environment you prefer to work in. Perhaps a private home office or studio fits the bill for deep work, which often requires solitude. But for socializing, collaboration, and even low-focus articulation work, you may prefer to be among others who are working like you. A coworking space can do the trick.

Ryan's preferred space was Caveday, where I first met him. But Anywhereists who are Seekers or Wanderers would be better served by an in-person location. According to one study, nine in ten workers report being happier after joining a coworking space. For work, it's a boon. The vast majority say their coworking space expanded their business network and made them more productive. Half said coworking led to new work opportunities.[16]

That was the case for Esther Inman, an Anywhereist who moved to Bali while her husband, a marine, was deployed. Part of the draw was Bali's extensive coworking culture. It seemed like practically all the expat entrepreneurs and digital nomads on the island gathered in a dozen or so coworking spaces.[17]

Esther found the energy there electrifying. "You're in a place where everybody is doing cool things," she said. "So that disbelief of 'Oh, I can't do that. That'll be too hard. No one wants to listen to me'—a lot of that goes away when you're surrounded by a community of people who are like, 'No, yeah, totally.'"

In a way, an active coworking space can become its own micro entrepreneurial ecosystem, with people validating each other's ideas and providing instant mentoring on the fly. It's proof of concept, right at the desk next to yours, that if you work hard, you too can do cool things.

Working amid so much hustle and ambition was not only emotionally empowering for Esther, but practically helpful. She'd been running an online placement agency for virtual assistants but was considering switching her focus to building an online training course. At her Canggu coworking space, her fellow digital nomads were enthusiastic. Many of them had built online courses themselves. "Everybody's like, 'Yeah, you should do that. Here's all the reasons why. Here's how we can help you. I have this resource. You should go on her podcast,'" Esther remembered. "Whereas [in America], who would I have even talked to about that? Maybe a virtual Zoom with my mentor? It's just very different."

Generous resource sharing made the impossible feel doable.

One of Esther's friends in Bali launched a fashion line, despite knowing very little about the industry, because fellow coworkers knew a good factory down the road.

Some coworking spaces are so good at nourishing innovation that they function more like informal incubators or accelerators, organizations designed to help businesses launch and grow. With so many entrepreneurs and big thinkers working in close quarters, the community makes everyone think a little larger and work a little harder.

For Wanderers like Esther, coworking spaces also become, in the parlance of sociologist Ray Oldenburg, "third places"—not quite the office (because people choose to be there), not home either, but something in between that nurtures connections and creates community.[18] In Bali, Esther relied socially on the friendships she formed at her coworking space's nightly talks and networking events.

Now living slightly reluctantly in Asheville, North Carolina, Esther still runs the online program she created in Bali, Virtual Assistant Internship. Over four thousand students have enrolled. She's also actively working to foster the same kind of community she enjoyed overseas. She chose Asheville in part because it had an active community of entrepreneurs and a network of coworking spaces she could join.

Things might not be the same in Asheville, she knows. But if they aren't, she'd consider opening her own coworking space. She'll make it just like the one she loved in Canggu.

FRIENDSHIP IS LIKE DATING

When Anywhereists work together, they're more likely to be successful. They're also more likely to be social. A substantial 83 percent said that coworking made them less lonely. More than half said that they were hanging out with coworking colleagues after work or on the weekends.[19]

That's not insignificant, because according to a survey by insurance provider Cigna, loneliness is on the rise, with 61 percent of American adults saying they feel lonely always or sometimes.[20] The toll is both psychic and physical. In a summary of several studies, a team of Brigham Young University professors came to the alarming conclusion that chronic loneliness and isolation can be as dangerous to your health as obesity, alcoholism, or a pack-a-day smoking habit, ultimately shortening your life span by about five years.[21]

Not everyone who's alone feels lonely. Loneliness creeps through the gap between the level of connection you want and the level of connection you have. Depending on your personality and your system of social support, being a remote worker or freelancer Anywhereist may make you miss the contact of regular human relationships—or not.

In general, though, loneliness is increasing for most of us for factors as varied and pervasive as social media (73 percent of heavy users of social media say they feel lonely), mental health challenges, uncertainty, and life transitions like divorce, retirement, or, ahem, moving to a new town.[22] Being a remote worker can exacerbate the feeling too.

In 2010, execs at Chinese travel agency Ctrip wanted to see if they could save the rent they were spending on the company's pricey offices in Shanghai by transitioning employees to working from home. About 125 call center workers volunteered to beta test the idea.

After nine months, the remote work group proved to be about 13 percent more productive than their colleagues in the office, with fewer breaks and sick days and more calls completed. Ctrip's executives were over the moon! Look at the millions they could save by sending everyone home!

Then came the bad news. Half of the home-based group—all of whom had a spare room to work in and no children or roommates at home—wanted to go back to working in an office. Why? According to study leader Nicholas Bloom, an economics professor at Stanford, "loneliness was the single biggest reason."[23]

One in five remote workers was already saying loneliness was their biggest challenge before the pandemic.[24] During the pandemic's enforced isolation, things predictably got worse, with more than half of the workers in a British survey citing loneliness as the reason they wanted to return to an office. "I think young people in particular really need that connection," said Matt Bradburn, the cofounder of London-based People Collective, the human resources consultancy that conducted the survey.[25]

We're all prone to loneliness—Wanderers because they're rarely in a single place long enough to develop sturdy social ties, Seekers because they may be facing the major life transition of moving and then reestablishing networks in a new place. Even Settlers have to beware that their investment in their existing social network doesn't keep them from expanding their circle from time to time.

As an Anywhereist, you have to be intentional about building and maintaining an in-person social network for yourself where you live. Strictly online just won't cut it. Without friends who'll team up with you for trivia night at the bar or neighbors who'll feed your dog when you go out of town, you'll struggle to feel at home anywhere.

Tiffany Yates Martin jokes that there should be a Match.com for friends. An Anywhereist writer and editor, she moved to Austin in 2007 and within a week met her future husband, Joel. Yet she still remembers it as a relatively lonely year.[26]

Every other time Tiffany had moved, she'd had a built-in work, school, or social community waiting for her in the new location. Austin was the first city she'd moved as an Anywhereist simply because she wanted to. That meant "I was just literally starting from scratch," she said. "And it took some time."

Tiffany learned she had to be proactive if she wanted to expand her tiny social network. To start, she focused on finding people with whom she had a common currency, often other writers. In the *Austin Chronicle* weekly newspaper, she found a calendar listing for a writing critique group, and she joined up. Later she was assigned to copy edit the book of a local author, who became one of her best friends.

She even joined the Austin chapter of the Romance Writers of America. "I'm not a romance writer, but I do write women's fiction," Tiffany said. "It was a near match." Her work interests dovetailed enough with her personal interests that connecting around work led to genuine friendships.

What Tiffany has learned: even for the ultrafriendly, social connection in a place doesn't simply happen on its own. It may require joining an existing mini network, like a church or a volunteer organization, friend-stalking people who interest you, attending a meetup, or arranging your own. Tiffany has plenty of local friends now, but she's always on the lookout for more at parties and at work events. She even hangs out with the neighborhood moms, despite having no children of her own. She just likes them.

Like dating, friendship requires feats of bravery—to invite someone you've met for coffee or a hike. To show up to a meeting where you don't know anyone. To be the new person.

You won't be the new person forever. Lately, Tiffany and her husband have been thinking about moving to escape Austin's oppressive heat and to find a lower tax rate, perhaps to a state like North Carolina. Her biggest hesitation is abandoning the dense network of friends and acquaintances that surrounds her in Austin.

She already has a plan if they do. First, she'll find the local chapter of the Women's Fiction Writers Association, of which she's already a member. "That would be a super easy way of just going, 'Hi, I'm new to the area, and we have a thing in common,'" Tiffany said.

Purple Politics

Some Seekers want to move to a new place because they no longer fit in politically where they live. One disgruntled Alabama resident told me that escaping her conservative town and moving to a deep-blue city was the number one factor in her location strategy.

The impulse is both understandable and unfortunate. A 2019 study of political partisanship in the United States shows that whole swaths of the country are becoming intolerant of political views different from their own.[27] Since Americans in general move to counties with their same party preference, the self-sorting threatens to continue unabated.

It's healthy—for you and the nation—to have at least some

friends who disagree with you. If political leanings are part of your place strategy, consider swing states that don't reliably go for the same party every election. Or look for a county that has a history of voting purple. Outcomes well divided between Democrats and Republicans signify tolerance.

LET'S LIVE TOGETHER

We are all, it is clear, looking for community and belonging, both at work and in our places. "Home is where the community is," wrote futurist Vanessa Mason.[28]

Literally. She predicts that in the future, we'll create belonging in a fractured world by living together. "Coliving takes on an entirely new life as the delay to marriage and pressures of the modern workplace all but kill the nuclear family as a viable socio-cultural organization."

What Mason means by coliving (or cohousing) is probably not the hippie commune you're thinking of. She describes young people finding a sense of rootedness in otherwise nomadic lives by purchasing homes on the same block, renting apartments in the same building, arranging collective child care, or investing in micro estates that they pool their money to afford.

One of WeWork's offshoots is WeLive, a newfangled sort of apartment complex where residents can rent private studios in a building that prioritizes shared amenities like a lounge, a gym, and a game center.[29] For Anywhereists who are spending a few months in a particular place, the setup provides an even deeper level of companionship than you'd find at a WeWork coworking space, but they have similar roots.

A company called Common takes the approach that remote workers might want to quell their loneliness by living together. Common rents out private rooms in homes in nine HCOL U.S. cities, from New York to San Francisco to Seattle. The shared-suite atmosphere mimics an upgraded college dorm. It's cheaper, yes, but most residents choose it for its work-live-play-together experience.[30]

Collective housing is what Maria Selting opted for in Stockholm, Sweden. She'd organized a camp called 100 Tjejer Kodar (100 Girls Code) in Barcelona in September 2016, and she'd loved the summer camp vibe so much that she began traveling with a group of digital nomads called WiFi Tribe. The connection with the fellow tribe members was that 100 Tjejer Kodar feeling all over again.[31]

As an Anywhereist who worked for a fintech company based in Stockholm, Maria formed a mini economic cluster with her WiFi Tribe friends. Not that they did exactly what she did. They were content creators, developers, freelancers, small business owners, and musicians. But they became de facto coworkers, and from them, she discovered a new way to work. "I've always been this super disciplined good girl," she said. "You know, setting the alarm to get up and go to the gym before work." Her motto had been "coffee solves it."

Now she learned new rhythms. Get enough sleep. Wake up naturally. Limit your time at the desk. Take a walk when exhaustion hits. Time your work sessions to match your peak energy. Amazingly, she was more productive than ever with fewer hours butt-in-chair.

So it was a loss when COVID hit while Maria was abroad, and

she had to abruptly fly home to Sweden. Her empty apartment was lonely. Maria missed the tribe and "feeling that human connection with people that I feel like I belong to," she said.

To replicate that 100 Tjejer Kodar vibe one more time, Maria moved into a cohousing community in Stockholm. Cohousing is not uncommon in Sweden, where real estate prices have shut out millennials and Gen Zers from buying homes. (A Swedish word, *mambo*, describes the single twenty- and thirtysomethings who still live with their parents because they can't find their own flat.)[32]

Maria also knew that, as one of the more individualistic countries in the world, Sweden's loneliness levels are high. Coliving allowed her to re-create the social life she'd loved as a Wanderer while being a Settler in a city where her roots run deep. Obsessed with thinking about the pros and cons of her new situation, she even started a podcast about coliving and plans to develop her own coliving space down the road.

Coliving isn't a perfect substitute for WiFi Tribe. In the tribe, "everyone's checking in the same day and checking out the same day. So you're always in the same phase, and everyone wants to know each other at the same time and experiences things together." When Maria moved into her coliving place, some residents had already been there two years. (Plus: pandemic. Ruining things as always.)

Yet Maria values learning from other people—not just the semidisinterested colleagues of her workplace, but a true "hodge-podge family" of friends who can show her a way forward in her work, energize her, and inspire her. She'll continue trying to build that for herself in Stockholm.

In August 2020, the coliving company Common announced the next phase in its business model: creating "remote work hubs" that act like coliving apartments combined with offices for young Anywhereists. Projects are in development in New Orleans; Bentonville, Arkansas; Ogden, Utah; Rocky Mount, North Carolina; and Rochester, New York.[33]

Working and living wherever you want with other people who want to work and live there too. Sounds like the Anywhereist anti-loneliness holy grail.

THE SEED OF A COMMUNITY

The year 2020 clearly changed the equation for how people work together. That's why as small-town consultants Deb Brown and Becky McCray advise rural communities about how to attract people who can work from anywhere, they typically recommend three things: better internet connections; more gathering spaces for remote workers, including coffee shops, libraries, and dedicated coworking spaces that double as third places; and activities that help Anywhereists build connections among themselves.

Deb points to a friend who created a remote work community in Round Rock, Texas, by inviting people to simply gather and work on their own projects in an atmosphere of collective productivity. "Some weeks it was just her," said Deb. "Some weeks it was a big group. That's the start of a community."[34]

These are the kinds of things Kate Schwarzler was thinking about when she started charging $300 a month for a large desk at Indy Commons in Independence, Oregon.[35]

Not everyone agreed that a coworking space was what the small town needed. Some locals told her she'd never succeed—that as a big-city outsider from Denver, she didn't belong here anyway. That unless she installed a fax machine, no one would come.

Kate set the bar low and told herself that filling sixteen desks in two years would be a win. Still, the early days were super slow. "And I knew it would be, not to say that made it any easier," she said. "A lot of it was just educating people on what I was about."

One day, Donna, a lawyer in private practice who'd moved to Independence from Minnesota, joined Indy Commons so she could have a place to work besides her kitchen table. A guy who builds websites took a desk too. More lawyers came, along with a man who owns his own blasting company and the representative for the local House district.

Kate knew that people didn't pay the $300 a month just for free coffee and Wi-Fi. They were there for the community. You could get feedback or an instant pep talk. Sometimes a couple of members in totally unrelated industries would start chatting, and one would make a mind-blowing suggestion that solved the other's problem. Once, a member asked Kate, "I have to ship a bunch of things. Is the post office the best option?" From a faraway desk came a faint but emphatic "No!" along with a walk-through of a website that made shipping easier. "It's that kind of thing where sometimes it just feels good to be around other professionals or just other people," Kate said.

For Indy Commons members, simply being in a dedicated workspace unleashed a certain focus that intensified success. "Marginally more productive and slightly less unmoored" is how one *New York Times Magazine* writer described his experience joining WeWork.[36] And if that's all we can ask from working among neighbors, that's probably enough.

Kate's thinking bigger, though. Recently, she moved Indy Commons to an old restaurant so she could offer more amenities, like a podcast room and a separate space for events. In the shared commercial kitchen, local growers can turn five hundred pounds of leftover tomatoes into a private-label sauce brand or teach classes on how to preserve your own food. On a small scale, that creates an economic cluster that better equips its members to weather the ups and downs of a fickle industry. "It's all about how can this community help support each other and help make sure that we're stronger together?" said Kate.

Ultimately, she hopes to help farmers, business owners, community members, and Anywhereists in rural communities find profitable and self-sustaining livelihoods. If all goes well, Indy Commons will model a way for small towns to end their dependence on a single industry or a single employer by whose success an entire town lives or dies. It'll become a resilient place where Anywhereists can "create a really good quality of life in a place that they love." Even in a town called Independence, she believes they're in it together.

During COVID, Kate used Indy Commons's nonprofit arm, the Indie Idea Hub, to qualify for CARES Act funding, which she used to help Independence entrepreneurs build e-commerce websites to put their products online. Digital matters, she knows.

But so does in-person human connection among people who live in the same place. She's not taking any chances on people deciding to work elsewhere. Kate recently ordered a Kegerator for the coworking space.

- -

Location Strategy Session: Connection
Without a standard office, Anywhereists have to be more

intentional about building their own work and social communities where they live. But feeling connected in your place, to friends as well as mentors and de facto coworkers, can increase your profession-people-purpose satisfaction and make you happier to stay in your town. Here are ways to find your people:

1. **Join a coworking space:** Communities that boast coworking spaces show they're serious about hosting Anywhereist workers. A town-owned coworking space like the one in Harbor Springs, Michigan, indicates that local government is on board.

2. **Discover your social entry point:** If you're not going to an office, you need other ways to quickly make friends in a new town. Figure out what that might look like for you in a town on your short list. Joining a parks and rec rugby team? Signing up for the Newcomers Club? Planting a plot in a community garden?

3. **Follow your family:** During COVID, a large number of people moved to be closer to family.[37] That doesn't eliminate the need to make other kinds of connections, but it does help.

4. **Start a Slack channel for local remote workers:** One in Burlington, Vermont, offers a virtual water cooler for the many residents who live in town and work online. Membership soared in the pandemic. They use it to set up in-person get-togethers too.[38]

5. **Join a networking group:** Networking may not be your jam. (Is it anyone's?) But almost every town has

the equivalent of a young professionals network, and it makes a great starting place when you're trying to feel like you're part of a new community.

6. **Plan a meetup:** Creative Mornings is a monthly breakfast lecture series for creative professionals with branches worldwide. If one isn't already in your city, you might start a chapter—or another kind of meetup for people in your place who do what you do: fellow programmers, graphic designers, farmers, whatever.

7. **Tag along to (or start) a business crawl:** Think bar crawl for shopping, usually in a downtown's locally owned retail shops. It's a way to create community around supporting local businesses.

8. **Take Neighboring 101:** The classes are offered in communities around the country, including online through University of Missouri Extension. You'll come away with a better sense of why neighborhoods are always good starting points for building relationships.

Place Study: Lansing, Michigan
Population: 117,000

- **Weather:** About 46 inches of snow falls annually (you've heard about Michigan, right?), but BestPlaces.net ranks its weather 6.7/10—more pleasant than most other places in the state.
- **What's here:** Michigan's domed and spired Capitol Building. Lansing is also home to Michigan State University, with nearly forty thousand undergrad students.
- **Why it's a great place to find a work community:** Because of the Fledge, a coworking space/business incubator/

community center built in a ninety-six-year-old church.

- **What you'll find there:** Twelve thousand square feet of artist studios, maker spaces, and meeting rooms, where up to nine events a day happen for teens and adults, from a coding club to a sword-fighting workshop. The Fledge is the brainchild of Jerry Norris, a former software entrepreneur who wanted to give back to the city where he grew up. Poverty levels in the neighborhood are high, and as Jerry believes, "Genius is lost in poverty." At the Fledge, which opened its Lansing location in 2018, project-based learning, hands-on help, and group brainstorming has translated into an estimated six hundred businesses, nonprofits, and community projects so far.[39]

- **Motto:** "We say yes." Whatever idea you have, someone at the Fledge will help you make it happen, whether you want to start an electric bike delivery service to compete with Grubhub, launch an app that rewards ex-offenders for meeting the terms of their parole, or sell digital art on blockchain. One of the Fledge's foundational ideas is radical inclusivity: no matter who you are, Jerry wants you to find your happiness. Even if you're a seventy-year-old guy who dreams of building a perpetual motion machine (there have been six of those so far), Jerry and the members of the Fledge community are down to help. In fact, the center is named the Fledge to represent birds who fly in formation, taking turns to lead the flock.

- **Why it's a little crazy:** Because they're hacking e-scooters by putting lasers on the front for jousting battles, but also because Jerry believes a little chaos is part of the process.

"When the economic development people and the artists council don't know what to do with somebody, they send them to us. And that person will succeed or learn." Money is a little piecemeal too, coming from fundraisers, grants, and recently, a $25,000 prize from the Small Business Administration and National Science and Technology Council for "creating a more inclusive R&D innovation ecosystem for the future."

- **Big place idea:** "We believe that we can build our own future," said Jerry. "We don't have to buy it from the East Coast or the West Coast or China. We have everything we need within a few mile radius of us."

YOUR CITY HAS AN INNER ARTIST

Location Strategy Value: Creativity

The aerialists soar above the stage on silken ropes. Fog mists in, illuminated by golden lights. At one point, a giant snake puppet slithers in as the floating pas de deux plays out thirty feet above the stage, and you're like, "Huh?"

Beauty, drama, and a solid helping of absurdity. Totally on brand for Cirque du Soleil.

It was 1984 when former street performers Guy Laliberté and Gilles Ste-Croix launched Cirque du Soleil in Quebec, Canada, and no one had seen a circus like this before. No animals. No ringmaster. A marvel of creativity. The cirque mixed dancing, music, gymnastics, and storytelling in a wholly original blend.

And it likely wouldn't have come together anywhere but Quebec.

That's because the French-speaking province of Canada didn't have a 250-year history of family circuses and circus schools the way Europe did. So no one had set-in-stone expectations around what a circus would look like. Things were new. That allowed the founders of the cirque to make it up as they went along by gleaning the best of arts and culture in Montreal. Street performers who juggled or breathed fire. Actors from the national theatre school. Dancers from the O Vertigo dance company. Cutting-edge musicians from the city's jazz festival. Costumes inspired by Montreal's up-and-coming fashion industry. All of it got mixed in a blender and poured out on stage.[1]

One early participant told researchers Deborah Leslie, a professor of geography at the University of Toronto, and Norma Rantisi, a professor of geography, planning, and environment at Canada's Concordia University, that "for years and years, circus artists were doing tricks, and they were in a certain way cutting or closing the doors to other arts influences. Now they see, they feel how much theatre can bring, how much music can bring, how much dance can bring... It is much more integrated."[2]

Even better for the birth of Cirque du Soleil: the provincial government valued and financially supported arts and culture as public goods. Cirque du Soleil's first big contract, for $1.3 million, came from the Quebec Ministry of Culture, which hired the brand-new circus company to perform as part of the national celebration of French explorer Jacques Cartier's arrival in Canada.

The next year, when the Cirque went on a national tour, more than half of its $3 million budget came from government grants and subsidies. On a trip to Los Angeles in 1987 for its first foray into international touring, Cirque du Soleil performers were seen as quasi ambassadors of Canada.

According to the field of evolutionary economic geography, there are a couple of explanations for how creative endeavors like this, or virtually any business, come into existence. First is path dependence, which hinges on the idea that long-term economic destinies are shaped by the cumulative effects of decisions and investment over time.

Imagine an entrepreneur discovers local wood that makes beautiful furniture. As demand grows for the furniture, other artisans start making furniture too. Soon woodcutters move to the area, teachers develop classes to train carpenters, and the furniture makers develop new techniques to expand production. Over time, an entire community—an economic cluster—has grown up around making wooden furniture.

That's path dependence. With every new investment, a community narrows in on an economic path forward.

There's a second explanation, and that's place dependence. As with path dependence, the cumulative effects of strategies and innovations matter. But it's more about the spatial dimensions of economic evolution, said Rantisi, "how institutions and resources are anchored in a place."[3]

The economic evolution of Cirque du Soleil has elements of both, but Leslie and Rantisi prefer to interpret the circumstances that led to the creation of Cirque du Soleil as primarily place dependent. The meeting of historical influences, able suppliers (like costume designers or musicians), government support and policies, and a culture of openness and risk-taking could only have happened in this little corner of Quebec. A particular place led to the Cirque's existence.

Now, Cirque du Soleil is a global corporation, with more than three thousand employees, $850 million in annual revenue, offices in Asia and Europe, and permanent shows in Las Vegas, Mexico, and Disney World.[4]

It's a juggernaut of creative energy that is singularly Quebecois.

SCENIUS AND SUCCESS

For many Anywhereists, creativity is central to who we are and how we work. An estimated one-third of Americans work in creative fields, as authors and artists, designers and architects, scientists and engineers, entrepreneurs and professors. It powers our daily lives too. Tasks from thinking of what to cook for dinner to crafting an Instagram post that will bring in the likes are all fueled by your individual well of creativity.

There's something inexplicable, almost supernatural, about it. How do we become creative? Why are some people so much more creative than others?

The Greeks credited bursts of creative insight to the Muses, and the process is still enough of a mystery that it's halfway believable. Whatever is happening when you develop a new recipe or draft a screenplay for a movie feels like it must be some divine gift.

Meanwhile, musician Brian Eno imagines creativity more like a chocolate chip cookie.

As an art student, Eno learned about great artists—Picasso, Kandinsky, Rembrandt, Giotto—who seemingly popped out of nowhere to spark their own one-man artistic revolutions. The way the subject was taught, it was as if these greats were created ex nihilo. They just appeared.

Later, Eno realized that wasn't the true picture. "What really happened," he explained at a Sydney music festival in 2009, "was that there were sometimes very fertile scenes involving lots and lots of people—some of them artists, some of them collectors, some of them curators, thinkers, theorists, people who were fashionable and knew what the hip things were—all sorts of people who created a kind of ecology of talent. And out of that ecology arose some wonderful work."[5]

The ecology of creativity is what Eno renders as looking something like a line drawing of a chocolate chip cookie. The circle of the cookie represents a place. And inside are the chips—people floating around among a lot of other chips. Just like you don't have a chocolate chip cookie with one chip, you don't have an artist without a whole support system enveloping them.

The people we think of as lone geniuses actually existed in a fertile crescent of community members who cocreated and sustained their art in some way. Rembrandt may have had a gift, but he also had his collectors, managers, and agents as well as other artists or thinkers who nurtured his ideas, primarily in the place where he lived and worked.

It's a concept that Brian Eno calls *scenius*, a mash-up of *scene* and *genius* that indicates the collective intelligence of an entire group of people. "Let's forget the idea of 'genius' for a little while," he said. "Let's think about the whole ecology of ideas that give rise to good new thoughts and good new work." The chocolate chip cookie.[6]

Scenius used to be entirely a product of a concentrated local geography. Consider Harlem in the early twentieth century, when an influx of Black thinkers, artists, and activists produced a fusillade of creative work. In Harlem, writers cooperated to produce literary magazines. Social gatherings put them in the right place to meet gatekeepers who could bring their work to a wider audience. At one famous 1924 book launch party, young poet Langston Hughes mingled with some members of New York's publishing world, after which mainstream magazines like *Harper's* began publishing his work.

As Harlem's reputation as a generative place for Black creatives grew, more artists migrated there from other parts of the country, and the critical mass increased everyone's chances of success. Novelist Zora Neale Hurston relocated to Harlem straight out of Howard University and, before that, a childhood spent in Florida. Langston Hughes was actually something of a Wanderer, traveling the country and taking guest teaching positions at various universities, from Chicago to Atlanta. But when he scraped together enough money to buy a house in the late 1940s, he settled in Harlem.

This was prime scenius, and similarly creative ecosystems have flourished all over the world at various times, from Athens to Florence to New York City. The right people come together in the right place to create something larger than themselves.

In his book *Geography of Genius*, Eric Weiner describes how creative geniuses sometimes respond to an inner GPS that draws them inexorably toward the environment that will help them thrive. For Beethoven, Mozart, and Haydn, that was Vienna, a city that offered composers the time, workspace, patrons, and access to audiences that let their genius flourish and be recognized.[7]

But you don't have to be a genius to benefit from or contribute to scenius. "Being a valuable part of a scenius is not necessarily about how smart or talented you are, but about what you have to contribute—the ideas you share, the quality of the connections you make, and the conversations you start," wrote Austin Kleon in his book *Show Your Work!*[8]

These days, the place where most of us share ideas, make connections, and start conversations is the internet. When I started out as a writer, I didn't know many people in my own geographic community who did what I did, but I found them by the hundreds online, happily posting in writing forums and constructing a scenius that propelled us all to more success than we could have mustered on our own.

If you're a creative, you've probably found your own digital scenius in Twitter's community of thinkers and writers or in Instagram's inventory of visual artists. The online world is a massive twenty-four-hour buffet of ideas and resources that isn't just local—it covers the entire world.

So why would you need a creative community where you live? Hasn't the internet rendered the idea of geographic scenius obsolete?

WHAT MAKES A COMMUNITY CREATIVE

Actually, we're combo packs of inner resources and outer influences. We behave in different ways when we react to our immediate environments. So in a practical way, being in the same physical place as other creative people may have the power to nurture your work in ways that being online doesn't.

No one's figured out how to order up a pixie dust that will make everyone in the vicinity think deep thoughts or write really funny *New Yorker* pieces. Yet it's clear that certain environments create a kind of scenius of group creativity, where everyone around comes up with more interesting, boundary-pushing ideas.

Creativity fermented in a bar in Oxford where J. R. R. Tolkien and C. S. Lewis met weekly as they worked on the Lord of the Rings series and the Chronicles of Narnia.

Creativity cropped up in a hotel in Manhattan, where a group of authors that included Dorothy Parker and Robert Benchley created the literary salon known as the Algonquin Round Table.

Innovative thinking made itself manifest at the University of Chicago, whose halls are roamed by six Nobel Prize in Economics winners.

Gunnar Tornqvist, a professor of human geography at Lund University in Sweden, suggests that "new ideas are built upon a capital of experiences gathered through interaction with one's surroundings."[9] Some hallmarks of geographic scenius include the following:

- **Rapid exchange of tools and techniques:** When one person develops a new way of doing something, they don't hoard the idea. In sharing, ideas flow quickly from one person to the next, benefiting the whole community, according to Kevin Kelly, one of the founding editors of *Wired* magazine.[10]

- **Mutual appreciation:** Creativity thrives among a group that applauds one another's innovations. There's enough friendly competition and peer pressure that you feel compelled to continue innovating and achieving.

- **Shared success:** As one person achieves, the entire community feels the psychological benefits of their success. There may even be an influx of capital to a community because of it (say, because someone won a MacArthur genius grant or got a big contract for software development).

- **Openness to novelty:** Some places resist change, but communities of scenius encourage their members to try new things and buffer them from disapproval from the outside. Renegades and mavericks are protected by the group. Frequent failure is encouraged.

- **Workers in a variety of fields:** Economic clustering means that you're more likely to live and work among others who do more or less what you do. But creativity thrives when people interact outside their field, so ideas can combine and recombine to create something new.

- **People from many backgrounds:** When different cultures and backgrounds intermingle freely, it creates the sort of fireworks that lead to new fashions, styles, technologies, and ways of thinking.

- **Creative markets:** No matter what creative field you're in, the presence of marketplaces for creativity—theaters, galleries, indie movie houses—signifies that there are local people and places that recognize creative production and push it into the limelight.[11]

Creativity is unpredictable. Sometimes it requires solitude, sometimes togetherness. When Lainey Cameron quit her career in tech to finish her novel in a thirty-three-foot RV, she hadn't counted on never being able to escape the distractions of her husband, Eric, in such a small space. To find the quiet that helped her achieve flow, she ended up renting a house with an office in San Miguel de Allende, Mexico.[12]

Then there was the daily challenge of putting her butt in the seat and working (the part of creativity that's not so mystical). For that, Lainey joined an in-person writers group that meets every Wednesday in San Miguel's city center. "Everybody states what their intention is, and then you just write in peace for two hours, and then you all share how it went," explained Lainey. "There's no critiquing, just a mutual energy for focusing and writing."

Lainey has plenty of online relationships with other writers; she's joined and formed highly niche groups for, say, authors of women's fiction. But in the artist colony of San Miguel, she's physically immersed in an expat community that supports an annual writers conference and literary festival that's hosted the likes of Margaret Atwood and Isabel Allende. Lainey volunteers at the festival, fixing tech snafus in a ballroom. Scenius is why we attend things like writers conferences in the first place.

And it may be why, as part of a location strategy, we look for things like art festivals and art galleries in our chosen communities— signs of local scenius. That's what reassured Julianne Couch when the all-remote English instructor for the University of Wyoming fell in love with Bellevue, Iowa, a town along the Mississippi River she'd encountered while researching a book.[13]

Her husband's a painter and she's a writer, and the aesthetics of the place bowled them over—the limestone cliffs like Dover's, the light on the river. So did the presence of the local arts council, which Julianne started volunteering with while they were still fixing up their 1880 house. Having resources like that for artists denoted that artists lived in Bellevue, that their work was valued, and that there would be scenius here.

Julianne's also an amateur musician—"not a very good one," she was quick to say—and finding a group that she could jam out on guitar with helped her feel at home. Creativity in general is like a jam session. A bunch of not-so-good musicians sit around and pluck out tunes, responding to the interplay of the notes, coaxing one another along. That's what a creative place can provide for you.

Whatever kind of creative work you do—writing, painting, DJing, inventing, running a small business—finding scenius can be part of your location strategy. You can locate and harness the elements that feed your creativity and help you succeed.

FIND ONE THOUSAND TRUE FANS

The internet makes it a lot easier to make a living as a creative. Kevin Kelly famously suggested that one thousand true fans is all you need if they're each willing to pay $100 a year to support your work—a prospect made even more likely today when someone in Sri Lanka can PayPal you for an illustration they spotted on Behance or for a song you uploaded.[14]

Offer premium content and community your customers can't get elsewhere, and you may be able to get by with just one hundred true fans, suggested venture capitalist Li Jin.[15] Virtually none of them, needless to say, will live in your neck of the woods. That geographic boundlessness is a seemingly beautiful development for creators, craftspeople, musicians, photographers, animators, app makers, and entrepreneurs, as well as for the people who want exactly what those creators are selling.

So is cultivating a local market of clients even a thing anymore? For artist Catherine Freshley, it was how she found her one thousand true fans.[16]

A military spouse, Catherine lived for a time with her Air Force pilot husband in Enid, Oklahoma. Enid was the middle of nowhere, a thousand physical and emotional miles from lush Portland, Oregon, where Catherine grew up.

Yet the beauty grew on her. On drives through the countryside, Catherine took pictures with her phone of scenery and sunsets, then took them home and started to paint them.

It was a departure for her as an artist. After years of painting abstracts, now her work turned into bright, realistic representations of the local landscapes. Skies were her thing. She washed the canvas in photorealistic images of Oklahoma's sunsets, with wisps of cotton-candy clouds over furrowed fields.

Catherine's smart about both her craft and her business, and she knew that her Oklahoma images would do well in the community. After making connections at Enid's First Friday art gallery walk downtown, she was invited to hang some of her work in a local coffee shop. Townspeople loved these paintings that reflected familiar places. "It was pretty easy to get some attention for that," she said. To make it clear what she was up to, Catherine even gave her paintings localized place names, like *South on I-35* or *Going to Stillwater*.

At a festival in Oklahoma City in the spring, with an estimated 750,000 people walking through over six days, she did about $12,000 in sales at her festival booth. For the next three years, she'd bring a little more inventory and raise her prices a little each time. By 2019, she sold almost $25,000 of art in six days.

Catherine may not have been Oklahoma born and bred, but

she was holding up a flattering mirror to a place that a lot of other artists ignored, and the state's art fans eagerly adopted her as one of their own. This was the scenius of collectors and gallery owners, the chips in Brian Eno's cookies all talking together and raising Catherine's status. "I would have so many people say, 'Oh, I went to my friend's house, and I've noticed that they have one of your paintings,'" Catherine said. "To this group of people, it seemed like I was everywhere."

When her husband left the military, the couple decided to return to Portland, Oregon, their hometown, in February 2020. She's thrilled to be working in a light-drenched studio there.

But she's glad she didn't have to launch her art career in Portland. "I think it was really helpful to be in a smaller town, because that allowed me to get opportunities that I don't think I would have had otherwise," she said. "And now I have those things on my résumé. And I have that experience that can help me go after similar opportunities in a bigger city."

Catherine's intention remains to paint what she sees around her. Her photorealistic paintings now bear titles like *Late Summer over Portland* and *Mt. Hood in Cherry Season*. Surprisingly, she's still selling her work to collectors in the Midwest, who happily follow her online.

"People on the West Coast probably tend to pooh-pooh Oklahoma, but they are so supportive of the arts," Catherine said. "They actually walk the walk." They are her one thousand true fans.

CRAFT VS. COMPETITION

Places, like creativity, are a bit mysterious. They have their own energy and beauty that inspire us to new levels of artistry.

That's certainly been the experience of Kristine Arth, the founder and principal designer of the branding agency Lobster Phone. She spent the summer of 2018 in France doing TypeParis, an accelerated master's program focused on typography that, she said, alerted her to one of the biggest geographical differences in creativity: Europeans cared more about craft. Americans cared more about competitiveness.[17]

In San Francisco, where Kristine is based, "the mindset here is all about, *I've got to be better than X, I've got to produce more than X, I've got to give more keynote speeches than X, and I have to create bigger things and launch better and be in X places.*"

In France, the most talented people simply wanted to create something beautiful. Her European friends were more collaborative, and after work, they liked to talk about things other than work. Their feeling was that a breadth of interests and inputs fueled their craft.

Unlike her San Francisco colleagues, hopped up on seventy-hour workweeks, Kristine's European friends picnicked, went to museums, even raised chickens. At the end of the day, it seemed to make them better artists.

Kristine finds value in both approaches. An Anywhereist Wanderer, she hopes to split her time between San Francisco and Paris, the two cities that represent the two selves she wants to bring to her design work. Her Paris self hones her craft and creates beautiful things. Her gritty San Francisco self knows that beauty alone isn't enough. "If it's not making money after I design it and brand it and name it and put it out in the world, then I failed," Kristine said.

There's a balance to making art and making money with art

that Kristine is familiar with. So is filmmaker Justin Litton, who boomeranged home to West Virginia after film school in England.[18]

His friends were surprised, assuming he'd become a cinematographer in Hollywood or New York. "Everyone assumes that, you know, there are some limitations to staying in West Virginia," said Justin. "And if you want to do big things, you don't stay here and do that." But what Justin wanted was a creative career, and living in small-town West Virginia made that possible.

His cinematography skills are unusual there. The company he started specializes in high-end corporate and commercial video work, and they rarely compete with other filmmakers for work. The creative pool is so limited that he and his team often take on every aspect of a project, from writing a script to casting a commercial to directing and producing it. Sometimes that's overwhelming, but mostly it's pleasurable.

Justin is practical about his work. Yes, he's making commercials for local banks, not Oscar nominees. But he still gets to indulge in the very real creativity of deciding camera angles and storytelling approaches. "If I'm behind the camera, I'm in my happy place."

Plus, creative inspiration is always right outside his door in the wild mountains of West Virginia. "Even if I go on a hike, for example, and don't have some idea for a video, it's at least grounding me in a place that when I get back to work, I'm balanced as a human being."

Science agrees. A Danish study found that for creative professionals, spending time in nature enhanced their creativity by making them more curious, more flexible in how they thought about problems, and thus more able to generate new ideas or new approaches to old ones.[19]

Nature is famously a boon for restoring attention as well. In a Finnish study, hikers found themselves agreeing with statements like "My concentration and alertness increased," and "My thoughts were clarified" after a trek in the woods.[20] Time in a natural space is great for incubating the aha moments that constitute great moments of creative insight.

One town over from where Justin lives in Scott Depot (population eight thousand) sits the Blenko Glass Factory. Men in flannel shirts blow glass using tools that were made by hand. Justin has filmed at the glass factory and felt a kinship with their industrious and expressive labors. "To me, that's a very Appalachian thing," he said, "where I'm surrounded by people who do amazing work, and they're using their hands and they're just diving in and getting dirty."

Craft is a place value here. In a state whose economics have historically revolved around coal mining, blue-collar work is seen as a craft you take pride in. It's why Justin named his business Mountain Craft—to honor West Virginia's legacy of potters and glassblowers, weavers and painters. Video production might feel like a different kind of art, but like his forebears, Justin cares about doing it well.

- -

Location Strategy Session: Creativity

The right scenius can act as a fire starter to your creativity, igniting your ability to produce art and ideas (and make money from them) with resources, support, and a collective will to succeed. Here are a few ways you can dig into the arts scene in your place.

1. **Find your arts council:** These can be government entities or nonprofits, with a regional, state-wide, or hyperlocal base. But if your area has an arts council, it gives you a place to apply for grants. And simply its presence is an indicator that this community cares about supporting the arts.

2. **Attend a studio tour:** Once or twice a year in places like Carson City, Nevada, artists and artisans, from glassblowers to jewelry designers, open up their creation spaces for public tours. It's a great way to see who's actually creating in your town and, if you're a creative artist, to join in.

3. **Hang out:** Creativity is "a relentlessly relational experience," said Joshua Wolf Shenk, the author of *Powers of Two: Finding the Essence of Innovation in Creative Pairs.* Several studies have found that the background noise of your average coffee shop can increase creativity for people who work there; plus, it's motivating to work alongside someone who seems to be putting in as much effort as you are.[21]

4. **Move into artist housing:** Paducah, Kentucky, runs an artist relocation program that offers 100 percent financing for artists who want to buy and refurbish a house in a blighted neighborhood. If they'd rather build new, the vacant lot is free. Since Lower Town is an enterprise zone, construction materials are tax-exempt, and it's zoned for both commercial and residential use, allowing artists to live, work, and run a mini gallery out of their home. So far, forty artists have moved in,

investing millions in the area. Other communities offer discounted housing or studio space for artists.[22]

5. **Buy local art:** If you want to foster a creative community, buy art from local artists. A First Friday event, where main street galleries stay open late, can be a good place to find them. In some towns, work by local artists decks the walls of restaurants, coffee shops, and small businesses.

6. **Reserve creation space for artists:** When vacant storefronts proliferated in Newcastle, Australia, landlords began letting artists and artisans use the empty spaces for free in exchange for maintaining the properties and paying utilities. Animators, photographers, and web developers started working in about seventy-four properties, freed to pursue their passions by the low financial risk. The mere presence of the artists decreased neighborhood crime. The program, sponsored by Renew Newcastle, also raised incomes. Artists who participated made on average an additional AU\$20,941.[23]

7. **Vote for a local art tax:** In 2020, Jersey City, New Jersey, passed a two-cent property tax hike whose proceeds go toward a trust fund to finance local arts organizations. Locals take pride in the fact that they passed the measure during the pandemic. "This should slam the door on anyone thinking that the arts is an extra, a bonus, the first thing that should be cut," said Robinson Holloway, former chair of the Jersey City Arts Council.[24]

8. **Support new ideas:** Creativity requires nurturing ideas, so beware the tendency to shoot down the unfamiliar as it arises in your community. Volunteer your own ideas as well by, say, writing an email to a city council person.

Place Study: Seagrove, North Carolina

Population: 229

- **Nickname:** The Handmade Pottery Capital of the United States.

- **What it's like:** Scattered in and around Seagrove's bustling downtown and acres of farmland are more pottery studios per capita than anywhere else in the country. Thank the first English and German immigrants, who settled Seagrove in the eighteenth century and immediately started making pots from the just-right local clay. Soon Seagrove pottery was a thing. Now there about fifty family-owned pottery shops in the area about forty minutes south of Greensboro and more potters coming all the time.[25]

- **Why the living is easier here:** The downtown Dollar General stands cheek by jowl with a host of studios, museums, and galleries. The annual festivals the weekend before Thanksgiving attract thousands of tourists. Pre-COVID, there was so much foot traffic that some artists never bothered to sell their work online. Cooperation trumps competition, and with lots of potters in one area, Seagrove has become a destination for art lovers.

- **The perks of collective action:** Creative types are not known for groupthink. But when they manage to get on board together (there's an association for local potters for that purpose), they make stuff happen, like pooling their cash to market the region collectively, sharing how to build a following on Instagram (check out the hashtag #SeagrovePotters), and planning events to bring in tourists. Plus, they share resources. When a potter gets their enormous wood-fired kiln going, they'll invite their neighbors to throw in some pieces too.

- **How side hustles thrive:** Working potters David Hernandez and Alexa Modderno moved here in 2005 and opened a studio-cum-gallery shop and an Airbnb. Then in 2020, they remodeled the old general store into an airy, industrial bar called the General Wine and Brew. (David also happens to be the mayor of Seagrove.) The mix works—they get to stay mostly full-time artists.[26]

- **How the place helps:** Seagrove's North Carolina Pottery is part museum, part shop, with space for artists in residence, kilns, wheels, and other equipment potters need. There are plenty of places around town to sell work. And a nearby community college's ceramic arts program trains apprentices.

- **The creativity boost:** "That collective group, it's inspirational all the time," said Alexa, who said her friends' styles and techniques sometimes seep into her own work. It's not stealing, more like cross-pollination—and most people are happy to share. "It's an amazing influence every day," she said.

WHEN YOU'D RATHER
LIVE EVERYWHERE

Location Strategy Value: Adventure

The wrong place ruined Nandita Gupta's life. The right places remade it.[1]

She'd been working as a college admissions counselor in the San Francisco Bay Area when she met her husband, a winemaker. Because her work was portable and his was literally planted in the soil of Napa Valley, she moved in with him—and was miserable.

Everyone thought Napa must be paradise. But Nandita, an off-the-charts extrovert, was lonely. Entire days would pass and she'd see no one, talk to no one, except the high schoolers she was advising on how to get into Stanford. Growing up in New Delhi and New York City, she'd always loved the feeling of being part of a throng. "And then I move to a place that's so rural, I don't see human beings," she said. "Like, I look out my window, and there's no people."

The place ultimately broke their marriage. She and her husband still loved each other, but Nandita could no longer stay somewhere that felt so wrong for her.

For a year after the divorce, she lived with her parents in New York to heal and regain some of the twenty pounds she'd lost grieving. Then she decided to become a digital nomad.

She called it her *Eat, Pray, Love* tour. Whereas Elizabeth Gilbert's postdivorce travels famously took her to Italy, India, and Bali, Nandita would try twelve cities in twelve months—in South America, Central America, Asia, Europe, and Africa—through the program Remote Year, a company that arranges long-term global travel for groups of Anywhereists. Nandita hoped her year of travel would be a chance to recover a sense of possibility and joy, "to reboot my life a little bit," she said.

Her first revelation: Seeing how the rest of the world lived was like entering Bizarro World. So you didn't have to work sixty hours a week? Or own a three-thousand-square-foot house to be happy? "If there are seven billion people on earth, there are seven billion different ways to live life," said Nandita.

New places gave her permission to see the American culture she'd been living in as just that—a culture. A choice. Different choices were okay.

Second revelation: Traveling with other people offered a living, breathing antidote to those long, solitary Napa Valley days. "I need people 24/7," Nandita said. "Or maybe let's say 23/7. The community was so key for me, and Remote Year totally delivered on that."

Third revelation: Doing her Anywhereist work from new locations made her like her job again.

Becoming a college admissions consultant, advising high schoolers on how to get into Ivy League schools, was more an accidental career than an intentional business, something she fell into after a friend asked her to help on her kid's college application. Word spread that she was good at it. Even though Nandita was making six figures, it didn't feel like a real career. Had she really gone to an Ivy League school to tell high school seniors how to get into an Ivy League school? In her family, people were doctors.

When she found herself luxuriating in a glorious southern hemisphere summer in Cape Town in February, those feelings evaporated. Whatever career shame she felt, whatever apparatus of office life she had sometimes craved as a solopreneur—the happy hours, the office retreats, a boss to make some decisions for her—all that was forgotten in Nandita's joy at having a career that let her go on a round-the-world trip without even FYI-ing her clients. *Oh my God*, she thought. *My job enables me to do this amazing thing. This is the best job for me.*

The ability to restructure your life from scratch, Nandita knows, is a privilege that not everyone has. But more people have it than think they do.

We're just low on imagination, high on a willingness to put up with an existence that doesn't really satisfy. "I think sometimes it does take a bold step to realize how much you are tied down to accepting in your life what actually you don't need to accept. Sometimes you've really got to shake things up to see what is very necessary for you and what isn't."

For Nandita, the divorce ended up being her big step. At the time, it felt like the worst thing that ever happened to her. Ultimately, "it gave me this gift to be able to redesign a life completely from my imagination and my inspiration from the world," she said. "It's like, wow, this beautiful thing came out of this thing that I thought was just scorching."

SHOULD YOU BECOME A WANDERER?

In 2015, in a presentation at an international conference, Dutch entrepreneur Pieter Levels made an eye-watering prediction: by 2035, there would be one billion digital nomads in the world.[2]

He explained his thinking. More people are freelancers. Internet speeds are rising rapidly. Fewer people are taking traditional steps like getting married or buying a home; they don't even want to. And plane rides? Faster and cheaper, to virtually anywhere in the world.

The progression would go like this: First, freelancers would work from home. Then they'd work in a coffee shop. Then at a relative's house in a different state. All of a sudden, they'd be sipping coffee in Vietnam with a view of the rice fields, thinking, *This is pretty cool. I could do this.*

It wouldn't take much, Pieter said, for there to be one billion digital nomads traveling and working all over the world.

To many of us, the idea of digital nomadism is keenly attractive. According to a 2018 study by MBO Partners, 11 percent of American workers confidently declared that they planned to become digital nomads in the next few years; an additional 27 percent said they might.[3]

At the time, only about 4.8 million Americans actually *were* digital nomads, about 1.4 percent of the population, suggesting that most people were simply talking a good game. As Elaine Pofeldt put it in *Forbes*, digital nomadism was mostly an "aspirational spectator sport."[4]

All that may have changed with the pandemic. By July 2020, the number of Americans who referred to themselves as "digital nomads" had grown to 10.9 million, a 120 percent increase from two years earlier.[5] So many workers had been unleashed from traditional office jobs that claiming digital nomadism was an easy next step.

But what did that even mean? Digital nomads don't have a single definition. Some are more or less standard expats, living in foreign countries for years at a time. Some are globetrotters, flitting across borders every few weeks to temporarily settle down in a new spot. Some are vanlifers or RVers, traveling across the continent with their house on their back, so to speak. Others do shorter workcations or sabbaticals, working from a far-flung resort for a few weeks or months.

According to MBO, what unites them is "a passion for travel and new adventures" as well as an ability to work anywhere they can connect to the internet.[6]

The pandemic added a twist. Just as more people were working from anywhere than ever before, travel got hairier. Nomads like Esther Inman, whom you met in chapter 7, returned from abroad, reluctant to be trapped overseas for an extended period of time, while people who'd never given a second's thought to a nomadic lifestyle suddenly saw it as their best option for a bad year.

Paige and Chip Severance, parents of five from Knoxville, Tennessee, had the aha moment in the summer of 2020. Chip's IT services firm was doing well all-remote. Their kids weren't going back to regular school anyway. Why not do something interesting?[7]

They ended up buying a used forty-foot motor home for around $30,000 and tooling to the national parks. First stop: Great Smoky Mountains National Park, then Mammoth Cave in Kentucky. After that, who knew? "We don't necessarily have everything planned out 100 percent," Chip said, noting that they intended to carry on their adventure for about a year.

During the pandemic, most digital nomads were, by necessity, doing all their travel domestically. Some digital nomads had been doing that all along.

Sandra and Julio Peña have been living in an RV with their four kids since the end of 2017, when they acknowledged they could never afford a house in exorbitant San Jose, California. Rather than upgrade to a two-bedroom apartment for $4,000 in monthly rent, they undertook full-time RV life.[8]

An online jewelry resale business keeps them earning on the road, and they've learned to game their location to their advantage. The first time they went to Arizona, they shopped for turquoise before realizing "you can't buy cheap turquoise in Arizona," said Sandra. You can, however, buy cheap diamonds. Now they hunt for whatever is affordable locally, resell to a national online market, and watch their profit margin increase. "That's another beautiful thing the road has done," Sandra said.

Digital nomadism is peak Anywhereist fantasy—not just *I can live anywhere* but *I can live everywhere*. As John Steinbeck once said, "Perhaps we have overrated roots as a psychic need. Maybe the greater urge, the deeper and more ancient is the need, the will, the hunger to be somewhere else."[9]

It's so enticing because it seems like the antidote to everything we hate about our lives in an office or our lives in general. On days that stretch into tedium, the idea of chucking it all and buying a plane ticket for foreign climes has a certain glamour to it. Suddenly all your work days become social media–worthy. (Hey, look at me, sending an email from the base of an Icelandic waterfall!)

The idea of constant or near-constant travel also speaks to some of our most powerful human desires.

You're more autonomous. More in charge of your own life. You don't have to hoard vacation days or endure office drudgery to see beautiful places once a year. Now they're outside as your everyday environment.

You're flexible. You set the schedule and the destinations. You choose when you'll work and when you'll abandon work to go check out a nearby museum.

You experience novelty more frequently, mixing it up to dispel tedium and stimulate your brain.

You get to explore, all the time, in a way that allows you to derive some meaning from what you're doing. To experience foreign cultures that cast new light on the life you've been living. To witness awe-inspiring sights that intensify everyday experiences. To also see poverty and struggle in a way that inspires more gratitude or compassion.

Writer Chris Guillebeau calls the passion for adventure the core of a person's soul and said that "nothing is more damaging to the adventurous spirit within a man than a secure future."[10] Which a lot of Anywhereists, by definition, don't have.

I'm the ultimate armchair spectator, and even I can see the allure of digital nomadism. If you're an Anywhereist, is this what you should be doing with your location freedom? Should you, in fact, become a Wanderer?

THE NOMAD INDUSTRIAL COMPLEX

Lauren Razavi, a remote work strategist and author of *Global Natives*, told me that deciding to be a digital nomad, even temporarily, is about deciding what kind of life you want for yourself. "In my experience, a lot of people I went to university with get very stuck in this kind of rat race of like, 'Okay, I just want to get the more expensive car, the bigger house, the highest salary.' And I think nomadism is quite a different approach to all of that, where you're actually saying, what is the amount of money that I need in order to live a satisfactory life?"[11]

Lauren measures her work life and decides which writing and consulting assignments to take based on how much money she needs to go where she wants. Six months in Amsterdam costs a lot more than six months in Portugal or Kuala Lumpur. Thailand can echo the sunny beaches of Los Angeles for less. Money has become a means to an end for Lauren, a way to experience what she wants in the world.

Where Lauren sees savings, others see money to be made. If Pieter Levels is right about one billion digital nomads, that means the market to cater to them will be huge.

They'd need apps! Software! Services just for them! Better places to stay! Travel companies! The global digital nomad space is turning into a billion-dollar industry, with its own personal coaches, conferences, websites, and crowded coworking or coliving spaces in places as far flung as Bangkok and Ubud.

Matt Dykstra, a Wanderer who's spent the past several years in Russia, started his Digital Nomad 2020 conference to help newbie nomads figure out what he had to learn the hard way—things like how to handle taxes or what to do about his cats.[12]

He'd been attending conferences, listening to podcasts, and feeling frustrated when speakers only shared 15 percent of what he needed to know "and you needed to pay several thousand dollars to come back and get the rest of the information. I wanted to help people out. I wanted to make this something people could do."

About 60 percent of attendees at the conference, held virtually during COVID, were already digital nomads or remote workers. The rest were trying to figure out how to make it work. "I think we attracted a lot of people who suddenly realized they were locked in their houses, and they can watch Netflix, or they can build a future and keep that income coming in," Matt said.

People don't always realize that they can afford to become a nomad because, like travel, your paths to do it can veer luxurious or basic.

Hostels and cheap rentals fit the bill, but for the discerning Wanderer, at least one boutique hospitality brand caters to digital nomads. Funded by $100 million in venture capital, Selina plans to build forty properties worldwide, a range of upscale hotels and hostels with coworking spaces and yoga and meditation rooms— "incorporating everything a nomad may want and need into a space to stay," according to Condé Nast Traveler.[13]

A helpful tool to figure it all out is the website Nomad List, which has thousands of paying members and millions of visitors annually. When Pieter Levels created it, he was a digital nomad himself, in the middle of a year-long "twelve start-ups in twelve months" project. Nomad List was project #7, a way to document which cities worldwide were best for nomads.[14]

If you're moving every few weeks, your location strategizing never ends. You're constantly choosing the next place to go. The stakes are lower for nomads than they are for people who plan to stay, yet they're not insignificant. They require money, time, and effort. If the investment doesn't pay off, work and plans can be disrupted. How could digital nomads identify the cities that were best—or at least best for them right now?

In a public Google spreadsheet, Pieter began collecting data on factors like cost of living and quality of life for fifty global cities. Soon friends added columns for their preferred indicators, including safety, coffee shop density, and LGBTQ-friendliness. Over time, Nomad List became a holistic index of around two thousand cities and towns that Anywhereist Wanderers or Seekers might consider living. Nearly three hundred filters help sort them, from basics like cost or weather to more idiosyncratic factors like "low in racism," "great for dogs," "fast-growing economy," or "vegan food," to name a few.

More filters get added all the time. In 2020, "few Corona deaths" made the filter list. Cities earn an overall score based on various factors. It changes frequently. Last I checked, Lisbon, Portugal, was #1.

Wanderers tend be thoughtful about where they end up moving, as they're thoughtful about a lot of things. It's still a counterculture choice to travel the world rather than settle down in a single location. Questioning standard decisions is part of the gig, Lauren Razavi said, calling her friends "hackers who were like, 'How does this work? Why aren't people doing this? Would this be fun?'"[15]

On Nomad List, Anywhereists can get clinically specific about what kind of place experience they're interested in having. Metropolis vs. small town? Palm trees vs. mountains? Rowdy or quiet? For a Seeker, rummaging through the filters is a helpful exercise in refining your location strategy, since you're forced to make repeated choices about your place preferences.

When I experimented with Nomad List's filters, I said yes to fast internet and safety and indicated a preferred cost under

$2,000 a month, the midrange for Nomad List. I got sixty-seven results. With a few additional filters—good food, high density of places to work, walkable, and clean—the website coughed up just three cities, all of which happen to be in Taiwan: Taipei, Taichung, and Kaohsiung.

Would I ever move there? Doubtful. But it's nice to know I could.

LEGALLY GRAY

Alongside figuring out where you're going as a Wanderer, you have to figure out your visa, the official authorization from a foreign country to live, work, or travel there long term. Maybe that hasn't been high on your list of location strategy considerations, but Estonia has been waiting for this to cross your mind, and it wants to say hello.

A country of 1.3 million across the Baltic Sea from Finland, Estonia's been engaged in a multiyear effort to wire up the nation into a "digital republic." Need to do your taxes? To vote? To bank? For a citizen of Estonia, every bit of that data is linked across a single national platform, allowing them to do it all with the click of a button.[16]

Lately, Estonia has had its eye on digital nomads. The country offers e-residency, which allows anyone to become a "citizen" of Estonia's digital nation. You get a digital ID card that lets you register a company 100 percent online (you'll still have to pay taxes in your home country), make electronic bank transfers, digitally sign documents, and access other all-online services from anywhere in the world—helpful for nomad entrepreneurs who carry their businesses with them.[17]

In August 2020, Estonia went one step further, offering a digital nomad visa that allows remote workers to live in Estonia and legally work for their employers abroad for a full year.

Why is that such a big deal? Because back when most countries developed their rules for visas, Anywhereist workers didn't exist. Visas were either for tourists or for long-term expats, so most digital nomads would sign up for the short-term tourist visa and work in a kind of legal gray area. When the visa lapsed, typically in 30 to 180 days, they'd make a "visa run" to another country to apply for a new tourist visa, then start the clock all over again. The process was expensive and inconvenient, and if a nomad skipped it and overstayed their visa, they could incur a fine or get kicked out.

The whole process "has been quite a barrier," said Lauren Razavi. "I think that a lot of people just wouldn't want to in any way be in a gray area when it comes to matters of immigration." As a result, digital nomadism has stayed primarily a fringe movement of early adopters who don't mind living on the legal edge.[18]

Recently, responding to the expected tidal wave of digital nomads and remote workers, a growing handful of countries and territories began offering long-term visas, including the following

- Albania
- Anguilla (UK Territory)
- Antigua & Barbuda
- Bali
- Barbados
- Bermuda
- Cayman Islands
- Costa Rica

- Croatia
- Czech Republic
- Estonia
- Georgia
- Germany
- Hungary
- Iceland
- Malta
- Mauritius
- Mexico
- Norway
- Portugal
- Spain
- United Arab Emirates[19]

Usually lasting a year, these remote worker visas are a country's way of shouting "welcome" and taking a swipe at talent attraction and retention of digital nomads. Not that these Wanderers intend to stay for long, but as Bermuda's minister of labor explained when he announced the island's new digital nomad visa, remote workers "will promote economic activity for our country without displacing Bermudians in the workforce."[20] Win-win.

There are still kinks to be worked out, like a $100,000-a-year income requirement in Cayman Islands, a British territory known for scuba diving and tax evasion, or the $2,000 fee for Barbados's twelve-month digital nomad visa—more than ten times what a typical visa costs.

But in general, the trend toward digital nomad visas and international remote worker programs heralds a whole new

digital nomadism 2.0, with different demographics than the earlier version. The millennials and Gen Zers who have been the
most common nomads will be joined by older adults in more
senior positions. There will be more room for different kinds of
Wanderers too, including slow travelers who stay in a place for
a month before moving on or going home. "I think that [digital
nomadism] is going to be much more mainstream," said Razavi.[21]

GOLDEN HANDCUFFS

Maybe the easiest way to try digital nomadism out is through a
group that arranges where you go and with whom you travel (not
to mention handles all the visas). Like Remote Year, the Chicago-
based company that Nandita Gupta used for her *Eat, Pray, Love*
tour.

Founder Greg Caplan created Remote Year to solve a specific
problem—in this case, that the then twenty-five-year-old wanted
to travel and work remotely after selling his fashion blogging platform to Groupon for $250,000 but couldn't find friends to join
him. "The biggest issue is traveling alone," he said in 2015. "I
thought it'd be lonely. I wanna go travel but I wanna do it with a
community and in a more structured way."[22]

With Remote Year, Anywhereists signed up for a year-long
work-travel experience, with destinations, apartments, coworking spaces, and sometimes outings arranged by the company. The
cost: a $3,000 deposit, plus around $2,000 a month, or $27,000
for a year. The concept of working from anywhere was still so
unusual then that Remote Year offered to match would-be participants with entry-level remote jobs. (They no longer do that
but will coach you on how to bring up the idea of working from

anywhere with your boss.) The quirky mélange of travel agency and employment service tapped into the emerging Anywhereist zeitgeist with a "have your cake and eat it too" scenario—a way to be both a self-supporting adult and a vagabond.

There were growing pains. In the first Remote Year cohort of sixty-eight Anywhereists, not everyone actually had a job, creating a partier/worker divide that left the people who had to actually, you know, work seething with FOMO.

Practical elements sometimes proved problematic. Participants complained so loudly about their lodging in Hanoi that Remote Year waived the monthly fee.

Ugly American moments cropped up too. Joyce Lin, an LA-based project manager in the group, explained the dynamic to Atlas Obscura: "If I travel on my own, I am forced to be in the position of the learner. People are not going to cater to me. I'm the minority, I'm forced to learn how the local culture is, and I'm forced to blend in with that, right? But then when we are in a group we have this presence that changes the way we interact with the places we are going into."[23]

Despite these challenges, the program has been transformative for people like Sarah Aviram, a human resources manager whose desire to travel nagged at her through stints at Fortune 500 companies like PepsiCo and Avon. She fantasized about taking a trip around the world, "but I didn't want to have to stop my career," she said. "I didn't want to have to use all my savings, which wasn't that much. I didn't want to go by myself. And I didn't want to plan it."[24]

Remote Year ticked all the boxes. She paid the $3,000 deposit and talked the CEO of the New York City–based tech company where she worked into letting her take her job on the road as an experiment in the future of work.

A human resources specialist, Sarah couldn't help but look closely at how her cohort of lawyers, software engineers, social media marketing professionals, consultants, ad agency employees, graphic designers, musicians, and entrepreneurs saw their jobs. For some, the year of travel was a Band-Aid to cover the fact that they hated their work but felt powerless to change it. "They had the classic golden handcuffs," said Sarah, "like, 'I get paid too much to do something else.'"

One day, Sarah led a career development workshop for her Remote Year group. Most people, she explained, have six core motivations that drive decisions around career: money, identity, routines, growth, impact, and ultimately joy. To stay happy in your job, you have to minimize friction related to the first three—by repaying debt, reducing expenses, using geographic arbitrage, ignoring outside expectations about the kind of work you should be doing, or reconsidering habits that keep you stuck on autopilot. After that, you can create a vision of what you really want to do *now* (not what you wanted when you were twenty-two) that expands your idea of what's possible for yourself. Sarah had done that just a few months before by convincing her boss to let her work from the road—her version of Nandita's big step of divorce.

With Sarah's encouragement, one disgruntled lawyer on Remote Year quit his job and became a vlogger, traveling around the United States in an RV.

Sarah has since left her job too, after a week back in her windowless New York City office prompted an existential crisis. "I actually kind of dreaded coming back into a corporate job after having the freedom that I had," she said. "I was like, 'I used to work on the beach in Bali.'"

Geographic arbitrage worked in her favor. Living on about $2,000 a month while earning her $200,000-a-year Manhattan salary, Sarah stockpiled cash during Remote Year; she even managed to pay off her business-school debt. That money gave her the freedom to leave corporate human resources and launch her own career consulting business, centered around the guidebook she wrote for remote workers, called *Remotivation*.[25]

At thirty-eight, Sarah's still figuring out what her remote life will look like going forward. Six months in New York, where her family lives, and six months elsewhere? Time in Shanghai or Thailand, where a delicious dinner costs $5? She spends a lot of time on the Remote Year Slack channel, talking to other people who are asking the same big questions about life, work, and location. Whenever she's ready to say, "I'm thinking about Costa Rica. Who wants to come?" she knows she'll have fellow Wanderers to go with her.

A BUNCH OF WEIRDOS

Living on the road has a way of doing funny things to your relationship with work. It can reinvigorate you, like it did for Nandita. Or make you pivot, like Sarah did. Or convince you, like Lauren, to cut back and earn only as much money as you need to keep traveling.

Rick Graham, a nomadic software engineer, met the cofounder for his blockchain-based events and tickets platform while traveling in Bulgaria. "I didn't know anybody in my network who was really willing to commit what it takes to start a business," he said. Then, at a digital nomad networking event called Silicon Drinkabout, he met a Bulgarian with the skills and the interest to help him move forward.[26]

For Marco Piras, a remote job as a growth product manager for a San Francisco–based company gave him control over his life as an expat. He's originally from Sardinia, Italy, and had done stints in Dublin and Copenhagen, but his dream job was the one that let him settle in Barcelona, Spain.[27]

According to a 2018 FlexJobs survey, about half of digital nomads make the same income or more as when they worked in a traditional office. One in six earn more than $75,000, but only 40 percent of nomads reported making more than $50,000 a year, perhaps because the fields that lend themselves to nomadism, like writing, education, customer service, data entry, and marketing, are lower paid to begin with. About a third of nomads had to get outside financial help from friends or family to make ends meet.[28]

When Hannah Dixon started out as a nomad, she scrounged odd jobs wherever she happened to be. She did a lot of bartending. She worked at a fashion house on Savile Row in London. She was a sales clerk at Macy's in New York City for a few months. She trained husky dogs for sled races. She did permaculture gardening. She volunteered on farms across Europe as part of WWOOF (Worldwide Opportunities on Organic Farms) in exchange for room and board. Once, she served drinks at a gentleman's bar.[29]

Money was never her object until she met a woman who worked online from home. This was 2013, and Hannah had no idea that online jobs you could do from anywhere existed. "I was like, 'Tell me everything I need to know.'"

Together they started a web development company, with Hannah offering virtual assistant services to beef up their income. Hannah was making more money than she'd ever seen. Friends started asking about her virtual work, and over a few weeks in Italy in late 2016, she put together a new website called DigitalNomadKit.com to train digital nomads, about twelve thousand of them from seventy-five countries, to make money as virtual assistants.

"Digital nomad" is not a term Hannah's always identified with. Most of the nomads she knew in her early days of travel were "very much young, straight white men hanging out in Chiang Mai living on $500 a month and bragging about it." At digital nomad meetups, she'd often be the only woman being preached at about hustle culture by a group of bro marketers who spent their days in hammocks. Cringey. Where, she wondered, were the women, the people of color, the queer people?

Some of them have gathered in Hannah's Digital Nomad Kit Facebook group, which she affectionately calls "a bunch of weirdos." The digital nomad community is slowly becoming more diverse; a third are now female, and more than half are over age thirty-eight.

There's still a dearth of people of color. Tykesha S. Burton, founder of MommaWanderlust.com, a travel site for Black families, said that may be because "as African Americans, we're still taking care of the basic needs... I didn't inherit a home; I didn't have my college paid for. I owe $80,000 in college debt. I have to work 40 hours. I could find a remote job, but that's not where I am yet."[30]

Figuring out how to combine work and wandering is the trick here. Hannah's entire cohort of virtual assistants are people who hope to be hired to do online odd jobs for someone else. Some of them lost traditional jobs in the pandemic and are freelancing to make ends meet. They're not all digital nomads, but they could be. FlexJobs found that about 18 percent of digital nomads own their own businesses, along with 28 percent who freelance and 35 percent who are employed by a company.[31]

Entrepreneurs and Wanderers have at least one thing in common: they're risk-takers with high levels of self-efficacy, a fancy term for a belief in your ability to accomplish a task. Though she hates the woo-woo sound of it, that's what Hannah Dixon said defines most successful digital nomads. They believe in themselves.

If you want to be a digital nomad, maybe try it out for a month or two first, Hannah advised. See how well you do working outside your normal environment. Save some money in a travel fund. Don't do it if you can't afford it. "You know, it's really nice to fantasize about, 'I'll just go to Budapest and figure it out.'" But speaking from experience, Hannah said, "That was hard work."[32]

Location Strategy Session: Adventure

An unbeatable benefit of location independence is the freedom you have to see the world without derailing your career, draining your savings accounts, or maxing out your vacation days. It's not for everyone, but if you're a Wanderer at heart (or want to be), you can try it for a season with these tips:

1. **Use geographic arbitrage:** Balancing time spent in a more expensive country, like Switzerland, with time

spent in a less expensive country, like Vietnam, can let you see the world affordably.

2. **Find a cohort:** Travel buddies make nomadism more enjoyable (and arguably safer). To find them, try a program like Remote Year or WiFi Tribe. Or join a coliving space designed for digital nomads, like Roam, whose big-city locations come with access to a shared kitchen for $1,800 a month, or Outpost, with coliving spots in Bali and Cambodia that start at $63 a night.

3. **Get reenergized:** When you're in a new place, even regular things require extra mental focus. "There's this opening of your brain that just happens where you're like, Oh, I need Band-Aids. Where do I go to get Band-Aids?" said designer Kristine Arth.[33] That next-level focus can juice creativity. The search for Band-Aids (or whatever) in an unfamiliar town pushes you headlong into new sights, new sounds, and new things in the grocery aisle.

4. **Apply for a digital nomad visa:** Slow travel can be a better way to experience a new country than fly-by-night tours. With a longer-term digital nomad visa, you can stay in most countries for up to a year without worrying about pesky visa runs.

5. **Attend a digital nomad conference:** There are dozens, including Digital Nomad Summit and Digital Nomad Festival DNX. Look for sessions that both inspire and cover the nitty-gritty, like how to get e-residency in Estonia or start a profitable blog.

6. **Hire a nomad coach:** If you're still not 100 percent sure how to get started as a digital nomad, a coach who's been doing it for a while can advise you on how to pick a country, manage your work life when you're living abroad, and make money as an Anywhereist. Or look for an online course that can walk you through the basics.

7. **Find a place to work:** Joining a coworking space abroad can help you network with risk-taking, big-thinking Anywhereists. (Like you.) A monthly membership to CoPass gives you access to 950+ work spaces worldwide, wherever you happen to be.

8. **Pare down and move online:** Prep for a digital nomad life by moving as much of your work life as you can online, including banking and document signing. Eliminate physical possessions by selling furniture online and giving away excess to a local thrift store or nonprofit that can use it. Joshua Fields Millburn and Ryan Nicodemus's website TheMinimalists.com can get you started. Try their thirty-day minimalism game.[34]

9. **Explore locally:** Maybe you like daydreaming about digital nomadism but you're never going to actually do it. That's okay. One of the things about being a Wanderer is that the novelty of it provides an energy and creativity power-up. Add novelty to your Settler life by arranging weekend trips to nearby places, exploring what your town has to offer, even varying your daily routine so you don't feel stuck.

10. **Manage time zones:** Because Nandita Gupta's clients are mostly North American, during her year abroad, she'd sometimes have to schedule phone calls for three in the morning. Other remote workers who had to clock in for nine-to-five remote jobs would start work at 10:00 p.m. and finish at 6:00 a.m. "We called it the night shift," Nandita said. If your job requires you to be available during certain hours, do the time zone math before you pick a place.[35]

11. **Live your dream:** Sixty-three percent of millennials say that financing travel is the main reason they hold down a full-time job in the first place, well ahead of things like saving for retirement or paying off debt.[36] Anywhereism lets you combine the two in a way that can give more purpose to your work, as long as you can remember the distinction between being a Wanderer and being on permanent vacation.

Place Study: Funchal, Portugal

Population: 111,000

- **Why it's cool:** Lisbon, Portugal, has been one of Nomad List's top spots for ages ("It's great if you're woke, young, and artsy," says the website). For someplace smaller and slightly more exotic, a two-hour plane ride away is the Portuguese archipelago of Madeira, whose capital city, Funchal, cracked Nomad List's top ten with its friendliness, low cost of living, and fast and free Wi-Fi.[37]

- **How digital nomads stay:** Portugal offers a temporary stay visa for independent workers and freelancers who earn at least 635 euros per month (that comes out to slightly less than $10,000 USD a year). That lets you live in the country for a year, then renew for two more years. It's a bargain 75 euros. Want to stay longer? Maybe even become a permanent resident? There are a few pathways for that too, including the Golden Visa for people willing to invest in Portugal.

- **Where to work:** Once you've toured Funchal's white-washed cathedral and ridden the cable car to the Monte Palace Tropical Garden, settle down to work at CoWork Funchal, a super modern space inside a colonial downtown building. A desk for a week costs 43 euros.

- **Why nomads like it:** Because Madeira is working hard to be liked. Thirty minutes up the coast from Funchal, the village of Ponta do Sol launched Digital Nomads Madeira in early 2021, creating a nomad community with a nomads-only Slack channel, swag bags, and free workspace in the local cultural center. (Score a desk on the terrace for stunning views of the sea.) Within a couple weeks of the program launch, over four thousand nomads from around the world had registered online, and more than one hundred had made the move to Ponta do Sol.[38] As remote work consultant Gonçalo Hall told CNN, "With many people leaving big cities right now, we wanted a village in a smaller place where people can create deeper connections than in a city."[39]

- **Getting to know you:** American educator Jenn Parr and her husband were already remote working in Portugal, but they trekked to Madeira for the double action of mountains and oceans as well as the chance to be around other

Anywhereists. "It can be inspiring to meet people who are entrepreneurs or have found ways to create more freedom in their lives and follow their passions," she said. They locked in a three-bedroom apartment between Funchal and Ponta do Sol that cost about $2,200 a month and filled the other bedrooms with nomad roommates.[40]

- **Small perks:** The upside of being in a smaller place is that connection is easier. Even with face masks and social distancing during the pandemic, Digital Nomads Madeira organized communal yoga classes, group hikes, and other opportunities for Anywhereists to network and learn from each other. In places like Ponta do Sol, which draws comparisons to the villages of Italy's Amalfi Coast, you may run into program participants just by stepping outside your house.

10

SMARTER PLACES

Location Strategy Value: Learning

The state of Utah had a crisis. Young adults were moving away from rural counties in the southeastern part of the state because there weren't enough jobs to go around. Coal mining was dying, replaced by limited pockets of employment at a few schools, hospitals, ranches, and tourist destinations like Arches National Park. In some rural counties, up to 35 percent of the workforce had been laid off, and local populations were declining as a result.[1] The Settlers couldn't stay settled if they couldn't make money where they lived.

In 2018, the Utah legislature authorized $2.2 million for a potential solution: the Rural Online Initiative (ROI), a program to train rural residents for remote work.[2] "The entire premise was using the mobility of jobs to bring opportunity to the people, instead of the people having to move to go to the opportunity," said Laurel Farrer, CEO of Distribute Consulting, who helped lead the project.[3]

It's not unusual for states and cities to introduce workforce development projects to prep special groups—people with low incomes or disabilities, workers who have been dislocated—for jobs. But Utah's ROI program was unusual because the end goal was upskilling workers so they could keep living where they were living while working jobs elsewhere, potentially even outside the state. In other words, this was a program to help Settlers become Anywhereists so they could stay Settlers.

The idea was brand new, and Laurel figured getting locals to participate would be the biggest obstacle. If you're a former coal miner or a cattle rancher's wife in Blanding, Utah, what could they say or do to get you to care about remote work?

But the pushback Laurel braced her team for never materialized. In most communities, once the mayor or another local influencer got on board, word of mouth did the rest. The town halls that ROI leaders held in local community centers were always packed. "The adoption rates were astronomical," Laurel told me. She and her team were hoping to sign up five hundred participants the first year. They reached five hundred in the first month.

Most of the participants were women, often homemakers reentering the workforce for a secondary household income. Family ties or a family ranch had brought them here; they typically loved the quality of life but hated being chronically underemployed. One had a PhD but earned $10 an hour as a secretary at the local elementary school. In ROI's online remote work certification course, they learned to identify potential Anywhereist career paths, develop and market their remote-ready job skills (like telling potential employers that you know C++ coding language, not just that you make websites), and practice applying and interviewing for jobs.

One ROI grad began doing remote patient intake for a New York City therapy clinic. A landscape architect from Sanpete County found long-distance gigs on Upwork. After the Utah Office of Economic Development sweetened the deal by offering a $5,000 bonus to Utah businesses that hired employees from rural counties, Whitley Potter, a stay-at-home mom to three kids in Tabiona, Utah (population 134), landed a job as a project manager with Utah-based Tephra Solar. It doubled her household income.[4]

For some Settlers, access to remote work gigs and knowledge about how to get and keep them is the only way to stay financially afloat when you live outside a major job market. For Anywhereist Seekers, the existence of a program like ROI telegraphs a message: this place is willing to do what it takes to help you grow here. No small thing, considering that professional growth—through training, education, upskilling, and mentorship—is one of the motivations that kept Facebook's workers satisfied in their jobs.

And it happens to kill two birds with one stone. That's because good help is hard to find these days. A 2018 survey by ManpowerGroup of nearly forty thousand employers in forty-three countries found that nearly half were struggling to find the right kind of workers for open jobs—the worst talent crunch in a decade.[5] The problem persisted through the pandemic. In 2021, 40 percent of C-suite and human resources leaders worldwide complained that talent scarcity was hampering their business.[6]

Like Chamber of Commerce exec Jessica Heer does for Dallas, some communities simply poach the talent from other places. More and more, though, that's a zero-sum game; there just isn't enough talent to go around. "With record talent shortages around the world, it's no longer a question of simply finding talent," said

Jonas Prising, chairman and CEO of ManpowerGroup. "We need to build it."[7]

Businesses obviously want to, but places are in on this too, offering education and training programs that do one of two things: turn residents into highly skilled remote workers, or equip residents with skills to fill local jobs. As Anne-Marie Slaughter, president and CEO of New America, has said, "Every place has a distribution of talent. Stop attracting and start lifting up."[8] As always, you are the talent—or could become the talent with a little investment from the place where you live.

DREAM DISTRICT

"Small towns but not small minds" was Laurel Farrer's mantra during her own recent place search. Like so many of the people she helped through Utah's ROI program, Lauren relishes the fact that remote work—she's also a consultant and president of the Remote Work Association—allows her a slower pace of life in a place she chooses herself. "We kind of think that living in New York and Silicon Valley is the dream that everybody's chasing after," she said. "And it's like, no, that's just where the high-paying jobs are. So if you can have the high-paying job and still have that nostalgic quality of life living in Mayberry, that's kind of the sweet spot."[9]

She wanted rural, but she didn't want uneducated, especially for her kids. Like most parents trying to execute a location strategy, school quality was high on the list, and she and her husband analyzed school rankings and fretted over electives in service of giving their kids the very best possible start in life.

Not for nothing either. Research by Raj Chetty, the Harvard economist who studies economic mobility, found that as early as kindergarten, teaching quality can affect outcomes far off in the future, including whether students go to college or how much they earn afterward.[10] Nationwide, there are huge disparities in education spending. In 2019, average spending per K-12 student, adjusted for regional price differences, was $12,756. But that figure hides a surprising range: Vermont was spending $20,540 per child, while Utah came in at just $7,635.[11]

Even within the same city, school quality can vary dramatically, pushing place decisions down to neighborhoods. No pressure for Seekers, who have to try to find the best classrooms where, by the way, homes are affordable. That in itself feels like an impossible task. According to a 2016 study by Realtor.com, homes inside well-ranked school districts cost 49 percent more than the median national home price, thus feeding a cycle of inequality: property tax revenues are higher in areas that cost more, so more expensive neighborhoods are intrinsically linked with better (or at least better financed) public schools.[12]

Some people escape the struggle by opting to live in areas that prioritize school choice, putting their money into private school rather than real estate, or home schooling. But for most Americans, geography and education remain tangled. When big swaths of the country shifted to online school during the pandemic, some Americans made long-distance relocations to other states or countries to get their children an in-person schooling experience.[13] Others became Wanderers, RVing the country with children in tow now that they didn't have to be in a single location for school.

Laurel Farrer's place search ultimately landed her family in rural Connecticut, where her kids attend well-ranked local schools and she runs her remote-work consulting business out of her home. Small town, not small minds—exactly what she wanted.

For now, at least. Because the relationship between geography and educational outcomes doesn't stop with twelfth grade. Where you live may also determine the kind of higher education options your family has access to and how much they cost.

For instance, a handful of states, including California, Delaware, and Maryland, have made community college free for state residents, at a potential savings of nearly $10,000 for an associate's degree.[14] Meanwhile, if your child wants to attend one of *U.S. News & World Report*'s top-ranked public universities—UCLA, UC Berkeley, University of Michigan, University of Virginia, or University of North Carolina—you can expect to pay on average $31,416 more in tuition and fees each year if you live out of state.

Moving to California with the dim hope that one day your kid will both get into UCLA *and* want to go there isn't exactly the wisest location strategy. But at that price point, you're not crazy for at least gauging which states might give your kids the best shot at attending a great school without drowning in debt. (The cheapest in-state tuition in the country: the University of Wyoming, only $4,620 a year.)

Education is an investment that places make in their residents. The bigger the investment in you and your family's knowledge, talent, skills, job readiness, and potential as a human being, the bigger the payoff for choosing the right place.

CRADLE TO GRAVE

To solve the talent crisis and retain the residents they've got, communities are starting young. Really young. Envision your preschooler whooshing through sixteen or so years of steadily intensifying STEM or leadership or otherwise specialized education, eventually emerging perfectly prepped to fill a local job opening. The idea of a cradle-to-grave talent pipeline may sound a little Orwellian, but it's happening already.

In Virginia, for instance, a key piece of the proposal that won Amazon's HQ2 business was the promise that the commonwealth would dump $25 million into improving STEM and computer science curriculums in K-12 classrooms statewide, literally "at every grade for every student," with after-school programming like coding camps and work-study programs. Ideally, all that early STEM education will lead more Virginia high schoolers to study computer science in college, producing the thirty thousand additional STEM grads that Amazon predicts it will need over the next two decades.[15]

Certainly Amazon would love more computer science graduates right now. But as the proverb goes, "The best time to plant a tree was twenty years ago. The second best time is now." (Or build a time machine. Probably in the works over there.) Virginia is playing the long game.

Other places with current or anticipated worker shortages are making more immediate interventions. Some high schools offer in-school workforce academies, with classes that teach the skills local employers need most, like technology, management, operations, or public speaking. Other communities run apprenticeship programs for teens. In Newfoundland and Labrador, Canada, an internship program pays fifty high school students $15 an hour to take full-time summer jobs with local tech companies, more than they can make scooping ice cream or mowing lawns.[16] The hope is they'll get interested enough in the business that they'll keep learning—and return to the province for full-time jobs after college.

College and adult education programs are where the talent pipeline really kicks in. Boot camps to prep participants for local biotechnology jobs. Tech hub trainings in data visualization and analysis. The problem for local talent pipeline programs is that a newly upskilled software developer is now a potential Anywhereist who can get a job in all those other cities that want tech talent too. Dallas. Tulsa. The Shoals. What's to keep them in the community where they started?

Well, nothing. But places like rural Crawford County, Ohio, make sure all their grads at least know what kinds of opportunities are waiting for them in their hometown. As part of the WAGE (Workforce Awareness for Graduates and Educators) Tour, every eighth grader in the school district hops on a bus for a field trip to some of the largest local businesses. Maybe a middle schooler who hears the CEO of Arctic Cat explain how they make snowmobiles in rural Ohio will decide his future dream job is in his hometown, not bigger cities like Cleveland and Columbus.[17]

There's something a bit disturbing about the effort to train a small child for the workplace, but realistically, people need jobs and employers need workers. The system is pleasingly symbiotic. Anyway, cynics would counter that's what free public school education has always done. It's just that the jobs have changed. Now, instead of funneling workers toward a factory line, school programming preps them for the lab or the tech start-up, often for free or as part of the everyday curriculum.

If you add learning and growth to your location strategy,

you can look for local programs that benefit you and your family. Internships. Mentorships. An after-school coding camp at the elementary school. Even training that makes you a better Anywhereist.

Relocation U

According to the American Communities Project, about 18.6 million people live in counties that are home to colleges and universities.[18] For Seekers, college towns can tick a lot of boxes for good quality of life:

- Plenty of university-related things to do, from sporting events to theater productions to films to concerts
- Chances for ongoing learning, either officially as a student or more recreationally through lectures, seminars, and speaker series
- Better K-12 educational opportunities, like student-run preschools, after-school programs, and summer camps
- Walkability and good public transportation, since college towns cater to students on foot
- Better healthcare facilities typically, especially if there's a medical school nearby
- Diversity, as universities often draw students and faculty from across the country and overseas
- A larger work ecosystem should you want a job locally
- More economic stability, since the university acts as an anchor institution
- And if you lived in this college town as a student, more place attachment, bolstered by a plethora of happy memories

---

RIPPLES

If Anywhereists are people who, at a certain moment in time, have to make a tough decision about where to go next among the multitude of locations open to them, then nowhere has more Anywhereists than a college town right before graduation.

Maybe you remember the feeling of cramming for your last-ever finals while burbling with an acidic mix of fear and excitement about your postcollege destination. Maybe you packed your car with your laptop and your dirty laundry and drove off into the sunset, pretty sure you'd find your dream entry-level job in your dream city.

The vast majority of students don't stay in their college communities—most don't even try to stay. They're happily off to major metros whose prestige seems to validate the massive debt they incurred in school. Perhaps it's easier to convince your parents that your life choices make sense when you have a fancy new job title in Atlanta.

But it's a perennial heartbreaker for college communities that pour resources into the ultradesirable eighteen-to-twenty-five crowd only to see them toss their caps at graduation and disappear without a backward glance.

Nebraska, for instance, ranks tenth in the nation for net migration of college-educated adults out of state, losing about sixteen hundred young adults with bachelor's degrees every year to states like Colorado, California, Texas, and Iowa that seem to hold more opportunity or sex appeal.[19] Dave Rippe is determined to keep a few more of them.

Dave is the born-and-raised Nebraskan director of the Scott Scholars program at Hastings College, in Hastings, Nebraska.

Scott Scholars is a new initiative with a goal of turning about seven top-notch students a year into what Dave thinks of as "builders"— leaders who have a desire to create something, anything, bigger than themselves. "Builders of places, builders of business, builders of community, builders of whatever," Dave said.[20]

According to Peter Kageyama, author of *For the Love of Cities*, only 1 percent of the residents of a given community are wired to be builders, a number that Dave, as a builder himself (he's the former economic development director for the state and develops projects in downtown Hastings), finds strangely comforting.[21] It means that in a town like Hastings, with a population of 25,000, about 250 people in the community are going to be natural-born builders, whether they're entrepreneurs or leaders or the master-minds behind cool new projects.

To make Hastings better, you don't have to attract a whole bunch more people. You just need a few more builders. Even twenty-five more builders in Dave's hometown could launch a flywheel effect of cumulative wins that create momentum and energy. So he runs the Scott Scholars program like Builders 101, first hand-selecting smart students with proven leadership potential, then spending four years showing them exactly what being a builder looks like. If he can get them to envision themselves becoming builders in Nebraska par-ticularly, maybe they'll stay put after graduation.

It's a long shot with students like nineteen-year-old Emma Enochs, whose full-ride Scott Scholarship convinced her to enroll at Hastings but who admits that Nebraska is the state she's mocked all her life.[22] "When I first started coming to school here, I hated all things Nebraska," Emma said. Driving into the state from her hometown of Lebanon, Kansas, she would pass the welcome sign that says "Nebraska...the good life" and snark to herself, "Is it though?" (If there's anything I've learned about places, it's that everyone has to have another place to mock.)

She may be starting to waver. During the 2020–21 school year, Dave Rippe tapped his bulging contact list and set up some high-level field trips and meet and greets for Emma Enochs and the other members of the first cohort of Scott Scholars at Hastings College. CEOs, mayors, entrepreneurs, state senators, and nonprofit directors all spoke with them. Even the governor of Nebraska. Emma gushed about the governor.

Most impressive to Emma was meeting the billionaire who funded her scholarship. Walter Scott, the former CEO of an Omaha-based construction and engineering firm, looked Emma in the face and told her she was a great investment for his money. She was going to do wonderful things. Ideally in Nebraska. "That totally shifted my world," Emma said. "Not only do these people want me to succeed, but their skin is in the game too. They want me to stay in their state. Like, [the governor of Kansas] never told me that I was going to be a Kansan for life."

Other states and cities are coming up with their own approaches to retaining their talent after graduation. In Philadelphia, losing college grads was a prime industry for years. At least fifty postsecondary institutions in the area, from the University of Pennsylvania to seven community colleges, grant about ninety thousand degrees every year. But only about 28 percent of the students who came from out of town for school stayed to work locally after graduation.[23] Often the Philadelphia region wasn't even on the short list of places to look for a full-time job.

To change those numbers, in the early 2000s, Philadelphia's Commerce Department started an organization called Campus Philly to connect students with job opportunities in the city. The organization sponsored career fairs and created a single, one-stop website that listed local jobs and internships. Campus Philly also sponsored dozens of career development events each year, from panels about jobs in biotech to grad student happy hours. During the pandemic, YouTube interviews with young locals talking about how they got their jobs were a regular thing.

The plot twist was Campus Philly's second mission: to get students to fall in love with Philly so they wanted to stay. "You have to get students off campus, so they even have a concept that there's a city beyond their campus borders," said Deborah Diamond, a former director of Campus Philly.[24] To that end, Campus Philly puts on an annual CollegeFest to welcome students to the city. And their website features an Explore Philly guide, with city event listings, neighborhood guides, and discounts to theaters, museums, and sports leagues, the kinds of activities that could make a nonlocal feel like they belong there.

In the Anywhereist moment that is college graduation, most young adults are paying closer attention to place than to jobs, but intertwining the two has yielded success stories for Campus Philly. Philadelphia now retains a sizable 54 percent of its college grads, who generate an additional $394 million in tax revenue each year. Other cities have started their own Campus Philly–style programs, including Greensboro, Cleveland, and Rochester.[25]

Most university towns have never assumed that their students would stay for life. Amid gladiatorial relationships between full-time residents and student populations or endless squabbles over big parties and noise violations, some people barely consider college students bona fide residents; they exist in this odd limbo— not from here, not *not* from here. (When I tell people about my own college town, Blacksburg, I usually feel compelled to mention that I'm not sure how many students are included in the population count of forty-three thousand.)

Yet college students are predisposed to love where they went to school. If you're thinking of a place to boomerang back to, your college town might end up on the list. "I think people realize this more and more in this generation, and probably postpandemic, that you kind of have to look at the 360 of your life," said Deborah Diamond. "Sacrificing friends, a livable apartment, and a neighborhood you enjoy for that perfect job just does not make sense anymore. It never did."[26]

With the 360 in mind, Emma Enochs, the Hastings College Scott Scholar, is thus far firm about her plan to go back home to Kansas to practice medicine in the same town where her parents and grandparents live. "Dave's great at making a Nebraska commercial," she admitted, "because it is a wonderful state." But that's as far as she's willing to go.[27]

BOOMERANGS

College towns want to retain their grads. Other communities want to attract them back. Whatever Emma Enochs ends up doing in the future, she's not alone in her plans to boomerang. On average, 25 percent of new residents who make the move to rural communities are boomerangs in their thirties and forties, former residents who have gotten a taste of urban life and realized what they're missing.[28] Right at the age when adults start marrying and having kids, they come back, said Ben Winchester, a rural sociologist with the University of Minnesota Extension, who said indicators point to "brain gain," not drain.[29]

One part of the value proposition in returning to the place where you came from is that it may make you better at your work. In a study by Harvard Business School professor Prithwiraj Choudhury, who regularly researches the impact of place on workers, an Indian technology firm randomly assigned new entry-level employees to one of eight locations across the country.[30] Over the next few years, the farther the worker was from their hometown, the worse their performance fared. Being a fish out of water made them suck at their job.

The biggest toll came during the festival of Diwali, the most important holiday in the Hindu year, akin to Christmas for Christians. If Indians workers were too far away to travel home, the emotional and cultural toll made the quality of their work product decline. Choudhury suggested that employers solve the problem by offering more flexibility and vacation time so far-away workers don't miss Diwali at home, but an even more obvious solution is that the workers move closer to home. If they're Anywhereists, they can.

Like college students and tech workers, boomerangs have become a hot commodity in the talent attraction and retention game. Greensboro, North Carolina, has a website aimed at enticing them, with stories of people who used to live in Greensboro and came back, including a jet-setting New Yorker and a Portland, Oregon, executive chef, along with contact info for "Greensboro Gurus" willing to point you to all the cool things you've missed out on while you were gone.[31]

Other places offer boomerang-specific financial incentives. The Come Home (Reverse) Scholarship program gives college graduates with STEM degrees $10,000 to help pay off student loans if they get a local job or create their own business back home in the thumb of Michigan's mitten.[32] The point was to attract contributors to the local economy. In Dave Rippe's words, builders.

There are challenges for Anywhereists moving back to their hometown, acknowledges Winchester. Are you going to have to explain to your old high school chemistry teacher what you do for a living? Will your mom want you to come by every time the garbage disposal isn't working? Unfortunately, boomerangs are sometimes hit with commentary from community members like, "Oh, so you couldn't make it in the real world."

But if you can get past that, you can focus on the appeal of boomeranging, which centers around family values, nostalgia, and a place attachment that already runs deep. One Iowa boomerang who'd worked in Chicago and Santa Monica, California, explained it this way: "There are certain traditions and values here that are different than both coasts. I loved California, but I didn't want to have a family out there. I wanted my parents close by, and I wanted my kids to have the same memories I have."[33]

Even Dave Rippe, who desperately wants talented kids to stay put in Nebraska, is okay with that. "It would be so incestuous to think that we should have every kid stay here and that we should wrap our arms around them and never let them leave," Dave said. "I think that the true aspiration would be, 'Get out of here, go see the world, but then ultimately see the value proposition to come back here and be a change maker.'"[34]

Dave likes to tell the Scott Scholars how much Nebraska needs them, how much it's open to their input, how much of a difference they can make living in the state. "The ripples that you make in the center of the water can reach the edge here," he said.

Location Strategy Session: Learning

Offering ways for residents to upskill, intern, pivot careers, and find the next job is part of how cities are attracting and retaining the next generation of talent, including you and your kids. Here's how your family can take advantage of the resources on tap.

1. **Learn more:** Most Anywhereists regularly need to upskill or reskill, and you may be able to find free training or resources where you live. In Connecticut, for instance, you can get a free 180-day license to more than five thousand courses in the online Metrix Learning catalog to develop your skills, while the city of Austin offers a free full-stack development boot camp to residents. Search online for "workforce development" and the name of your town for programs and resources you might qualify for.

2. **Join an upskilling challenge:** Louisville, Kentucky, partnered with Microsoft to offer free online coursework from groups like Google Analytics, Cognitive Class, Microsoft Learn, IBM, and General Assembly, with a thirty-day challenge to earn a tech-centric certification that would make you more employable. To motivate a 2021 cohort, participants were entered

for a weekly raffle of a free laptop. The program was sponsored by the Louisville Future of Work Initiative, but a similar program has popped up in New York.[35]

3. **Help your teen find an internship:** To build a talent pipeline early, smart companies make room for high schoolers—and it arguably looks better on their résumé than a mission trip to Africa. Your child's counseling department or the local economic development office may have leads.

4. **Think regional:** A small town may not have everything you're looking for. But if you're at the epicenter of a two-hour region, what do you have access to then? You can likely meet all your needs, including the need to get a nonremote job in the future.

5. **Account for schooling:** To completely escape the tyranny of geography vis-à-vis education, you're going to have to homeschool your kids, and there are abundant options to help you do that. If you'd rather not, remember that test scores aren't the only indicator of school quality, and you can find a good fit for your child most places. Ben Winchester pointed out that in his small-town school district, his child gets more opportunities to participate in extracurriculars like sports simply because the programs need bodies.[36]

6. **Teach your kids what they can do locally:** Ultimately, you want your children to choose the best paths for themselves. But don't write off the area you live in because you believe they need to fly elsewhere to have a good experience. One Michigan town gives

high school seniors a mailbox as they graduate. The
message: No matter where you go, you'll always have
a place here.[37]

Place Study: Burley, Idaho

Population: 10,313

- **Geographic oddity:** Way closer to the Utah and Nevada borders than it is to its own state capital in Boise, two and a half
hours away.

- **Closest Costco:** forty-five minutes west in Twin Falls.

- **Why people live here:** Often because they're from here.
Mike Ramsey and his wife boomeranged to Burley after
college to open a work-from-anywhere marketing firm,
Nifty Marketing. "It was super, super high risk moving back
to Burley," Mike said. "But I felt like it was the right thing to
do." Their families still lived there, and they wanted the kind
of life where they had built-in babysitters and Sunday dinners with their extended families. Mike and his wife broke
ground on a new house the day Mike quit his day job to
start a new business.[38] Like Cortés burning the ships, there
was no going back.

- **Local pride:** The vast majority of Nifty Marketing's clients
aren't local. Most of them have no idea where the company is based. Yet in the early days of Nifty Marketing,
Mike downplayed just how small a town he worked in, fear-
ing that it would make him appear less serious. Over time,
being in Burley became a positive differentiator—a way to
embody small-town values. As Mike explained, "We began
to embrace it."

- **The pitch:** Despite his initial worries, it's actually been fairly easy for Nifty to attract talent. Mike matches the salary they would make in a city like Boise and points out how much farther their money goes in Burley, how quickly they can be hiking or kayaking the Snake River, and how great life is for families with kids. "There is a type of person who absolutely eats it up and is very happy to be able to have a job that's more of a city job in a place where it's a total lifestyle," Mike said. Some employees originally hail from the area, but the ones who don't still tend to buy their own homes and get involved in the community. That makes Nifty more resistant to the constant churn that dogs similar companies elsewhere. Employees who want to stay in Burley will probably stay at Nifty.

- **Revitalizing Burley:** In a town as small as Burley, a company with twenty-five employees has a big impact. A few years ago, Mike bought a run-down building in Burley's fading 1940s downtown to house Nifty's headquarters. The effect was catalytic. Now multiple projects are in the works, and other entrepreneurs are buying and restoring long-empty real estate. Someone's putting in an upscale restaurant; there's a new real estate office and a call center. A few of his employees have even spun off marketing companies with different slants. To Mike, they don't represent competition but a growth industry in Burley.

- **Future students:** If Mike's four kids want to go to state universities, they have a handful of choices, including the University of Idaho, whose 2021 in-state tuition was $8,300 a year. But as part of the Western Interstate Commission for Higher Education, Idaho has reciprocal agreements with fifteen western states—Alaska, Arizona, California, Colorado, Hawaii, Idaho, Montana, Nevada, New Mexico, North Dakota, Oregon, South Dakota, Utah, Washington, and Wyoming—so students can get reduced tuition at over 160 public universities and colleges.

- **How to end brain drain:** Nurturing home-grown entrepreneurship is key, Mike thinks, to saving small towns like his. Burley's high school graduates around two hundred seniors a year who typically go elsewhere; the other rural schools in the community do another two hundred. That's four hundred seniors a year that the area loses on an annual basis. If you could convince a few of those to remain—or come back—and "start and build things, then that's how you grow and save small-town USA," Mike said.

BEING THE GOOD WHERE YOU LIVE

Location Strategy Value: Purpose

In 2016, Amanda Staas and her husband, Luke Uncapher, were waiting for a table at Brewfontaine beer bar, in downtown Bellefontaine (pronounced Bell-Fountain), Ohio. They wandered down the street to a former five-and-dime that had been converted into a kind of old-fashioned brick mini mall called the Marketplace. A handful of stores—a salon, a bank, a café—were tucked inside. One, Amanda saw, had a "For Rent" sign in the window. The second they claimed a table in the brewery, she emailed the person listed on the sign to say, "I'm interested in this space."[1]

Amanda and Luke had been in Bellefontaine (population 13,370) only a handful of times before. They'd moved into an old house nearby, but their jobs—hers in e-commerce at the Express corporate office, his as plant manager for a tooling company—were still in Columbus, more than an hour away if traffic got thick. "My hours were just insane, and then I had to drive on top of it," Amanda said. "We knew once we had children, that was not going to be an option. I would literally never see them."

Her exit strategy was to start her own boutique closer to home, and she'd been casually making calls about retail storefronts for lease in nearby Marysville, jotting down the details that realtors gave her: *twelve hundred square feet. $800. Electric included. Thanks for calling.*

When she talked to the landlords about the spot in the Marketplace, things hit different. They were *thrilled* she wanted to put a boutique in the empty store. They told her that was exactly what they'd had in mind for the space—that in fact they had already installed high-end lighting to show off clothes. Amanda's plan to keep her full-time job for a while as she launched the boutique didn't faze them. "We're flexible," they said. "Whatever you need."

"I felt the support from them immediately," Amanda remembered. "They were invested right away, and I got the feeling like, 'Oh, they care.' It's not just a Realtor being like, 'Give me my $800.'"

The landlord at the Marketplace was a thirty-nine-year-old guy named Jason Duff, who'd grown up working in his dad's construction business and his mom's Hallmark shop in a nearby town. After earning a business degree at Ohio Northern University, he moved to Bellefontaine and got his real estate license right before the 2008 economic crash hit. He never sold a single piece of real estate. He started thinking about buying instead.[2]

Like a lot of small towns in the Rust Belt of Ohio, Bellefontaine was a once-thriving agricultural and manufacturing community that struggled to find its footing over the past thirty years. Some residents wanted to demolish downtown Bellefontaine's beautiful old buildings to make room for parking lots. Jason couldn't stomach the thought of wasting all that potential. So in 2010, he bought an 1890 brick building from the town's land bank for $1.[3]

His model became this: Buy buildings. Renovate them. Then

recruit the best people to run the businesses he wanted to see inside them, with the help of the development firm he founded in 2011, Small Nation. Jason and his team understood instinctively that to reverse Bellefontaine's trajectory, they'd have to create a town whose amenities echoed the ones folks loved in big cities. "Once I came back [to small-town Ohio]," he explained, "I wanted to create a reason why other people like me would want to come back."[4]

Into that 1890 brick building across from the courthouse, Jason and Small Nation installed a gourmet, brick-oven pizza restaurant, convincing a five-time world pizza champion to leave her restaurant nearby and open Six Hundred Downtown. After nearly thirteen hundred Google reviews, it's still averaging 4.7 stars.

Next, Jason thought Bellefontaine needed great coffee. He was visiting Leipsic, Ohio, a village of two thousand people about an hour and a half north of Bellefontaine, and started chatting with an especially passionate barista at a coffee bar downtown. When it turned out Braydon Campbell had grown up near Bellefontaine, Jason invited him to come for a tour.

On the appointed day, Jason staged a recently purchased building with some used furniture to make it look like an ersatz coffee shop. The high production values convinced Braydon, and he boomeranged back to Bellefontaine and started Native Coffee. He's been selling hand-roasted organic coffee there for five years.

Bellefontaine's size and its leaders' openness to revitalization made Jason's dollars go further. Decisions were made quicker. There was less red tape. "In eight years, we've renovated more than forty historic buildings in this town," Jason said. "If I was in Columbus, maybe I could do two or three with that same amount of money."

Over and over, Small Nation flipped empty downtown spaces to create the Bellefontaine people wanted to see. Jason convinced the members of Bellefontaine's beard-growing club to open a craft brewery. He went on Etsy and invited the most successful sellers in Ohio to see what a brick-and-mortar storefront in Bellefontaine could be like. If they hesitated, he talked them into doing a pop-up booth in the Marketplace for the holidays, telling them, "I believe your sales are going to be so good for the months of November and December, you're going to want to have a storefront here."

Retired people. People with unusual skills. Closet entrepreneurs. Small Nation made it easy for them to get a business off the ground by providing cheap spaces, start-up capital, ongoing training, coaching, mentorship, and cheerleading. Often, Small Nation provided proof of concept—creating the shell of a coffeehouse so that prospective retailers would believe a coffeehouse could exist there. In an empty storefront where they were dreaming of a bakery, they put vinyl graphics on the window of doughnuts and muffins so people walking by would say, "Wouldn't that spot make a great bakery?"

On Facebook, Small Nation pumped up the excitement: "Vote! Do you think a bakery would be great here? What kind of bakery would you like to see?" People would tag their friends who had a side hustle baking cakes, and someone from Small Nation would assiduously follow up on all the leads.

Bellefontaine's downtown is like *The Secret* in action, as if Small Nation is manifesting desirable things into existence. A sports bar? Yes. A coffee shop? Yes. No to payday loan businesses, tattoo parlors, and CBD stores, which Jason saw as not in keeping with his vision for an upscale, family-friendly downtown

Bellefontaine. Intentionally and incrementally, Small Nation shaped Bellefontaine into a hipster destination.

A huge reason why Jason's approach with Small Nation works is that Bellefontaine had basically hit rock bottom. "Things had to get so bad here economically for someone like me to be able to come along and actually acquire buildings and make a positive change," Jason said. A confluence of cheap real estate, access to capital, minimal regulation, and willing community partners helped too.

But you can't underestimate the value of having a vision. In the clothing store Amanda Staas opened, in the exact spot where Jason had imagined a clothing store, business did so well that in 2018, Amanda quit her job and moved Hanger Boutique to a storefront down the street with almost double the square footage. That building, it goes without saying, is also owned by Jason.

NOT JUST THE MONEY

In Small Nation's ten years, its eleven-person team has brought in $28 million of public and private investment, buying and renovating forty buildings. Downtown, there are seven new eateries and event spaces, twenty-six loft apartments, and fifty specialty retail tenants that weren't there before. That's created 121 new jobs. All in a town of fourteen thousand.[5]

"I think the secret sauce is, you have to have people who have a love for that town," Jason said. "And you have to have people that are willing to work really, really hard."[6]

I don't want to be too idealistic here. Jason Duff may have turned Bellefontaine around, but he's also in this for the money. Small Nation's annual revenue exceeds $1 million, and its real estate portfolio has grown to more than sixty properties.

But he's not in it *only* for the money. If he were, he likely would have stuck with his first development project, building a self-storage facility on the outskirts of Bellefontaine, something his banker recommended as a way to build a track record before buying a historic building. A different kind of guy might have stopped there. A low-cost, low-energy moneymaker? What's not to love? Build self-storage units, make easy money, repeat ad nauseam.

Except Jason could see a future for his town that didn't start and end with self-storage units. By aiming to make the experience of Bellefontaine better for him and everyone else who lived there, he also happened to become a powerful change agent for the local economy.

Maybe too powerful, critics would say, considering how much of Bellefontaine's development Small Nation has driven in the past ten years, even though Jason's not an elected official. Not everyone's a fan of change (we sometimes call them CAVE people—citizens against virtually everything).

Jason protests that he had to own enough of the Monopoly board to make a difference, but his goal is not to be "the big Walmart Goliath of owning every building in town." His plan is to transition ownership of his buildings to the business operators in them as fifty-fifty partners.

Anyway, most residents are believers. A few years ago, an older woman approached Jason and said, "Thank you for helping me fall back in love with my town again." Jason had a moment of realization. "Okay, this is working. This is meaningful. This matters."

To feel like our jobs tap into some larger sense of purpose is one of the key payoffs most people—including the Facebook employees that Adam Grant, Lori Goler, Janelle Gale, and Brynn Harrington surveyed—want from their work. Once upon a time, it would have been enough to build widgets and make money and go home. Now we want to feel like we're contributing value to the world.

Maybe as an Anywhereist, you have a job that feels meaningful already. You're putting out life-altering blog posts or podcasts, coaching clients into positive change, developing software that makes work easier for everyone else.

Or maybe you're just making widgets. That's okay too.

We want meaning from our work, but frankly, not all work is meaningful, or it requires a serious amount of mental gymnastics to make it seem so. (The wine spritzer I'm marketing makes people...happy?) What if instead we found meaning by having an impact in our places?

CHANGE AGENT

For some lucky people, like Jason Duff, work and helping the community are one and the same. His day job has a visible effect in his town, changing it for the better right before his eyes.

Even Amanda Staas, who after all was only trying to shorten her terrible commute when she opened the Hanger Boutique, feels a profound sense of impact in Bellefontaine. Hers is one of the businesses that draw people into downtown, helping it grow. Amanda regularly contributes time, energy, and money to community events, business groups, and school fundraisers. Her store's success and the town's are knotted together.[7]

Often you build community with your work skills, like Darcy Maulsby, the Settler in Iowa who writes marketing copy for small towns, or Justin Litton, the West Virginia filmmaker who shoots beautiful videos to help other small businesses succeed.

A lot of Anywhereists, though, have jobs that exist entirely in the cloud. If you're working remotely or freelancing for global clients, there's likely no clear intersection between your work and your place. It barely exists in the physical world! You're not even as impactful as the guy who owns the storage units! (Before I wrote *This Is Where You Belong,* the only time people in my town even knew what I did for a living was when someone spotted a *Reader's Digest* article I'd written at a dentist's office. *Reader's Digest* magazines apparently exist solely in dentist's offices.)

The good news: You don't have to physically work in your place or own a business there to be a force for good in your town. Simply living there lets you enter and influence the economic life of your community.

Some of that happens naturally: you live here, you pay rent, you eat at restaurants, you buy groceries, and you help the local economy shuffle along. As Adam Ozimek, chief economist at Upwork, points out, being able to work from anywhere may increase economic efficiency and spread opportunity out from major cities. When you take a flyer on living in an unexpected place, you bolster its economic foundations.[8]

You also, just by living there, become set up to be a local change agent—as a volunteer, a community activist, a neighbor, or just a random person who shows up for the annual watermelon festival and buys cookies from the Girl Scouts. Engaging in intentionally community-minded behaviors increases your personal sense of place attachment, that feeling of belonging to and love for a particular place. That in turn can help you experience more meaning and purpose in your life.

If we learned anything from COVID-19, it's that the most

stable economy is the village economy, the one that supplies its own needs and cares for its own members. When community members rally to save a restaurant about to go under, or when places create virtual tip jars to support out-of-work hairstylists and baristas, it tells you something about what the village will do for you if you join the village.

It's tempting never to join the village, to remain a little place promiscuous as a Wanderer, a little place agnostic as a Seeker. In the age of burnout, avoiding entanglements with communities that demand something of you feels like the easier course—and the savvier one, freeing you up to focus on your core competencies of selling widgets and making money.

In work and in life, however, the more you connect to your place, the better off you are. In San Diego, a bookstore owner who needed open-heart surgery had several of his fellow bookstore owners—otherwise known as competitors—step in to help run his shop while he recovered.[9] The people in your place can care for you (and sometimes your livelihood) when life veers off course.

Community, writer Jenny Anderson explained, "is about a series of small choices and everyday actions: how to spend a Saturday, what to do when a neighbor falls ill, how to make time when there is none. Knowing others and being known; investing in somewhere instead of trying to be everywhere. Communities are built, like LEGOs, one brick at a time. There's no hack."[10]

When you're an Anywhereist and your town is your office, you worry less about extracting a sense of meaning and purpose from *what you do for a living* and more about deriving meaning and purpose from *what you're contributing to your place*. Your vocation becomes being a good citizen of where you live.

DIVERSITY WINS

Sometimes we shape our places even before we move there by what we demand from them.

Elham Watson fantasizes about North Carolina—specifically Charlotte, where a couple of her friends have settled and the average price per square foot is about $100 less than it is in her hometown of Sacramento.[11] Real estate in Sacramento, she'll tell you, is a frenzy of multiple offers, waived contingencies, offers thousands of dollars above asking (and the asking price wasn't so hot to begin with). "I'm tired of literally spending $3,000 a month to be in an apartment," she said.

Several years ago, Elham's job as a researcher for an investment firm went remote. Recently, her husband Matt's work as an environmental consultant did too. They became Anywhereists, free from place restraints just as California becomes more frustrating, politically charged, and expensive. A normal middle-class life there requires an upper-class income, Elham said. "We make decent money, but it feels like we're priced out." Now Charlotte beckons from across the country as something a little more reasonable.

Cheap is high on their location strategy list, but another of the place values they're prioritizing is diversity. Growing up as a first-generation Iranian in inner-city Sacramento, Elham remembered with pleasure how her school friends came from every race—until her family moved to a Sacramento suburb. Suddenly, she was in the minority. "I was like, 'Why am I so different?' Like, I had never experienced being so different. And I was very much treated that way." Her brother, who was in high school when 9/11 happened, fared even worse. "Those are the things that make me sensitive to diversity," Elham said.

A little under half the population of Charlotte is White, and 35 percent are Black. Elham, whose husband is White and whose kids are light skinned, worries about finding a place that's just the right mix. If they choose a community of color, could her children be treated like outcasts the way she and her brother were? If they live in a majority-White community, will they disengage from their Iranian heritage?

Most of us at least pay lip service to wanting to live in a diverse community where people of different races, religions, nations of origin, languages, income levels, sexual orientations, and gender orientations feel at home. According to a 2020 Livability survey, most millennials hunt for it as part of their location strategy. Nine in ten of all respondents from the West said they would be more likely to move to a place they perceived as diverse and inclusive. Eighty-eight percent of non-White respondents said the same.[12]

For places, diversity is a genuine marker of success. In his 2002 book *The Rise of the Creative Class*, sociologist Richard Florida ranked cities on a tolerance index that measured how many gay people, immigrants, and foreign-born residents lived there and how well racially diverse groups integrated. The cities that were the most welcoming to diverse groups were also the most successful, with higher incomes, more innovation, and greater well-being.[13]

Unfortunately, what we say we want and what we actually

choose aren't always the same. In workplace settings, employees are likely to say they value diversity while not actually wanting to factor it into hiring and promotion decisions. Most humans are subject to a strong in-group bias that unconsciously steers us toward places where people look, act, and think like we do.[14]

Diversity is on the rise, like it or not. In the United States, nearly 70 percent of the country's largest cities became more racially diverse in the last ten years. And since about half of Gen Z comes from communities of color, that trend is likely to continue.[15] Even rural areas are becoming increasingly diverse, albeit at a slower pace.[16]

Simply being conscious, like Elham, of the need to embrace diversity as a Seeker may help you fight your own tendency toward in-group attraction. If you're a Settler, you can become intentional about supporting community members who are Black, indigenous, or people of color (BIPOC) and BIPOC-owned businesses where you live. If you're a Wanderer, you can take a hard look at how you interact with people from other cultures.

Economic success isn't equitable and hasn't been for generations. Choosing to include diversity as part of your location strategy, then support it in your community, is a way to have an impact as an Anywhereist.

SMALLER AND BETTER

A steadily growing economy is the gold standard by which economists measure a city's success. More businesses, more output, more jobs, more revenue. More, more, more.

To a point, more money really can make your life better. A 2010

Princeton study famously found that $75,000 in annual income was the sweet spot for making individuals feel like their lives were going well; adjusted for inflation, that's $91,000 in 2021. After that, more money didn't add substantially to their well-being.[17]

The "bigger and better" model of economic development isn't helping communities be healthy, equitable, or sustainable either. As Bill McKibben pointed out in his wonderful book *Deep Economy*, "Perhaps the very act of acquiring so much stuff has turned us ever more into individuals and ever less into members of a community, isolating us in a way that runs contrary to our most basic instincts."[18]

We saw the evidence of economic inequities during the pandemic in the very nature of who got to become an Anywhereist. Overwhelmingly, it was white-collar workers who were able to hunker down with their families at home and service workers who had to keep showing up to jobs that offered very little in the way of financial security, health insurance, or protection against a new disease.

Even now, the benefits of remote work are continuing to leave behind the poorest Americans. According to a Redfin survey, 78 percent of people who moved reported having more disposable income despite having upgraded to a bigger house.[19] But if you were moving in the first place, chances are you were a well-paid white-collar worker. Ninety percent of people earning more than $100,000 per year expect to be able to work virtually in the future, compared to only 10 percent of those who earn $40,000 or less per year. "The folks who need low-cost housing the most have the least flexibility to move," pointed out Redfin CEO Glenn Kelman.[20]

Spreading wealth to make sure that everyone does okay has

never been one of the more successful functions of our economy. But in local communities, you see examples of Anywhereists who are trying to bypass old systems and set up a new world based on helping everyone do a little better.

Rudy Glocker built his outdoor apparel company, Burgeon Outdoors, in Lincoln, New Hampshire (population sixteen hundred) because he wanted to have an impact there. He'd fallen in love with the state spending summers there as a kid but had seen the ravages of economic fluctuations and shrinking populations in the White Mountains. "Unfortunately, a lot of jobs have migrated away from these communities, and I wanted to turn that around," he told me.[21]

Lincoln has some competitive advantages as an outdoorsy hub for skiers and hikers, but its tiny size was the bigger attraction for Rudy. "If I create ten jobs in New York City, no one even knows it," Rudy said. "If I create ten jobs in a community of fifteen hundred, wait a minute, you're a percent of the workforce now. If you want to make an impact, you've got to go to a place where your impact is going to be felt."

Surprisingly, it's tough to hire locals with the right skills for the work. The mills closed twenty-five years ago, so few people are left there who know how to sew. If Burgeon was in New York City or Boston, Rudy might have better luck finding stitchers, and he might be able to get away with paying them less. "But it never really crossed my mind, because that's not what we're trying to do," Rudy said. "We're not trying to create more jobs in Boston." The point is to rebuild a struggling community. The clothing company just pays the bills.

So Rudy, an economist with an MBA from Harvard Business School, provides his employees flexible hours, a livable wage, health care, and monthly sales bonuses. He donates 5 percent of sales to local nonprofits, like New England Disabled Sports. And the company made and gave away ten thousand masks during COVID. In its small way, Burgeon is making life in rural New Hampshire more livable.

In Wardensville, West Virginia (population 320), Paul Yandura and Donald Hitchcock have had a similar experience, albeit not quite so intentionally at first. They bought a second home there for weekends away from Washington, DC, where Paul ran a political consulting firm and Donald sold medical devices, till the day they decided they just couldn't go back. "Don and I were looking at each other, just saying like, 'Okay, we're done with Washington. What are we going to do?'" remembered Paul. They moved to their Wardensville cabin full-time and started selling real estate.[22]

Nothing much was there, just a 7-Eleven and a Dollar General. So when the old feed store came up for sale—their first commercial real estate listing—they bought it themselves and turned it into a funky, folksy store they called the Lost River Trading Post. Stocked with everything from craft beer to locally made incense sticks, with a bright-orange cow statue out front, the trading post took off, seeing double-digit sales growth every year since it opened in 2013.

By itself, a successful business in a small town makes a big economic impact in terms of revenue, property taxes, and visitors. Then two more things happened. First, Donald hung a rainbow flag on their house on Main Street, next door to the Lost River Trading Post. "It caused a huge stir," said Paul. Some of his neighbors, whose flag of choice was Confederate, bristled. Paul and Donald got death threats. Their property was vandalized.[23]

But the rainbow flag sounded a sharp note of diversity. Maybe Wardensville wasn't what you thought it was, it said. Attracted to the changes happening in the town, other DC expats have settled there and opened small businesses, saying, "If you can do it, we can do it." One woman driving through on a motorcycle met Donald and Paul, then ended up buying the town's old motel and renovating it into *Schitt's Creek* chic. (Paul loved the show, by the way; Donald didn't.)

Now the couple has real estate clients who are gay or Latino or Black and looking to buy in Wardensville. "So we're getting a diversity here that we've never seen before," Donald said.[24]

The saga of Wardensville's evolution isn't always pretty. Haters have been, well, hateful. But the second hopeful note is that Paul and Donald launched a nonprofit social enterprise—a farm, market, bakery, and kitchen that trains local young people in what Paul calls "living classrooms." At any given time, they employ eighty to one hundred people, a lot of them teenagers who otherwise would be working at Walmart or the chicken plant.

Funny, that's helped silence the haters too, Paul said. "A lot of grandmothers, grandfathers, fathers, nieces, nephews, uncles, they may say what they want [about us], but their kids are like, 'Shut up. We know them,' or 'Hey, I work for them, and they're actually pretty nice.'"

SAVE WHAT YOU LOVE

Can you make change in your community without doing something grand like opening your own business or nonprofit? You can invest in people who are. In Philadelphia, a group called the Circles of Aunts and Uncles pools their money and provides small-business loans to entrepreneurs, especially women, people of color, and people from low-income backgrounds who might not have easy access to other forms of capital.[25]

Their first low-interest loan, in 2015, went to Hanifah Samad, who ran a Haitian Creole–inspired boutique called Fason De Viv. Hanifah had just moved her store to Philadelphia's Old City neighborhood and needed capital for more inventory. The Circle of Aunts and Uncles stepped up.

Twenty-one other small business owners, including a small-batch ice cream maker, a café-charcuterie owner, a clothing designer, and a textile maker, have since been the recipients of the aunts' and uncles' largesse. They're not just loan recipients; they're considered "nieces" and "nephews" (and given advice accordingly).

If you want to make an impact in your town, invest in the people you want to see thrive and in the places that matter to you.

Maybe in a lot of towns, the place that matters is the local bar. Villagers in South Stoke were among eighty communities in England who saved their town pub, in their case by selling $600 shares to community members and recruiting volunteers to spend hundreds of hours sprucing up the place. When the Packhorse pub reopened, the whole town showed up. "We now have got 430 people who want it to work," said Dom Moorhouse, the local entrepreneur who led the Save the Packhorse effort. "They are our marketers."[26]

In rural Nyabing, Australia, the town saved its local pub with the income from a community crop. On fifteen hundred acres of town land, everyone plants (usually barley), everyone harvests, and the money they raise—often well into six figures—is used on infrastructure projects. Like buying and renovating the town pub and turning the Nyabing Inn into a gathering spot.[27]

We save what we love, and we love what we've saved, precisely because we saved it. Maybe it's odd to choose a place to live because it needs you. But if it's meaning you're looking for, low taxes and cheap housing aren't nearly as important as a sense of contributing to the community. If you can see your place's local economy as a collection of people, their livelihoods, and their desires, you're more likely to feel purpose by contributing to its success.

Location Strategy Session: Purpose

Purpose is one of the original three Ps (along with profession and people) that satisfy and motivate workers on the job. For Anywhereists, championing the success of the local economy can bring a deep sense of purpose in your community. Here are a few more ways to do it.

1. **Make community-smart decisions:** Become a little more intentional about where and how you spend your money. As Rudy Glocker put it, "These little incremental decisions that we all make every day create tidal waves of impact."[28]

2. **Invest:** Contribute to businesses you care about in a tangible way by participating in a micro loan group like Philadelphia's Circle of Aunts and Uncles. On the platform Kiva, you can make small loans to entrepreneurs all over the world, including, possibly, in your own town. Find small business owners in American communities (a gym owner in Springdale,

Arkansas, or a shoemaker in La Mirada, California) at Kiva.org.

3. **Buy and pay local:** When you shop at locally owned businesses, more of the money you spend will circulate locally than if you'd spent the same amount at a big-box store or another national chain.[29] To motivate residents to prioritize local, some communities have created their own currency. If your town has it on offer, consider investing.

4. **Welcome diversity:** Find the groups in your town that support economic growth for communities of color. For instance, nonprofit Mortar Cincinnati runs an entrepreneurship academy in which 87 percent of participants are people of color, and 67 percent are Black women. By supporting BIPOC-owned businesses in your community, you help create equitable wealth.[30]

5. **Live in the doughnut:** Kate Raworth, a senior associate at Oxford University's Environmental Change Institute, imagines the economy as a doughnut: in the "hole," a too-small economy fails to provide life essentials to every human being. Outside the doughnut, an economy of unchecked growth appears to thrive but destroys the planet. The sweet spot is the doughnut itself, where a healthy economy and a healthy planet coexist. Watch her TED talk about the "doughnut economy" for a dose of inspiration.[31]

6. **Act collectively:** Most problems in towns aren't solved by a heroic Lone Ranger but by a group of

committed citizens acting together. Figure out which groups already exist in your place with the goal of making it better. Join one of them, or invite friends to join you in creating your own.

Place Study: Thomaston, Georgia

Population: 9,000

- **Zombie love:** In the triangle formed by Atlanta, Macon, and Columbus, Thomaston is smack in the center, less than a ninety-minute drive to each, making it appealing for television location scouts taking advantage of Georgia's film subsidies. Scenes from *The Walking Dead* have been filmed in Thomaston's Sprewell Bluff Park.

- **Worth the trip:** The Rock Ranch, a working cattle ranch turned nostalgic agritourism playground founded by Chick-fil-A owner Truett Cathy. Come for National Pumpkin Destruction Day, when pumpkins get smashed by monster trucks, fired from cannons, and dropped off a fifty-foot forklift.

- **Pivot point:** The town lost five thousand jobs when the textile mills closed in 2000. Eighteen years later, the local electric cooperative sponsored a Vermont-based program called Community Heart & Soul. Volunteers canvassed neighborhoods, handed out surveys, and asked residents to share ideas about what they wanted to see in town—and what they already loved about Thomaston. They even hauled a chalkboard to a community festival so people could write their answers to "What do you love about our community?" in bright chalk: *The school. The friendly people. The family atmosphere.*

- **Diverse data:** To make sure the ideas they gathered represented the true diversity of the community, volunteers collected demographic data when they canvassed neighborhoods. Since Thomaston is 43 percent African American, they aimed to get 43 percent of their feedback from the Black community. At Thomaston's annual Emancipation Celebration, one of the oldest in the country, volunteers sat down with Black residents to record their memories of the celebration and the town before integration. "Out of the stories come things that need to be done or things that everybody values," said Community Heart & Soul coach Jenny Robbins.[32]

- **To-do list:** In the end, almost seven thousand residents piped up with their opinions about what would make Thomaston better. That led to twenty action items for the town, from "get a Chick-fil-A" to "start a farmers market downtown." COVID hit a couple of weeks after Community Heart & Soul wrapped up, but that didn't stop the momentum. A farmers market opened in a former cattle sale barn for summer of 2020. A Chick-fil-A is there now too.

- **Go for it:** People felt empowered by the program, so when litter started piling up during the pandemic, residents organized their own cleanup instead of waiting on government to take care of the problem. Within a few Saturdays, they bagged thirty-five hundred pounds of trash.[33]

- **Work in progress:** Next on the agenda is paving a thirteen-mile walking and biking path to link the Civic Center, the schools, and Sprewell Bluff Park. It'll cost a few million dollars, but the Community Heart & Soul feedback proves that people want it.

- **Putting down roots:** Artist Fawne DeRosia said, "I always kind of feel like, 'If no one else is going to do it, then why not me?'" So after moving to Thomaston when she got married, she joined the local arts council, organized the Easter egg hunt and the Christmas light parade, and opened her own retail space/art studio. Her twenty years in Thomaston are the longest she's ever lived anywhere, and because she's involved with everything, everyone knows her. "I went to Dunkin Donuts the other day, and they're like, 'Well, hey, Miss Fawne, what's up?' I have a community here that I haven't been able to build anywhere else. I think that maybe other people take that for granted, and I'm trying not to."[34]

HAPPY TO BE HERE

Location Strategy Value: Happiness

Choosing a new place as an Anywhereist is a marker of the life you want for yourself, a way you vote for the kind of person you want to be. For Amy Bushatz, moving to Alaska was a vote for an outdoorsy life—and a wild gamble at that.[1]

Amy is the first to tell you that she was not an outdoorsy person. Then in 2009, her husband, Luke, suffered a traumatic brain injury while serving in Afghanistan as part of the army. He left the military, and because Amy was the all-remote executive editor of Military.com, they effectively became Anywhereists.

For the first time in many years, Amy and Luke began to have long discussions about where *they* wanted to go. Santa Cruz, California, where Amy was from? Back to Seattle, a place they'd both loved when they lived there? As a parting hurrah, the military would move them anywhere in the United States for free. They felt compelled to make it count. "That was really paralyzing," Amy remembered.

One day, on a family camping trip to Kentucky, Amy noticed

that in nature, her husband, who had struggled with memory loss and organizational skills since his injury, seemed at ease for the first time in months. "It was like watching somebody take off a backpack of problems," she said. "I was like, 'Well, whatever we're doing, we need to do this some more.'"

Finding a place with easy access to the outdoors became a priority. When Luke decided to pursue a master's degree in outdoor education, they landed on Palmer, Alaska.

Neither of them had ever been there. They mentally associated the state with Sarah Palin's 2012 vice presidency run. Yet something about Alaska or, more honestly, the idea of Alaska spoke to them. Its wildness and remoteness. Its last frontier-ness. Few people, little traffic, and the outdoor-centric lifestyle they'd been thinking about. In 2016, they bought a house in Palmer after touring it via FaceTime. Boldly, they put all their chips on "the outdoors will heal us."

Healing did not happen automatically. Her first Memorial Day weekend there, Amy settled onto her deck with a copy of one of the Harry Potter books, determined to have a picturesque summertime moment. Cold rain drove her back indoors.

The moment presented a reality check. Summers were short and unpredictable in her adopted state. "Amy, this is it, bud," she told herself. There was no hoping for better weather, "so either get on the train or get off."

From then on, Amy challenged herself to get outside at least twenty minutes a day, no matter how uncooperative the weather. With rain gear she ordered from REI, she and her boys, then eight and five, undertook a 2.5-mile hike nearby. They got a little wet, but nobody froze to death, and the top of the hike rewarded their effort with a gorgeous view of a glacier rimmed by mountains. "Is this even real?" Amy wondered, awestruck.

When we spoke, Amy was up to twelve hundred consecutive days spending at least a little time out of doors in Alaska. Having made her commitment to Alaska, Amy committed to the reason she moved to Alaska in the first place. The place helped her operationalize her own transformation. She hikes, skis, snowshoes, and trail runs. She joined a Monday-night running group that runs together all winter long, even on nights when sixty-mile-an-hour gusts feel like free sandblasting on your face.

None of this happened organically just because she moved to an outdoorsy location. Actually becoming outdoorsy required developing daily habits of behavior, the way someone who wants a spiritual awakening might develop a practice of reading sacred texts. Said Amy, "I had to decide that this is what I'm going to do. And then I had to actually do it."

The effect of her time in nature has been so powerful that it has seeped into her career. In a closet in her house in Palmer, she records a podcast called *Humans Outdoors* that examines other people's ventures into nature; she's writing a book about it too. It's a path she never would have predicted when she and her husband chose their place.

SOMETHING BEYOND WORK

Of all the Anywhereists I talked to about their geography decisions, pretty much no one was like, "The only reason I moved to this town is for the great job opportunities." That's the whole point, right? When you're a remote worker, a freelancer, an entrepreneur, or a retiree, bounteous job opportunities are no longer of the essence. Yes, you should find a place that can nurture your work. But I don't expect that work will ever make the number one slot on your location strategy list.

Most Anywhereists intend it that way. As an Anywhereist, you know work matters, but you want to be in a place that inspires you to live a satisfying life beyond work, to escape the idea that the reigning yardstick for the worth of your life should be how many hours you put in, how productive you are, or how much you ship.

On the other hand, the transition to an Anywhereist life may be the perfect moment to reassess the role you want work to play for you. Is it your number one thing? What else does, or perhaps should, matter more to your happiness? Can you structure a life that prioritizes work and, simultaneously, something beyond work?

It doesn't have to be an either/or situation. In a Pew Research survey, 95 percent of teens described "having a job or career they enjoy" as an adult as "extremely or very important," more critical than helping people in need or getting married.[2] For most adults, working sucks up more time than almost anything else in your life except sleeping (if you're lucky). Practically speaking, you hope you like it.

But when you physically leave the workplace, as Anywhereists do, work starts to shrink a bit in the rearview mirror, allowing space for other priorities, values, and sources of contentment in both your life and your location strategy.

The place you settle can make you work better, smarter, and more lucratively. It can also maximize your potential for non-work-related joys, turning the well-chosen city into a symbol of what you want your existence to be. As writer Whitney Johnson put it, "When we make a conscious choice about where to be—what will surround us—we are powerfully reminded of what, how, and who we are trying to be."[3]

Some Anywhereists want to be more outdoorsy, like Amy Bushatz. Some want to have a closer relationship to the land, like Amy and James Hebdon (and their chickens).

Christine Schmidt, who has an Anywhereist job with a Washington, DC, nonprofit, spent the pandemic Wanderer-style, getting geographically and emotionally closer to family and friends, including her long-distance boyfriend.. "I feel like I really took advantage of the opportunity to be with people I love," she said. "I was looking back at 2020 and I'm like, I feel like this is one of the years I've been happiest. I feel like I laughed more than I otherwise would have when I was this person in this big city having all these different adventures." Her dominant place value, she realized, isn't urban adventure. It's family and friends.[4]

For Paul Liepe, it's historic preservation. Owning a home-based business made him an Anywhereist, and when he and he his wife decided to move, they prioritized practicalities like low cost of living, moderate summers and winters, and a big grocery store in their location strategy. What moved the needle on their decision was the visible, well-preserved history of Danville, Virginia—and the fact that it clearly mattered to residents. Now the executive director of his historic neighborhood group, Paul has centered his life on his passion for saving endangered homes.[5]

Andrew Phillips convinced the tech company he worked for to let him relocate from Washington, DC, to Minnesota after he visited Lakeville Brewing Company on a work trip there. "I can exactly remember the moment it happened," he said. "I get there, and it's this cute downtown district that I had never seen before. And there are kids playing in this backyard area that's part of this brewery, and there's a guy playing live music. And it's just like, people are happy." It occurred to him that maybe he could be happy there too. Turned out happiness was his dominant place value, and he didn't care if his employer fired him. He was going to move to Minnesota and get it.[6]

THE END OF THE RAT RACE

To believe that a place might allow us to live more fulfilled lives is more than wishful thinking. In 2020, Gallup surveyed respondents in 145 countries to answer questions about how frequently they had positive or negative emotional experiences. They asked questions like: Did you feel well-rested yesterday? Were you treated with respect? Did you smile or laugh a lot? Did you learn or do something interesting? Did you experience worry, anger, stress, sadness, or physical pain during a lot of the day? Did you experience enjoyment?[7]

There's a geography to happiness, the study found. Globally, residents of certain countries seemed to have—or at least acknowledge—more happy experiences. And they weren't the ones you'd think. Panama ranked highest, with a score of 85 out of 100 on the positive experience scale. Next came El Salvador, Guatemala, Paraguay, Colombia, Indonesia, Mexico, Nicaragua, China, Costa Rica, Denmark, and Honduras, all of which scored in the 80s.

As Gallup's study points out, "These scores strongly relate to people's perceptions about their living standards, personal freedoms, and the presence of social networks." They also likely reflect a cultural bias toward happiness that is part eat-drink-and-be-merry and part suck-it-up. In some communities, people simply seem to lean harder into contentment.

Meanwhile, in the United States, 55 percent of respondents to the 2019 survey reported feeling stressed, putting us 20 percent higher than the global average. We're above average for worry too.

Is that just part of who Americans are? Inheritors of a culture whose priorities are skewed enough that we're more stressed than happy, more worried than well rested? Confessing to "internalized capitalism," writer Katie Hawkins-Gaar acknowledged that "work is my answer for most everything. Feeling anxious? I distract myself with work. If I'm happy? It's a good time to work! Sad? I clearly haven't gotten enough work done."[8]

Shifting to remote, independent, or even flexible work can help redirect workaholics from an all-consuming nine to five (though, honestly, nine to five would be a relief for most of us). One University of Birmingham study found that higher levels of autonomy lead to higher levels of job satisfaction and well-being.[9] We feel happier when we get to be in the driver's seat of our own lives. Perhaps that's why so many traditional employees are clamoring for the ability to time shift by setting their own schedules, even with unconventional hours; step away for a couple of hours—to attend a kid's class play, for instance; cut back their workloads or switch to part-time; travel less for work—no more than four days a month on the road; and be location independent.

According to one 2018 survey, 96 percent of white-collar workers want more workplace flexibility, with the idea that it will make it easier to care for all the little things (you know, like kids and aging parents and doctor's appointments) that sometimes slip through the cracks otherwise.[10] For women, job flexibility is especially powerful, according to the Institute for Women's Policy Research.[11] When women don't have to choose between succeeding at work and showing up for their families, they tend to more efficiently break glass ceilings. (Good child care and maternity leave policies help a lot too.)

As it is, 39 percent of millennials say they're working so much that they don't exercise or eat right, and they suspect that increased flexibility might make them not only healthier and happier but also more productive, more likely to stay at their company, and more satisfied with their work.[12] Almost three-fourths of millennials and 66 percent of Gen Xers have considered quitting altogether for lack of flexibility.[13]

The fly in the ointment here is that when you can work whenever and wherever you want, work sometimes bleeds into every moment of the day. That the trade-off for picking up your kid after school may be checking work email in bed at eleven at night. (According to some studies, half of us do.)[14] When you don't have traditional boundaries between work and home—like that commute to an office—work time and home time can become indistinguishable.

But you're less likely to be consumed by what you do for a living if you're living beyond work. And the right place can pull you off the hamster wheel altogether.

Freelance designer and writer Paul Jarvis has worked with the likes of Nike, Microsoft, and Mercedes-Benz. He also lives with his wife in the middle of a forest on an island in Canada, which he writes about in his book *Company of One* as an intentional stepping away from the rat race. Their isolated location, unreliable internet and all, reminds him every day of what he cares about or hopes to: people, nature, breaking out his surfboard while the weather cooperates. He hasn't always been so zen or so willing to live rural, but he's since realized, "A lot of times, the life we *think* we want and the life we *actually* want are very different."[15]

Or maybe you knew all along what you wanted, but it wasn't until you became an Anywhereist that you were in a better position to achieve it. My friend Heather is a director with a nonprofit that implements public health programs all over the world. A lot of her work is in Africa, advising programs that fight HIV. Since her postcollege days as a Peace Corps volunteer, she's racked up a cumulative ten years living overseas.[16]

When COVID hit, she relocated to Utah to live with her mom. As an adult, trips home had always brought on fantasies of living there full-time. "It's so beautiful," she'd think. Then she'd reality-check herself. "What would I do here? International public health work in Utah?"

Once her job went remote and made her an Anywhereist, the move was a no-brainer. Because her boss is still on eastern time and because she's emailing with colleagues in Africa all day, she wakes up extra early. But by 2:00 or 3:00 p.m., the emails are tapering off, and she feels zero remorse about ducking out to fill the rest of her afternoons with snowshoeing, biking, or hiking. "I'm not a workaholic," Heather bluntly explains. "I never have been."

Even so, working in a Washington, DC, office subjected her to an invisible pressure "to have that butt time in the chair." The communal ambition of the place manifested itself in an expectation to show your face at all hours in the office, even if you didn't really need to be there to do your work. Heather rarely knocked off work early. Being geographically removed from that center of power, in a remote-work situation that allows her flexibility with her hours, has changed how she manages her time, which is really a way of managing what's important to her.

Work, yes. But also taking ski lessons for the first time in her forties. Remote workers report an extra 105 hours of leisure time a year, and for that reason alone, Heather has no intentions of moving back to DC.

"If what you really love doing is skiing, why wait until your hips are too old to take a hard fall and *then* move to Colorado?" wrote Jason Fried and David Heinemeier Hansson in their book *Remote: Office Not Required.* "If you love surfing, why are you still trapped in a concrete jungle and not living near the beach?... The new luxury is to shed the shackles of deferred living—to pursue your passions *now,* while you're still working. What's the point in wasting time daydreaming about how great it'll be when you finally quit?"[17]

The right place reminds us of who we are and what we love most.

HEALING PLACES

Our place choices are so influential to our well-being that they shows up in our bodies.

In ancient times, it was believed that certain places had healing properties, like the Roman baths in Bath, UK, or the Asklepieion sanctuary in Epidaurus, Greece, where the sick from around the country came for treatment and hopefully a miracle. Seventy miracles are on record at the Asklepieion, which housed a temple, a gym, and baths in a site dedicated to Asklepios, the Greek god of healing.

Modern research shows less divine but no less salutary effects. Living near the ocean calms you down. Walkable neighborhoods make you less depressed. Green spaces lift mood.[18]

In one study, adults with mental illnesses in Melbourne, Australia, identified "enabling places": a garden, a bookshop, a church, and a local thrift store ("my endorphins go sky-high here") that helped bring them peace, joy, hope, and connection. One man found that spending time in a cemetery inspired strikingly hopeful thoughts: "It's great to be alive."[19]

There's nothing magical going on here. We decide what our places mean for us and our well-being. As the researchers explained, "Enabling places are made or nurtured as much as they are discovered."

An enabling place changed things for Ria Talken. For most of her life, she's grappled with a variety of mental illnesses, including bipolar 1, ADHD, and eating disorders. Despite therapy and medication, she got sicker and sicker, eventually going on full disability from her travel industry job.[20]

When her husband's business started faltering, the couple sold their two-bedroom Oakland home, packed three suitcases apiece, and moved into a rented house in San Miguel de Allende, Mexico, a city that Ria describes as warm, brilliant, and bright.

Affordable as well. In San Miguel, they pay $1,200 a month to rent a three-thousand-square-foot house (the price includes utilities, five terraces, and a maid). Quality of life is high. They don't own a car because they can walk everywhere, from the grocery store to the International Chamber Music Festival. She said she and Glenn made more friends in two months there than they did in the States in twenty years.

The unexpected benefit to this simpler, more pleasant life was that Ria's mental and emotional fragility has gone on hiatus. She credits her new location, saying it's "as medicinal as a prescription."

In 1979, Israeli sociologist Aaron Antonovsky coined the term *salutogenesis* to describe an approach to health that focuses on enhancing well-being, not just eradicating disease. You're healthy when you have a sense of coherence, or a belief that your life is comprehensible, or structured, predictable, and explicable; manageable, meaning that most of your circumstances are within your control and you have the resources to meet life's demands; and meaningful, or full of interest and goodness, in a way that makes you care about the outcomes.[21]

Antonovsky recognized a number of dimensions that could impact someone's sense of coherence in their life, including one's immediate environment. In San Miguel, things seem to make more sense for Ria. Living in a town where life feels comprehensible, manageable, and meaningful takes away some of the daily triggers and stressors she confronted in the Bay Area. Ria still has ups and downs with her mental illness, but she feels better. Happier. "Here I can be my best self," Ria said.[22]

TRANSFORMATION

To build a location strategy as an Anywhereist is to decide what sorts of values will inform your life. You already worked through an exercise to identify some of your place values back in chapter 2, but consider how the values you identified might manifest in a place. For instance, if you value success, you could move to a high-energy city with abundant opportunities for networking or to a Zoom town where you won't have much to interfere with your focus.

If you value nature, you might move to a farm with lots of land for chickens or to the ski community where you've spent every winter holiday for twenty years.

If you value family, you might return to your hometown or find an LCOL town where lower overhead allows for less time on work and more time with growing children.

Ask yourself:

- What is most important in my life?
- How do I want to spend my time?
- What do I enjoy?
- What makes me feel whole and happy?
- What makes me feel valued?
- How much money do I really need?
- What portion of my life do I want to be taken up by work, and what portion of my life do I want to dedicate to other pursuits?

Getting clear on their own values helped Davida Lederle and her husband, Curt, make the difficult decision to leave San Francisco, a city they loved, where they'd lived for ten years, where they had family.[23]

Life there was increasingly unaffordable. The situation became more dire during COVID, as Davida and Curt pondered starting a family as housing prices rose ever higher. They were both Anywhereists—Davida operates the website TheHealthyMaven.com, and Curt is an independent software engineer—so when their landlord sold their rental house from under them, they packed up their car and drove to Minneapolis, where Curt's mom lives.

The original plan was simply to stay temporarily while they figured out next steps, but in Minneapolis, "it was like a weight was lifted," said Davida. Curt's old friends reached out to point them toward favorite coffee spots and the best restaurants to get takeout. In spite of not being able to gather because of the pandemic, "it just felt like people actually cared. Just all of a sudden, we were like, maybe this is our place."

The experience made Davida realize that her place value was community. After just a few weeks in Minneapolis, she felt a stronger sense of community than she had after ten years in California. In California, people were always so busy that plans with friends often didn't materialize. It felt like their friends were always on the hunt for a better offer. In Minneapolis, "we could spend six hours sitting on the couch with friends drinking wine or eating dinner together or watching a movie." This was the kind of casual social life she hadn't realized she was craving.

To be clear, Davida said that their values have changed over time. San Francisco was a perfect fit for their late twenties and early thirties, because they were just as busy and ambitious as everyone else in the city. But as she and Curt move into a new season of life in which they're focusing more on family, Minneapolis better matched their values. "Moving here was really the first time in my life where I actually felt a real sense of peace in moving," Davida said. "Maybe we were trying really hard to make our life work in so many different places. It doesn't feel so hard anymore. And that feels really good."

Places don't transform you just because you move there. But going through the process of thoughtfully choosing a place can be a marker of what you want for your life—an expression of who you are, what you value, and what kind of life you want to live.

Your town is a vote for the kind of person you want to be as well as a daily reminder of that choice. It won't change you fundamentally, but it can nudge you a little further down a path you're already on.

Quality Goods

People who chose to move to their area for its quality of life—nationally, about a third of residents—feel more strongly attached to it than people who moved for other reasons, according to a study by the Knight Foundation.[24]

What about local quality of life attracted them? First and foremost, the basics of safety, health, employment, and shelter. When Seekers and Settlers have access to safe places to live and work, high-quality health care, affordable, well-built housing, and local work opportunities, they're more satisfied with their community. A second tier of quality-of-life factors also proved important:

- Recreational amenities, like parks, playgrounds, trails, beaches, and lakes
- Family amenities, like libraries, zoos, community centers, youth camps, and sports leagues
- Good schools, from kindergarten to university
- Easy transportation, including public transportation
- Vibrant arts and culture, such as theater, museums, craft fairs, concerts, and classes
- Plentiful shopping, dining, and entertainment at restaurants and clubs

Location Strategy Session: Happiness

To prioritize joy, quality of life, relationships, and leisure is to realize that work is only one small portion of a happy life. Most Anywhereists seek places that help them keep nonwork values front and center. Here are a few ways to do that as you think about where to live.

1. **Know thyself:** Some of how we approach location decisions is aspirational. Like Amy Bushatz in her move to Alaska, we may search for a town that represents an idealized future version of ourselves (artsy, urbane, granola) rather than who we actually are. That's okay if you're willing, like Amy, to put in the work of becoming the person you hoped you'd be here. To avoid geographic buyer's remorse, a better tactic may be to focus on your current needs and not who you think you'd like to become.

2. **Don't monetize everything:** Places can help you achieve success, but they should also strengthen your nonwork values, like spending time on relationships, experiencing nature, or developing your talents. You don't have to monetize everything in your life.

3. **Include family:** Proximity to members of your family makes you less likely to move again. Some Anywhereists have happily settled in the communities where they were raised and where their families live. Others think that being a quick plane ride away from relatives is the happiest arrangement. What role do you want your parents and siblings to play in your life

and the lives of your children? How geographically stable are they? How would spending more time with them affect your family? How will you (and your children) feel about this in five years, ten years, twenty?

4. **Choose a fifteen-minute city:** In 2020, Mayor Anne Hidalgo announced a plan to turn Paris into a fifteen-minute city, where all residents can meet their needs on foot, by bike, or on public transit within fifteen minutes of their homes. It's a "city of proximities" designed to reduce carbon emissions and reinvent Paris as a place of gardens, bike lanes, and powerful neighborhoods. Try choosing a fifteen-minute city (or neighborhood) for yourself as a way to slow down your life. As an Anywhereist, your lack of a daily commute puts you light-years ahead. Now look at how easy access will be to other places that matter to you, like the supermarket, the library, the daycare, the doctor's office, or your church.[25]

5. **Make a decision that brings you joy:** A poem by Marie Howe recommends that when we have big decisions to make, including where to move, we should choose "whatever leads to joy...to more life and less worry."[26] *More life, less worry* is not a bad mantra for making a place decision.

Place Study: Great Falls, Montana
Population: 58,835
- **Median home cost:** $201,000
- **What people do for fun:** Bike the River's Edge Trail that skirts

forty miles of the Missouri River, go to concerts in Gibson Park, or take in the Montana Pro Rodeo Circuit Finals. Don't miss the art museums and an epic farmers market.

- **How it's a better life than New York City:** Stress levels go down a lot, according to Millie Whalen, who left her job as a public defender in New York City to take over Cassiopeia Books, a bookstore there that stocks seventeen thousand volumes.[27]

- **Why she moved:** Millie had visited Peace Corps friends in Great Falls several times. In 2019, one sent her a text. "The bookstore you love is for sale," she wrote. Cassiopeia is the adorable shop where Millie loaded up on paperbacks for the plane ride home. Though she knew nothing about running a bookstore, the opportunity was too good to pass up. "I really just sort of thought, life's too short," said Millie. At sixty-one, she figured out the finances, did a look-see trip, sold her Brooklyn apartment, and took the leap.

- **On living a Hallmark movie:** When Millie told her brother, a business owner, of her plans, he said, "That is the most cliché thing I have ever heard."

- **Cost of living:** Great Falls is an estimated 55 percent less expensive to live than Brooklyn. It's so much cheaper that the money Millie's financial advisor okayed for her to invest in this nutty bookstore idea became a three-year runway.

- **Good for business:** "People in this town are really committed to having an independent bookstore," Millie said. Despite a COVID closure and a storefront swap, residents were eager to buy local when Cassiopeia reopened. The Great Falls

Business Development Authority, which Millie met with before she bought the store, offers her all kinds of support, including workshops and classes on building a business plan, setting goals, increasing profitability, and creating an e-commerce site. Even though she's never owned a business before, that makes Millie more confident she'll succeed.

- **Why Great Falls is great for contentment:** It's beautiful. A few hours from Glacier and Yellowstone National Parks, it's small and quiet in a way that reminds Millie to breathe. "I can see the Missouri River, and I can see the Rockies out in the distance," she said. "And it's really peaceful and really calm. I don't hear sirens. I look up at the stars at night."

YOU TOO CAN BE AN ANYWHEREIST

There are lots of ways people become Anywhereists.

They ask their current employer to let them go remote.

They look for a new job with an all-distributed company.

They go freelance.

They start an online or otherwise portable business.

They start a business in the community they prefer to be in.

They choose a place they love and get a new job there.

They retire so they don't have to work at all.

They take a sabbatical or a gap year to try Anywhereism on for size.

They test a city that appeals to them with a few months of slow travel.

They decide where they want to live and just go there. They think, *Why am I waiting until I'm sixty-five to live the life I want?* They think, *There are better places for me right now.* They quit their jobs, pack up their lives, and they go. Which is the approach Rebecca Williams took, quitting her job at a university in Liverpool,

England and moving to the emerald coast of Ireland, where she'd been vacationing for years.[1]

Ireland's population is one of the most rural in all of Europe, with 42 percent of Irish people living in small, isolated communities, hundreds with fewer than twenty-five hundred residents.[2] Louisburgh, in County Mayo, has just 420 people, two cafés, a market, and a few pubs. But it's a gorgeous little village on the coast, surfers and cyclists always passing through. That's where Rebecca moved, barely believing she had done something so wildly out of character.[3]

She didn't have a job when she got there. An admin role she held briefly turned out not to be what she wanted. Some people suggested she might have to commute to Galway, a two-hour drive, for a good job, but she was a single parent with a daughter, and that felt like a no-go.

One day, her office manager said, "Have you ever thought about working remotely?"

Rebecca replied, "It's just not an option for me."

In her mind, remote workers were high-flying salespeople or software developers, not women with a master's degree in occupational psychology. Then she heard about a group called Grow Remote Ireland, whose Louisburgh chapter was holding an information session on remote work. Rebecca came away with a list of all-distributed companies that hired workers in Ireland, even in out-of-the-way places like Louisburgh.

One of the businesses on the list, alongside GitLab, Buffer, HubSpot, and Shopify, was Automatic, the parent company of WordPress. Rebecca had never heard of it, but after some research, she applied, and applied again, taking pointers from Grow Remote

Ireland. Within six months, she had a job in Automatic's human resources department. She's since given a talk to her coworkers about moving to where you go on holiday.

That's how people become Anywhereists.

Or it's one way. There are plenty of others. You could be like Kat Slater, the Londoner who heads up Grow Remote Louisburgh and invited Rebecca to that session on remote work at the coworking space she runs above a bookshop. Kat became an Anywhereist by going freelance as a behavior change researcher so she could move to the west coast of Ireland while her partner, a scientist, got a PhD nearby.[4]

Or you could do it like Rose Barrett, a freelance social media manager whose friend Tracy Keogh told her, "Nobody's catering towards remote workers in Ireland. There's potential here for our rural communities. Let's do something."[5] Together they organized Grow Remote Ireland, which was originally designed to connect rural Ireland's remote workers—and get more underemployed rural workers into location-independent jobs. Their tagline: "Making remote work local."

While the broader Grow Remote group offered classes, like Utah's Remote Online Initiative, to help rural residents prepare for and apply for remote jobs, there were also seventy local chapters around the country that served sort of as group therapy for remote workers—a way to hang out with other people who faced the same challenges of slow internet or managing a team that's hundreds of miles away.

In some cases, the chapters kick-started their own local talent attraction efforts. About a third of Ireland's population was crammed into the four largest metros: Dublin, Cork, Limerick, and Galway. *If you can live anywhere, why not live here?* these small communities asked. (Or as Rose put it in her lovely Irish brogue, "Lads, what about the rest of us?") Small towns began to market themselves to convince potential remote workers to rethink their life choices.

The town of Dingle, for instance, with a population hovering slightly over the two-thousand-person mark, offered what they called a "Town Taster." Would-be Seekers were invited to visit for the weekend, claim a free hot desk at the local coworking facility, then meet up for snacks and drinks at the local pub.[6]

Other small places followed suit. In Valentia, a 9.9-square mile island with fewer than seven hundred residents, two families that visited during the Town Taster event ended up moving there permanently.

There's an island off the coast of Donegal called Arranmore, and a couple of years ago, residents realized that if they couldn't increase the population fast, the local island school would be shuttered. They urgently needed to entice new people to move there or former residents to return. On an island of 469 people, the best way to do that was to promote remote work.

So island leaders partnered with the telecommunications company Three Ireland, which not only wired Arranmore for high-speed gigabyte internet and helped fund a coworking space but also created an ad campaign about it. In one commercial, amid shots of waves crashing on craggy rocks, islanders talk about their love for Arranmore and their desire to hear the sound of children there again. An expat talks about running his educational gaming company from the island.[7]

Since the ads debuted in spring 2019, Arranmore has increased its population by 10 percent. Nearly forty people have moved there or stayed when they otherwise might not have. On a visit to Arranmore, Tracy Keogh, the founder of Grow Remote, started chatting with a local young man in his early twenties who wanted to stay on the island but felt like he'd probably have to decamp for London for work. Tracy put out feelers in her network, and within a few weeks, he had eight interviews lined up for remote jobs that would let him stay in Arranmore.[8]

Though the impetus behind Grow Remote Ireland was to help remote workers feel less isolated, Rose and Tracy saw secondary benefits accruing to communities. Anywhereists typically made more money than was average for small Irish villages, and thus towns started to fare better economically. Then, because remote workers felt more financially secure and had more time, they became more engaged in the running of their places.

Other approaches to creating sustainable and viable rural communities, like advocating for entrepreneurship or universal basic income, might have also helped, Rose acknowledges. But Anywhereist work is compelling at a whole different level. "We want people to be able to have choice and flexibility to live where they want, and we also want to see community strengthened." Anywhereism ticks both boxes.

Advised by Grow Remote Ireland, the country of Ireland has gone on to adopt a national Remote Work Strategy.[9] And Rose, who's a community manager at Grow Remote, lives where she wants, which happens to be near Galway.

More and more Anywhereists are emerging all the time. Sometimes they stay where they are. Sometimes, like the more than 40 percent of Americans who wouldn't choose to stay in their current city given the choice, they go to a new spot.[10] That's the beauty of being an Anywhereist. Once you have that freedom to choose, you decide how to use it. Are you going to be a Wanderer, flitting from place to place? A Settler, who stays put? Or a Seeker, who develops a location strategy to zero in on what you're looking for, then relocates to a community whose values seem to reflect your own?

WHAT MATTERS NOW?

However you approach it, it's smart to remember the relationship between your work and your place. Even if you're not spending every day in an office, you hope for professional success and growth in your career, coworkers and bosses who will help you along the way, and a sense of meaning to make it all worthwhile. With smart planning, you find those same supportive qualities of profession, people, and purpose in your place too. When you can work from anywhere, the right anywhere can make you better at your work.

To help you factor in smart place values as you formulate a location strategy, here are a few more questions to think about:

- **Recognition:** Does this place offer incentives to move there? Are there recruitment efforts locally to attract remote workers? Are there programs to welcome you to the community or help you connect you with locals? Is there an easy way to contact the local economic development authority or the chamber of commerce to ask for advice? Does this town make it clear that they want you here?

- **Wealth:** Will geographic arbitrage help you in this new city? Is housing less expensive than where you live now? Will other expenses go up or down? What about your taxes? Are there other countries that might serve you better financially? How will moving costs affect your financial outcomes?

- **Entrepreneurship:** Will this city help you become more or less ambitious? More or less focused on personal growth and success? Is there an entrepreneurial ecosystem that encourages good ideas? Can you imagine bringing your own good idea to fruition here? Are there holes in the market you could fill? Will there be mentors to guide you? Sources of capital? Do you envision that the community here might rally around you? What resources are available for small business owners or remote workers?

- **Connection:** Are there coworking spaces in the city? Community gathering spaces? Are there people who do what you do for a living, or work in adjacent fields, who might become a support network? Are there networking opportunities or activities that help you build career connections, like writers' groups? Are there coliving spaces if you're interested in that? Do you have a plan for finding friends in this new place? Are there entry points into the community, like clubs or career- or hobby-related groups?

- **Creativity:** Will this place inspire your creativity? If you're in a creative field, are there local markets for your work? A community of fellow creatives? Is the focus on craft or on success? Are there mentors or others who can support your work? Housing for creatives? Places to exhibit work? Places to create work? An arts council to provide resources and support?

- **Adventure:** Are there interesting things to do here? Will you have chances to experience novelty and excitement in your daily life? Would moving to this place feel comfortable or adventurous? Can you imagine using your work flexibility to have fun and dispel tedium? Have you considered moving abroad? Is there a country offering a nomad visa that you'd consider living in?

- **Learning:** What is the per-student spending in this state or community? Are there resources for upskilling or reskilling if you need a career shift? Are there internship or work opportunities for your children? Do schools here prep children with career-readiness skills? Are there programs here that might help you become a more skilled remote worker or find a remote job? Are there good public universities that might make college more affordable for your kids? Will you be living in a larger work ecosystem, with career opportunities within a reasonable drive if you need or want them? Would you live in your college town?

- **Purpose:** Can you identify ways you'd like to have an impact here? Does this place need you? Would you feel comfortable getting involved here? Are there ways for you to use your work skills in service of your community? What kinds of needs do you envision having now or in the future that your community could support you through? How do you envision establishing that community? How diverse is this new community? In what ways will you add to its diversity? How can you help create more equity where you live? Are there things here that you'd like to save or invest in? Can you thrive here economically? Can others?

- **Happiness:** How will this place help you live your best life? Will you be able to keep your work in perspective? What would living here tell you about who you are and who you're trying to become? How will your place values show up here in positive ways? How will you find joy and perspective here? Rest? Positive experiences? How close would you be to family? How easily accessible are amenities? Are there therapeutic, enabling places to improve your well-being? Does this place feel manageable? Would it allow you to do the things that bring you the most pleasure in life?

THE CHOICE

By now, you should have a better sense of what you're actually looking for in a place and a life. You've analyzed your own values and translated those into a location strategy. Now, to turn your touchy-feely epiphanies into boots-on-the-ground decision-making, you can systematize what you've discovered. We'll be using a ten-by-ten grid. Create a small spreadsheet on paper or online, or download one at melodywarnick.com.

Along the top of the grid, write your ten must-haves—place qualities you can't live without. Big city! Close to an airport! An entrepreneurial community! Abundance of Thai food! If you're having trouble narrowing it down, here's a hint: when you think about living around these qualities, you feel comfortable, peaceful, or content. When you think about living without them, you feel marginally freaked out.

Next, along the spreadsheet's y-axis, add ten candidate places—cities you're curious about, towns you love or heard you might. If you've boiled it down to a handful of candidates already, that's fine, but if you're starting from scratch, go for at least ten places.

Verify that all the towns under consideration meet your deal-breaker requirements. Start Googling. Look at Facebook forums and City-Data.com. Eliminate any city that falls short. If none do, dig a little deeper, and add a few more qualities you care about. Keep going until you've narrowed the list to four or five cities you're really interested in.

Now visit. In person. At least once, possibly more. If you're a Seeker looking for a mostly permanent home, there's no substitute for showing up yourself and seeing how a place feels to you. Be a tourist, but also act like a resident. Explore neighborhoods. Ride public transportation. Look at problems (traffic, expenses) but also possibilities that might delight you (an amazing bar in a funky downtown).

The process of choosing a place is made exponentially more difficult when you need to agree with a partner. Location decisions are frankly revelatory, and finding out that your partner wants vastly different things from their geography can test the foundations of a relationship: How can we be together and want such different things?

Whatever process you've used in the past to come to consensus on serious issues will be helpful here, including therapy. Start by acknowledging that your firmly held beliefs about an ideal location may not resonate for your partner. Aim for mutual understanding, then consider compromise to end a decision deadlock.

One strategy is to create separate ten-by-ten spreadsheets,

populated with your own lists of ten must-haves and ten cities. You may find that totally different desires nevertheless got you interested in similar places. (You're excited about Boulder for building your business; your partner's excited about all that hiking.)

If not, take a step back by writing your ten most desired qualities on separate index cards—*great schools* on one card, *airport within forty minutes* on another, and so on. Do the same with the qualities you absolutely don't want. Lay them on a table in order of importance to you. Then look for overlap. Do you agree on anything? Can you create a stack that more or less reflects what matters to you both? What if you allowed each other one or two vetoes?

Worst-case scenario: You agree to a split decision that sends you to different cities, and you meet in the geographic middle every few weeks. Or like some couples do with naming their children, you take turns having your way: your partner gets to pick their favorite city for the next three years, then you do.

Ideally, it doesn't come to that, and you can identify a place that satisfies everyone. More or less.

YOU CAN MAKE A MISTAKE

The reality is, there is no perfect choice. The heady feeling of being a newly minted Anywhereist—something along the lines of *Holy crap, I can literally go anywhere in the world!*—may make you drunk with geographic power. You might, like grant writer and Anywhereist Margaret Vandergriff, be tempted to do something... rash.[11]

First, Margaret traded Austin for a tumbleweed-strewn town near Lubbock, Texas ("It's hard to describe just how awful it was," she said). Then on a road trip along Route 66, she and her free-lance writer husband, Ryan, fell in love with rural Iowa, a place so antithetical to West Texas that they were enchanted. The idea took hold: Why not move here? "Now I can look back and see it was totally ridiculous," Margaret admitted. "But at the time, we were swept up in it—this romantic idea of what it meant to live in a small town in the Midwest. We were just blinded by it."

The mortgage on Margaret and Ryan's drafty old farmhouse was cheap. Utilities, property taxes, and car registration turned out to be more expensive. Worse, after a brief honeymoon period when their neighbors brought them cookies, they had a tough time making friends. No one seemed to want them there. Perhaps the locals merely thought of them as the new people in the old house, one in a string of similar new people who had imagined their fortunes changing in small-town Iowa.

In retrospect, Margaret recognizes that in the rush of realizing they *could* move, they didn't think hard enough about if they *should*. They thought they could buy the house and figure the rest out later. Steeped in the glamour of their decision, Margaret and Ryan failed to do their due diligence.

Margaret has since become an advocate for making a location strategy. She and Ryan have had long conversations to discuss what mattered to them and what kind of life they imagined living as Anywhereist empty nesters. What made them happy? What did they need or want? They figured out their place values and examined their uncomfortable experiences in two small, conservative towns in a row to decide on priorities.

A spreadsheet of preferences slowly began to take shape. They wanted to be in a liberal-leaning small city, with all they thought that included: farmers markets, yarn stores, art galleries, movie theaters. As vegetarians, they wanted better restaurant options. Margaret also wanted to be closer to her eighty-seven-year-old mother, who lived in a rent-controlled apartment in San Francisco. She felt pulled to the ocean and to the West in general, where she'd grown up.

The two restrictions that seriously narrowed their field of candidates were (1) wanting to be in a state that had legalized marijuana and (2) wanting to be in a place that did not have tornadoes. (Ryan had had a close call with a tornado earlier in life and had no wish to repeat the experience.) By the end, they were looking at just two states, Oregon and Washington.

Despite all the online research, Margaret and Ryan had no intention of leaving anything to chance. This time, they bought plane tickets and flew to Eugene, Oregon, which topped their list of possibilities. They talked to strangers, drove all over, and explored. By the end of the trip, Margaret knew. "It was just like kismet," she said. "It was magical." Eugene was their next town.

The kicker is that they still haven't moved there. Not long after making the decision, COVID struck, and they had to resolve some family matters. But Margaret knows Eugene's out there, waiting for them, a town they chose not because of idealistic assumptions but because of hard data, research, and experimentation. A town they chose with a location strategy.

The experience of finding the right place was so life-changing that in 2020, Margaret launched a service called Your Place Finder to help other Anywhereists find their own best towns. She asks clients to think deeply and set place priorities, and Margaret hands them a short list of possible places, like a geographic matchmaker.

Strangely, her clients don't always feel like they deserve the place they really want to go to. They'll tell her that they ultimately want to land in Tennessee, but for now, let's look at Indiana. When they get burned by a new location, they move straight back to the old one they profess to hate.

Maybe there's a fatalism in a lot of us. Perhaps we fear being disappointed, like Margaret has been. We're scared of making a mistake. We want to hold a dream location in reserve, as something we earn when we've put in enough time in the salt mines of lesser places.

Margaret gently tries to steer people back toward what they most want. "It's like, if you ultimately want to be in this place, can't we just put this place front and center and go there? Let's just focus on this."

If you need permission to pursue living in a place that you're excited about, even if it doesn't meet all the criteria you've laid out for yourself with your location strategy, consider this your yes. I want you to be logical and clear-eyed about your choices, but I also want you to take joy in the chance to design your life.

Take your time. But in the end, move forward. As Eckhart Tolle wrote, "Any action is often better than no action, especially if you have been stuck in an unhappy situation for a long time. If it is a mistake, at least you learn something, in which case it's no longer a mistake."[12]

MAKE A MOVE

The good news is, there are great towns out there—places that feel like long-lost soul mates, places that fit a need right now, places that need *you*. Any one of them could be your future destination.

There are happy endings for Seekers too. Amy and James Hebdon, the couple who moved to Clarksville, Tennessee, absolutely love where they live now.[13] It took a lot of strife to get them to where they are, past unknowns, moments of indecision, changes of plans, doubts, a pandemic. Some things Amy did as part of building her location strategy helped, like joining Facebook groups around her interests (permaculture, aquaponics, backyard poultry) to prove that there were like-minded people in the areas she was considering. Some things didn't, like looking up state rankings or listicles about "Best States for Start-Ups." As she points out, there are probably more differences within states than between them.

But in the end, they pulled the trigger, bought the house in Clarksville, settled in, and got their chickens. It's not perfect, but it's home.

NOTES

- - - - -

Chapter One: When Anywhereists Rule the World

1 **where should we live?:** Amy Hebdon, in conversation with the author, December 2020.

2 **just because he could:** Ryan Mita, in conversation with the author, November 2020.

3 **like she is:** Grace Taylor, in conversation with the author, November 2020.

4 **the American workforce:** "Freelance Forward 2020: The U.S. Independent Workforce Report," Upwork, September 2020, https://www.upwork.com/i /freelance-forward.

5 **to the Netherlands:** Jessica Araus, in conversation with the author, January 2021.

6 **320 days of annual sunshine:** Ria Talken, in conversation with the author, February 2021.

7 **a work robot:** Anne Helen Petersen, *Can't Even: How Millennials Became the Burnout Generation* (New York: Mariner, 2020), xix.

8 **wherever that might be:** Jason Fried and David Heinemeier Hansson, *Remote: Office Not Required* (New York: Crown Business, 2013), 31, 40.

9 **workers grew by 140 percent:** Kate Lister, "Telecommuting Statistics," Global Workplace Analytics, updated June 22, 2021, https://globalworkplaceanalytics .com/telecommuting-statistics.

10   **some of the time by 2016:** Niraj Chokshi, "Out of the Office: More People Are Working Remotely, Survey Finds," *New York Times*, February 15, 2017, https://www.nytimes.com/2017/02/15/us/remote-workers-work-from-home.html.

11   **allowed remote work:** "The Modern Workplace: People, Places, and Technology," Condeco Software, 2019, http://www.condecosoftware.com/resources-hub/wp-content/uploads/sites/8/2019/05/Condeco-workplace-report-2019-Digital-Copy.pdf.

12   **and we discourage it:** Nikil Saval, *Cubed: A Secret History of the Workplace* (New York: Doubleday, 2014), 288.

13   **impromptu team meetings:** Charles Arthur, "Yahoo Chief Bans Working from Home," *Guardian*, February 25, 2013, https://www.theguardian.com/technology/2013/feb/25/yahoo-chief-bans-working-home.

14   **the perk that would tip the scales:** Shilpa Ahuja, "The Pros and Cons of Remote Work," Robert Half Talent Solutions, June 11, 2018, https://www.roberthalf.com/blog/the-future-of-work/the-pros-and-cons-of-telecommuting.

15   **during a global pandemic:** Carl Benedikt Frey et al., "Technology at Work v5.0: A New World of Remote Work," Citi GPS: Global Perspectives & Solutions series, June 2020, https://www.oxfordmartin.ox.ac.uk/downloads/reports/CitiGPS_TechnologyatWork_5_220620.pdf.

16   **RVs by 53 percent:** "RV Shipments Up 54% in July," RV Industry Association, July 2020, https://www.rvia.org/news-insights/rv-shipments-54-july.

17   **suitability for remote work:** Joan Verdon, "Work-From-Anywhere Isn't Going Away: 5 Ways the Hospitality Sector Is Monetizing the Trend," U.S. Chamber of Commerce, June 29, 2021, https://www.uschamber.com/co/good-company/launch-pad/hospitality-industry-work-from-anywhere-trend.

18   **one in ten Americans relocated:** Will Storey and Lilian Manansala, "One in Every 10 Americans Moved during the Pandemic," *Business Insider*, August 10, 2021, https://www.businessinsider.com/where-americans-moved-covid-pandemic-2021-8.

19   **reassess where they lived:** Crissinda Ponder, "Nearly Half of Americans Are Considering a Move to Reduce Living Expenses," Lending Tree, November 17, 2020, https://

www.lendingtree.com/home/mortgage/nearly-half-of-americans-are-considering
-a-move-to-reduce-living-expenses/.

20 **by up to 25 percent:** Diana Olick, "These Are the Five Hottest—and Three
Coldest—Markets for Home Prices in 2021," CNBC, January 21, 2021, https://www
.cnbc.com/2021/01/21/best-real-estate-markets-2021.html.

21 **option to work remotely:** "The Bay Area Exodus: Remote Workers Can Live
Anywhere. Will They Stay Here?," Zapier, May 26, 2020, https://zapier.com/blog
/bay-area-remote-work-report/.

22 **One in five already had:** "How Airbnb and Travelers are Redefining Travel in 2021,"
Airbnb, October 15, 2020, https://news.airbnb.com/2021-travel-trends/.

23 **until they retired:** "State of Remote Work," Buffer, 2019, https://buffer.com
/state-of-remote-work-2019.

24 **stay totally virtual:** Mary Baker, "Gartner Survey Reveals 82% of Company Leaders
Plan to Allow Employees to Work Remotely Some of the Time," Gartner, July 14,
2020,   https://www.gartner.com/en/newsroom/press-releases/2020-07-14-gartner
-survey-reveals-82-percent-of-company-leaders-plan-to-allow-employees-to-work
-remotely-some-of-the-time.

25 **ping-pong tables and snacks:** Brent Hyder, "Creating a Best Workplace from
Anywhere, for Everyone," Salesforce, February 9, 2021, https://www.salesforce.com
/news/stories/creating-a-best-workplace-from-anywhere/.

26 **new homes by 2030:** Eshe Nelson, "The City of London Plans to Convert
Empty Offices into Homes," *New York Times*, April 27, 2021, https://www.nytimes
.com/2021/04/27/business/city-of-london-apartments.html.

27 **levels in a decade:** Peter Eavis and Matthew Haag, "After Pandemic, Shrinking Need
for Office Space Could Crush Landlords," *New York Times*, April 8, 2021, https://www
.nytimes.com/2021/04/08/business/economy/office-buildings-remote-work.html.

28 **employees more content:** Laurel Farrer, in conversation with the author, February 2021.

29 **this way by choice:** "Freelancing in America 2017," Upwork, 2017, https://www
.upwork.com/i/freelancing-in-america/2017/.

30   **high-powered careers:** Amy Adkins, "Millennials: The Job-Hopping Generation," Gallup, accessed October 4, 2021, https://www.gallup.com/workplace/231587/millennials-job-hopping-generation.aspx.

31   **and moved there:** Janee Allen, in conversation with the author, March 2019.

32   **they were Anywhereists:** Katie Lincoln, in conversation with the author, January 2021.

33   **hover around $1,500:** Kevin and Dani VanKookz, in conversation with the author, August 2020.

34   **keep them there:** Darcy Maulsby, in conversation with the author, November 2020.

35   **The front range of Colorado:** Crystal Atkinson, "Currently in HCOL," Facebook, January 5, 2021, https://www.facebook.com/groups/womenspersonalfinance/permalink/2812840589004138.

36   **their towns as I'd been:** Melody Warnick, *This Is Where You Belong* (New York: Viking, 2016).

37   **municipalities on planet earth** Gregory Scruggs, "There Are 10,000 Cities on Planet Earth. Half Didn't Exist 40 Years Ago," *Next City*, February 12, 2020, https://nextcity.org/daily/entry/there-are-10000-cities-on-planet-earth-half-didnt-exist-40-years-ago.

Chapter Two: You Need a Location Strategy

1   **they loved it:** Lisa Comingore, in conversation with the author, February 2021.

2   **analysis paralysis:** Barry Schwartz, *The Paradox of Choice: Why More Is Less* (New York: Ecco, 2004), 99–220.

3   **FOBO is worse:** Patrick J. McGinnis, "Meet FOBO: The Evil Brother of FOMO That Can Ruin Your Life," PatrickMcginnis.com (blog), accessed October 30, 2021, https://patrickmcginnis.com/blog/meet-fobo-the-evil-brother-of-fomo-that-can-ruin-your-life/. Read more in Patrick McGinnis, *Fear of Missing Out: Practical Decision-Making in a World of Overwhelming Choice* (Naperville, IL: Sourcebooks, 2020).

4   **serious emotional labor:** Leah Love, in conversation with the author, January 2021.

5   **cataclysmic mistake:** Hebdon, conversation.

6   **areas do better:** Daniel Brancusi, "Starbucks Location Analysis," NY Data Science

Academy, August 23, 2020, https://nycdatascience.com/blog/student-works/starbucks-location-analysis/; Dhrumil Patel, "Site Planning Using Location Data," Medium, October 17, 2019, https://medium.com/locale-ai/site-planning-using-location-data-ae7814973521; Rong Dai, "Starbucks Site Selection Analysis Based on GIS Method," Barry Waite (blog), accessed October 4, 2021, http://www.barrywaite.org/gis/projects/fall-2015/Rong%20Dai.pdf (site discontinued).

7   **homes farther away:** Spencer Rascoff and Stan Humphries, *Zillow Talk: Rewriting the Rules of Real Estate* (New York: Grand Central, 2015), 49–56.

8   **the discount grocer:** Jake Rossen, "Living Near a Trader Joe's Can Increase the Value of Your Home—Here's Why," Mental Floss, July 28, 2020, https://www.mentalfloss.com/article/626950/living-near-trader-joes-can-increase-home-value.

9   **actually support one:** Jon Harris, "Here's What Trader Joe's Is Looking for in a New Location, and Why It's Not (Yet) in the Lehigh Valley," *Morning Call*, August 28, 2019, https://www.mcall.com/business/mc-biz-why-trader-joes-hasnt-opened-lehigh-valley-store-20190828-7icd2wpj25ezblyaci6ocoxsy4-story.html.

10 **affordable homes:** Jackie Gutierrez-Jones, "All the Right Moves: 5 Key Insights Into the Present and Future of Millennial Talent Attraction," Livability, accessed October 4, 2021, https://livability.com/wp-content/uploads/2019/01/Livability-Millennial-Trend-Report.pdf.

11 **make do with one:** Na Zhao, "Nation's Stock of Second Homes," NAHB Eye on Housing, October 16, 2020, https://eyeonhousing.org/2020/10/nations-stock-of-second-homes-2/.

12 **closest to home:** Anne Bogel, *Don't Overthink It* (Ada, MI: Baker, 2020), 52–53.

Chapter Three: Your Town Is Your Office

1   **actual location: Remote, Oregon:** Brian Feldman, "The Job Capital of America," BNet.com, February 26, 2021, https://bnet.substack.com/p/the-job-capital-of-america.

2   **in particular is irrelevant:** Daniel H. Pink, *Free Agent Nation: The Future of Working for Yourself* (New York: Grand Central, 2001), 261.

3   **work-here-or-anywhere Wanderer life:** Stephanie Storey, in conversation with the author, January 2021.

4   **not for your job:** "Future Workforce Pulse Report," Upwork, December 2020, https://wf-info.upwork.com/i/future-workforce/fw/2020.

5   **a medical device:** Alexander M. Bell et al., "Who Becomes an Inventor in America? The Importance of Exposure to Innovation," *Quarterly Journal of Economics* 134, no. 2 (May 2019): 647–713, https://doi.org/10.1093/qje/qjy028.

6   **California or Texas:** Raj Chetty et al., "Where is the Land of Opportunity: The Geography of Intergenerational Mobility in the United States," *Quarterly Journal of Economics* 129, no. 4 (November 2014): 1553–623, https://doi.org/10.1093/qje/qju022.

7   **seems fairly clear:** For instance, see Ann Owens, "Income Segregation between School Districts and Inequality in Students' Achievement," *Sociology of Education* 91, no. 1 (2018): 1–27, https://doi.org/10.1177/0038040717741180.

8   **outcome of exposure:** Bell et al., "Who Becomes an Inventor?."

9   **which he worked:** Robin Pogrebin and Scott Reyburn, "Leonardo da Vinci Painting Sells for $450.3 Million, Shattering Auction Highs," *New York Times*, November 15, 2017, https://www.nytimes.com/2017/11/15/arts/design/leonardo-da-vinci-salvator-mundi-christies-auction.html.

10 **matter more than that:** Paul Graham, "Cities and Ambition," Paul Graham (blog), May 2008, http://www.paulgraham.com/cities.html.

11 **happy and engaged at work:** Lori Goler, Janelle Gale, Brynn Harrington, and Adam Grant, "The 3 Things Employees Really Want: Career, Community, Cause," *Harvard Business Review*, February 20, 2018, https://hbr.org/2018/02/people-want-3-things-from-work-but-most-companies-are-built-around-only-one.

12 **positive contribution to the world:** Jim Harter, "Historic Drop in Employee Engagement Follows Record Rise," Gallup, July 2, 2020, https://www.gallup.com/workplace/313313/historic-drop-employee-engagement-follows-record-rise.aspx.

13 **order of importance:** Goler, Gale, Harrington, and Grant, "The 3 Things Employees Really Want."

14   **career paths altogether:** Amy Adkins, "Millennials: The Job-Hopping Generation," Gallup, accessed October 4, 2021, https://www.gallup.com/workplace/231587 /millennials-job-hopping-generation.aspx.

15   **unlock your full potential:** Brett and Kate McKay, "Craft the Life You Want: Setting Up Shop, or the Importance of Where You Live," Art of Manliness, February 15, 2011, https://www.artofmanliness.com/character/advice/craft-the-life -you-want-setting-up-shop-or-the-importance-of-where-you-live/.

Chapter Four: All the Towns Want You

1   **450 applicants for twenty-five slots:** Mackenzie Cottles, in conversation with the author, January 2021.

2   **for lack of work:** Austin Carr, "Inside Wisconsin's Disastrous $4.5 Billion Deal With Foxconn," *Bloomberg Businessweek*, February 6, 2019, https://www.bloomberg.com/news /features/2019-02-06/inside-wisconsin-s-disastrous-4-5-billion-deal-with-foxconn.

3   **HQ2 ring in 2017:** Derek Thompson, "Amazon's HQ2 Spectacle Isn't Just Shameful—It Should Be Illegal," *Atlantic*, November 16, 2018, https://www.theatlantic .com/ideas/archive/2018/11/amazons-hq2-spectacle-should-be-illegal/575539/.

4   **totaled $7 billion:** Dustin McKissen, "Guest Post: St. Louis Tried to Give Amazon More than $7B," *Silicon Prairie News*, May 9, 2018, https://siliconprairienews .com/2018/05/guest-post-everything-about-the-way-the-st-louis-region-recruited -and-responded-to-amazon-has-been-a-mistake/.

5   **generations to come:** "Amazon Selects New York City and Northern Virginia for New Headquarters," Amazon, November 13, 2018, https://www.aboutamazon .com/news/company-news/amazon-selects-new-york-city-and-northern-virginia -for-new-headquarters.

6   **it's totally flipped now:** Sarah Kerner, in conversation with the author, February 2021.

7   **new community and one another:** Tulsa Remote, accessed May 30, 2021, https:// tulsaremote.com/. See also Carel-Lee Bernard, "We Got Paid $10,000 to Move to a Flyover

State for a Year," Thrillist, February 3, 2021, https://www.thrillist.com/travel/nation/tulsa-remote-program-what-to-know.

8   **as part of Tulsa Remote:** Dale Denwalt, "Tulsa Remote Luring Out-of-State Workers with Cash to Buy a Home," *Oklahoman*, February 24, 2021, https://www.oklahoman.com/story/business/columns/2021/02/24/tulsa-remote-luring-out-of-state-workers-with-cash-to-buy-a-home/332990007/.

9   **moved to the area:** "Shoals Economic Development Authority Offers Remote Workers $10,000 to Relocate to Northwest Alabama," Shoals Economic Development Authority, June 4, 2019, https://www.seda-shoals.com/blog/shoals-economic-development-authority-offers-remote-workers-10-000-to-relocate-to-northwest-alabama.

10   **Anywhereists' preconceived notions:** Cottles, conversation.

11   **Walton Family Foundation:** "Talent Incentive," Finding NWA, accessed October 4, 2021, https://findingnwa.com/incentive/.

12   **bought a home:** Choose Topeka, accessed October 4, 2021, https://choosetopeka.com/apply/.

13   **north of Cincinnati:** Tiffany Pennamon, "Foundation Offers Recent Graduates $5,000 to Move to Ohio City," *Diverse Issues in Higher Education*, March 1, 2018, https://www.diverseeducation.com/home/article/15102109/foundation-offers-recent-graduates-5000-to-move-to-ohio-city.

14   **gifts from local businesses:** "Housing Initiative," Newton Economic Development, accessed October 4, 2021, https://newtongov.org/806/Housing-Initiative.

15   **stay longer:** "Work Remotely, Connect with Aloha," Movers and Shakas, accessed October 4, 2021, https://www.moversandshakas.org/.

16   **repay the money:** Helena Bachmann, "You Won't Believe How Much This Tiny Swiss Village Will Pay You to Move There," *USA Today*, November 30, 2017, https://www.usatoday.com/story/news/world/2017/11/30/you-wont-believe-how-much-tiny-swiss-village-pay-you-move-there/910922001/.

17   **Savannah Economic Development Authority:** Jared Lindzon, "Cities Offer Cash as They Compete for New Residents amid Remote Work Boom," *Fast*

Company, June 22, 2020, https://www.fastcompany.com/90517270/cities -offer-cash-as-they-compete-for-new-residents-amid-remote-work-boom.

18   **it dried up:** Dan D'Ambrosio, "Is Vermont's $10,000 Incentive Program for Remote Workers Working?," *Burlington Free Press*, November 18, 2019, https://www. burlingtonfreepress.com/story/money/2019/11/19/vermonts-10–000-pay -move-remote-worker-program-does-work/4189358002/.

19   **good the bait was:** Adam Wren (@adamwren), "Brutal Day for Indiana on the TL," Twitter, April 13, 2021, 4:50 pm, https://twitter.com/adamwren /status/1382117499244793861/photo/1.

20   **to come there:** D'Ambrosio, "Vermont's $10,000 Incentive Program."

21   **a huge problem:** Winona Dimeo-Ediger, in conversation with the author, January 2021.

22   **given proper recognition:** Marcel Schwantes, "A New Study Reveals 70 Percent of Workers Say They Are Actively Looking for a New Job," *Inc.*, December 4, 2018, https://www.inc.com/marcel-schwantes/a-new-study-reveals-70-percent-of-workers -say-they-are-actively-looking-for-a-new-job-heres-reason-in-5-words.html.

23   **in the country:** Joel Kotkin and Cullum Clark, "Big D Is a Big Deal," *City Journal*, Summer 2021, https://www.city-journal.org/dallas-fort-worth.

24   **accessible international airport:** Jessica Heer, in conversation with the author, December 2020.

25   **they were told:** Heer, conversation.

26   **human being is better:** Uri Berliner, "You Want To Move? Some Cities Will Pay You $10,000 To Relocate," NPR, December 20, 2020, https:// www.npr.org/2020/12/20/944986123/you-want-to-move-some-cities-will -pay-you-10–000-to-relocate.

27   **on their own:** Berliner, "You Want to Move?."

28   **things they cared about:** Dimeo-Ediger, conversation.

29   **decision-making factors:** Gutierrez-Jones, "All the Right Moves."

30   **reason to stay put:** Gutierrez-Jones, "All the Right Moves."

31   **and small towns:** Marie Patino, Aaron Kessler, and Sarah Holder, "More Americans Are Leaving Cities, But Don't Call It an Urban Exodus," *Bloomberg CityLab*, April 26, 2021, https://www.bloomberg.com/graphics/2021-citylab-how-americans-moved/; Anna Bahney, "People Are Snatching Up Vacation Homes," CNN, June 17, 2021, https://www.cnn.com/2021/06/17/homes/vacation-home-sales-increase-covid-feseries/index.html.

32   **their same metro area:** Patino, Kessler, and Holder, "More Americans Are Leaving Cities."

33   **spikes in remote workers:** Richard Florida, "Talent May Be Shifting Away from Superstar Cities," *Bloomberg CityLab*, November 18, 2019, https://www.bloomberg.com/news/articles/2019-11-18/why-superstar-cities-may-be-losing-their-luster.

34   **underdog locations:** Becky McCray and Deb Brown, "Zoom Towns: Rural Remote Work," Save Your Town, video, December 2020, https://learnto.saveyour.town/zoom-towns-remote-work.

35   **priced out of those:** Joe and Ana Kuykendall, in conversation with the author, March 2021.

36   **tip of the iceberg:** Marcus Andersson, in conversation with the author, December 2020.

37   **local ambassador programs:** "Marcus Andersson on Talent Attraction and Place Attractiveness," Place Brand Observer, July 30, 2015, https://placebrandobserver.com/interview-marcus-andersson/.

38   **That's talent attraction:** Tim Carty, in conversation with the author, January 2021.

39   **your new town:** Dick Hakes, "Wingman Program Gives Newcomers a Healthy Dose of 'Iowa Nice,'" *Iowa City Press-Citizen*, October 18, 2019, https://www.press-citizen.com/story/life/2019/10/18/wingman-program-helps-connect-new-residents-iowa-city-experts/4002163002/.

40   **things like that:** Heer, conversation.

41   **kind of intense:** Dimeo-Ediger, conversation.

42   **we got that here:** Joe and Ana Kuykendall, conversation.

43   **arts and culture and restaurants:** Barbara Stapleton, in conversation with the author, March 2021.

44   **marketing director:** Bob Ross, in conversation with the author, March 2021.

45   **ready to stay:** Shawn Wheat and Alyssa Willetts, "Topeka Partnership Responds to Colbert Criticism," WIBW, December 19, 2019, https://www.wibw.com/content /news/Topeka-Partnership-responds-to-Colbert-criticism-566335651.html.

Chapter Five: Everything's Cheaper in Panama

1   **lost their jobs:** Tommy Andres, "Divided Decade: How the Financial Crisis Changed Jobs," Marketplace, December 19, 2018, https://www.marketplace.org/2018/12/19 /what-we-learned-jobs/.

2   **one of them:** Susanna Perkins, in conversation with the author, December 2020.

3   **where to move:** Gutierrez-Jones, "All the Right Moves."

4   **the national average:** Sean Coffey, "New Research: People are Leaving SF, But Not California," California Policy Lab, March 4, 2021, https://www.capolicylab.org /news/new-research-people-are-leaving-sf-but-not-california/.

5   **in 2019 was $3,550:** Adam Brinklow, "San Francisco Market Rents Soar up to 105 Percent above Average," Curbed, October 2, 2019, https://sf.curbed.com/2019/10/2 /20895578/san-francisco-median-rents-market-census-september-2019.

6   **pressures where they lived:** D'Vera Cohn, "As the Pandemic Persisted, Financial Pressures Became a Bigger Factor in Why Americans Decided to Move," Pew Research Center, February 4, 2021, https://www.pewresearch.org/fact-tank/2021/02/04 /as-the-pandemic-persisted-financial-pressures-became-a-bigger-factor-in-why -americans-decided-to-move/.

7   **around 49 percent:** Joe Roberts, "US Cities with the Lowest Cost of Living," Move .org, November 10, 2020, https://www.move.org/lowest-cost-of-living-by-us-city.

8   **a lot less money:** Tim Leffel, in conversation with the author, April 2021.

9   **something better comes along:** Paulette Perhach, "A Story of a Fuck Off Fund," Billfold, January 20, 2016, https://www.thebillfold.com/2016/01/a-story-of-a-fuck-off-fund/.

10   **triple-A baseball team:** Mark Huffman, "New Study Finds Most Consumers Prefer Experiences over Things," *Consumer Affairs*, October 15, 2019, https://www .consumeraffairs.com/news/new-study-finds-most-consumers-prefer-experiences -over-things-101519.html.

11   **$1.31 in Bulgaria:** Lydia Belanger, "The Cheapest and Most Expensive Places in the World for a Cup of Coffee," *Business Insider*, March 28, 2018, https://www.businessinsider .com/the-cheapest-and-most-expensive-places-in-the-world-for-a-coffee-2018-3.

12   **family's annual spending:** "Consumer Expenditures—2020," U.S. Bureau of Labor Statistics, September 9, 2021, https://www.bls.gov/news.release/pdf/cesan.pdf.

13   **climb in fifteen years:** Sylvan Lane, "Housing Prices Rose Nearly 15 percent Annually in April," The Hill, June 29, 2021, https://thehill.com/policy /finance/560752-housing-prices-rose-nearly-15-percent-annually-in-april.

14   **income in a market:** Wendell Cox, "Demographia International Housing Affordability: 2021 Edition," Urban Reform Institute and Frontier Centre for Public Policy, February 2021, http://www.demographia.com/dhi.pdf.

15   **and St. Louis, Missouri:** Cox, "Demographia International Housing Affordability."

16   **the affordability ratio:** Cox, "Demographia International Housing Affordability."

17   **so...maybe not?:** Josephine Tovey, "Waiting to Borrow: Buying a First Home Amid Soaring Real Estate Prices Feels Grimly Beckettian," *Guardian*, April 11, 2021, https:// www.theguardian.com/australia-news/2021/apr/12/waiting-to-borrow-buying-a -first-home-amid-soaring-real-estate-prices-feels-grimly-beckettian.

18   **median household income:** Cox, "Demographia International Housing Affordability."

19   **house poor:** "The State of the Nation's Housing 2018," Joint Center for Housing Studies of Harvard University, 2018, https://www.jchs.harvard.edu/sites/default /files/Harvard_JCHS_State_of_the_Nations_Housing_2018.pdf.

20   **Our budget is $1.4 million:** Jeremy Gibbens (@afterglide), "House Hunters intro," Twitter, April 20, 2017, 10:55 a.m., https://twitter.com/afterglide/status /855072496554475520.

21   **over their heads:** "State of the Nation's Housing 2018."

22 **the poverty line:** Tom Lisi, "Plenty of Cheap Homes in Decatur, But Still Out of Reach for Many," *Pantagraph*, August 26, 2018, https://pantagraph.com/news/state -and-regional/plenty-of-cheap-homes-in-decatur-but-still-out-of-reach-for-many /article_0a1cd010-9371-5521-80aa-f2244b675c81.html?mode=comments.

23 **city of Henderson, Nevada:** Janie Sandberg, in conversation with the author, January 2021.

24 **declines as a result:** Conor Dougherty, "The Californians Are Coming. So Is Their Housing Crisis," *New York Times*, June 21, 2021, https://www.nytimes .com/2021/02/12/business/economy/california-housing-crisis.html.

25 **have ever dreamed of:** Melanie Allen, in conversation with the author, April 2021.

26 **high quality of living:** "The World's Best Places to Retire in 2021," *International Living*, June 29, 2021, https://internationalliving.com/the-best-places-to-retire/.

27 **#1 offshore conference:** "The World's #1 Offshore Conference," Nomad Capitalist, accessed October 5, 2021, https://nomadcapitalist.com/live/.

28 **his website NomadCapitalist.com:** Andrew Henderson, *Nomad Capitalist: Reclaim Your Freedom with Offshore Companies, Dual Citizenship, Foreign Banks, and Overseas Investments* (self-pub., 2018).

29 **hiring policies:** Andrew Henderson, "Nomad Flag Theory," Nomad Capitalist, accessed October 5, 2021, https://nomadcapitalist.com/flag-theory/.

30 **no estate tax, nothing:** Mike Huynh, "Living in the World's Lowest Income Tax Countries," *CEO Magazine*, November 28, 2019, https://www.theceomagazine.com /lifestyle/property/lowest-income-tax-countries/.

31 **based on your citizenship:** John D. McKinnon, "Tax History: Why U.S. Pursues Citizens Overseas," *Wall Street Journal*, May 18, 2012, https://www.wsj.com/articles /BL-WB-34630.

32 **rest of your life:** Taylor, conversation.

33 **from American taxes:** "Foreign Earned Income Exclusion," IRS, updated February 3, 2021, https://www.irs.gov/individuals/international-taxpayers/foreign -earned-income-exclusion.

34 **not the financial savings:** Taylor, conversation.

35 **attracting other scientists:** Enrico Moretti and Daniel J. Wilson, "The Effect of State Taxes on the Geographical Location of Top Earners: Evidence from Star Scientists," *American Economic Review* 107, no. 7 (2017): 1858–903, https://doi.org/10.1257/aer.20150508.

36 **hire other workers:** Jared Walczak and Janelle Cammenga, "2021 State Business Tax Climate Index," Tax Foundation, October 21, 2020, https://taxfoundation.org/2021-state-business-tax-climate-index/.

37 **moved to Singapore:** Kate Conger, "They Got Rich Off Uber and Lyft. Then They Moved to Low-Tax States," *New York Times*, May 9, 2019, https://www.nytimes.com/2019/05/09/technology/uber-lyft-low-tax-millennials.html.

38 **Hanover, New Hampshire:** "Federal Income Tax Calculator," SmartAsset, accessed October 5, 2021, https://smartasset.com/taxes/income-taxes.

39 **California has nine:** "California Tax Rates," H&R Block, accessed October 5, 2021, https://www.hrblock.com/tax-center/filing/states/california-tax-rates/.

40 **how cheap they are:** Seth Godin, "The Tyranny of Lowest Price," Seth's Blog, May 30, 2014, https://seths.blog/2014/05/the-tyranny-of-lowest-price/.

41 **one-fifth before the pandemic:** Laura Bliss and Sarah Holder, "What Happens When a City's Largest Employer Goes 'Work From Anywhere,'" Bloomberg CityLab, February 12, 2021, https://www.bloomberg.com/news/articles/2021-02-12/what-will-remote-work-do-to-salesforce-tower.

42 **we want for our families:** Wade Foster, "De-Location Package: Keep Your Career and Live Beyond the Bay Area," Zapier, March 17, 2017, https://zapier.com/blog/move-away-from-sf-get-remote-job/.

43 **job title in Brooklyn:** "Should Salaries Be Locally Adjusted for Remote Employees?," NoHQ, accessed October 5, 2021, https://nohq.co/blog/locally-adjusted-salaries-for-remote-workers/.

44 **than when she left:** Sharon Tseung, in conversation with the author, December 2020.

45 **28 percent off everything:** John Forberger, in conversation with the author, November 2020.

46 **three-thousand-square-foot house:** Perkins, conversation.

47 **$10,000 annually:** "June Transit Savings Report: Soaring Gas Prices Take Transit Savings to Highest Level of the Year," American Public Transportation Association, June 8, 2018, https://www.apta.com/news-publications/press-releases /releases/june-transit-savings-report-soaring-gas-prices-take-transit-savings-to -highest-level-of-the-year/.

48 **moving overseas:** Marian White, "How Much Does a Moving Company Cost in 2019?," Moving.com, August 23, 2019, https://www.moving.com/tips /how-much-does-a-moving-company-cost/.

49 **renting out the others:** For a good intro to house hacking, read Andy and Liz Kolodgie, "18 Ways to Retire Early by House Hacking," Financially Independent Millennial, accessed October 5, 2021, https://thefinanciallyindependentmillennial. com/house-hacking/.

50 **country in 2021:** Lynn Walker, "Report: Wichita Falls among Cheapest Cities to Live," *Wichita Falls Times Record News*, March 17, 2021, https://www .timesrecordnews.com/story/news/local/2021/03/17/wichita-falls-among-cheapest -cities-live-study-says/4736755001/.

51 **donate to community causes:** Debbie Dobbins, in conversation with the author, April 2021.

Chapter Six: Don't Move to Silicon Valley

1 **bakery in California:** Janee Allen, conversation.

2 **taken the leap:** "FreshBooks Third Annual Self-Employment in America Report," Fresh Books, 2019, https://www.freshbooks.com/press/annualreport.

3 **their first two years:** Timothy Carter, "The True Failure Rate of Small Businesses," *Entrepreneur*, January 3, 2021, https://www.entrepreneur.com/ article/361350.

4 **makes you an entrepreneur:** "One in Three Americans Have a Side Hustle," Zapier, January 14, 2021, https://zapier.com/blog/side-hustle-report/.

5 **a real company challenge:** "The 50 Best Workplaces for Innovators," *Fast Company*, August 5, 2019, https://www.fastcompany.com/best-workplaces-for-innovators/2019.

6 **their competitors do:** Michael Ringel, Ramón Baeza, Rahool Panandiker, and Johann D. Harnoss, "In Innovation, Big Is Back," BCG, June 22, 2020, https://www.bcg.com/en-ca /publications/2020/most-innovative-companies/large-company-innovation-edge.

7 **quality of life locally:** For example, see Kristian Kremer, "The Entrepreneurial Ecosystem: A Country Comparison Based on the GEI Approach," *DICE Report* 17, no. 2 (2019): 52–62, https://www.ifo.de/en/publikationen/2019/article-journal /entrepreneurial-ecosystem-country-comparison-based-gei-approach.

8 **you should try harder:** Graham, "Cities and Ambition."

9 **make a decent wine:** Colleen Gross, in conversation with the author, January 2021.

10 **the area as innkeepers:** Chris and Jenna Simpler, in conversation with the author, December 2020.

11 **in Kansas?" she asked:** Rani Navarro Force, in conversation with the author, January 2021.

12 **to do was ask:** Teresa McAnerney, in conversation with the author, January 2021.

13 **better person," he explained:** Ernesto Sirolli, "Want to Help Someone? Shut Up and Listen!," filmed September 2012 in Christchurch, New Zealand, TED video, 16:17, https://www.ted.com/talks/ernesto_sirolli_want_to_help_someone_shut_up_and _listen?language=en; Ernesto Sirolli; Ernesto Sirolli, *Ripples from the Zambezi: Passion, Entrepreneurship, and the Rebirth of Local Economies* (Gabriola Island, BC: New Society, 1999).

14 **start forty thousand businesses:** Leslie Brokaw, "'Want to Help Someone? Shut Up and Listen,'" *MIT Sloan Management Review*, December 4, 2012, https://sloanreview .mit.edu/article/want-to-help-someone-shut-up-and-listen/.

15 **abilities to solve problems:** Wouter Steenbeek and Veronique Schutjens, "The Willingness to Intervene in Problematic Neighbourhood Situations: A Comparison

of Local Entrepreneurs and (Un-)Employed Residents," *Tijdschrift voor Economische en Sociale Geografie* 105, no. 3 (July 2014): 349–57, https://doi.org/10.1111/tesg.12092.

16   **integral to quality of life:** Samuel Stroope et al., "College Graduates, Local Retailers, and Community Belonging in the United States," *Sociological Spectrum* 34, no. 2 (February 2014): 143–62, https://doi.org/10.1080/02732173.2014.878612.

17   **become entrepreneurs themselves:** Olav Sorenson, "Social Networks and the Geography of Entrepreneurship," *Small Business Economics* 51, (2018): 527–37, https://doi.org/10.1007/s11187-018-0076-7.

18   **Massachusetts, and New York:** Kim Hart, "Venture Capital Slowly Seeps outside of Silicon Valley," Axios, January 15, 2020, https://www.axios.com/venture-capital-midwest-growth-13ac8514-e8e2-498f-98b7-71026277e826.html.

19   **they won't invest:** Trung T. Phan, "The Story of Sequoia, a Silicon Valley VC Legend," The Hustle, November 25, 2020, https://thehustle.co/11252020-sequoia/.

20   **Birmingham, and Lexington:** "About Revolution," Revolution, accessed October 5, 2021, https://www.revolution.com/our-story/.

21   **cities in the first place:** Patrick Sisson, "The New Magnetism of Mid-Size Cities," Curbed, May 1, 2018, https://archive.curbed.com/2018/5/1/17306978/career-millennial-home-buying-second-city.

22   **for at least a year:** "Two Startups Awarded 1ST50K Grant," Codefi, accessed October 5, 2021, https://www.codefiworks.com/blog/two-startups-win-in-local-competition.

23   **foremost entrepreneurial ecosystems:** See StartupChile.org. Thanks to Marcus Andersson for drawing my attention to this program.

24   **living there these days:** Rina Patel, in conversation with the author, February 2021.

25   **$6,000 in five months:** Arianna O'Dell, in conversation with the author, January 2021.

26   **become a great asset:** Garrett Moon, "How 'Small Town' Entrepreneurs Can Use Location to Their Advantage," *Entrepreneur*, September 29, 2017, https://www.entrepreneur.com/article/300734.

27 **book *Startup Communities*:** Brad Feld, *Startup Communities: Building an Entrepreneurial Ecosystem* (Hoboken, NJ: Wiley, 2012), 49.

28 **threatened everyone else's:** Jordan DeGree, in conversation with the author, February 2021.

29 **she'd stayed in a city:** Alissa Hessler, in conversation with the author, January 2021.

Chapter Seven: The Colleague in the Neighborhood

1 **I want to live in:** Kate Schwarzler, in conversation with the author, March 2021.

2 **crowding in on market share:** Maya Kosoff, "How WeWork Became the Most Valuable Startup in New York City," *Business Insider*, October 22, 2015, https://www.businessinsider.com.au/the-founding-story-of-wework-2015-10.

3 **were shelved altogether:** Rebecca Aydin, "The WeWork Fiasco of 2019, Explained in 30 Seconds," *Business Insider*, October 22, 2019, https://www.businessinsider.com/wework-ipo-fiasco-adam-neumann-explained-events-timeline-2019-9.

4 **the growth of their company:** Jenna Wilson, "2019 Global Impact Report," WeWork, April 29, 2019, https://www.wework.com/ideas/newsroom-landing-page/newsroom/posts/2019-global-impact-report.

5 **pleased with their decision:** Steve King, "Coworking Is Not About Workspace—It's About Feeling Less Lonely," *Harvard Business Review*, December 28, 2017, https://hbr.org/2017/12/coworking-is-not-about-workspace-its-about-feeling-less-lonely.

6 **together in the same space:** Catherine Nixey, "Death of the Office," *Economist*, April 29, 2020, https://www.economist.com/1843/2020/04/29/death-of-the-office.

7 **more watercooler chat:** "What Employees Miss," Twingate Research, October 12, 2020, https://www.twingate.com/research/what-employees-miss/.

8 **five days a week:** Ariana Denebeim, "Smaller City Centers Are Poised to Win Tech Talent Post-Pandemic," One America Works, May 7, 2021, https://www.prweb.com/releases/smaller_city_centers_are_poised_to_win_tech_talent_post_pandemic/prweb17918871.htm.

9 **makes you more innovative:** Michael Storper and Anthony J. Venables, "Buzz:

Face-to-Face Contact and the Urban Economy," *Journal of Economic Geography* 4, no. 4 (August 2004): 351–70, https://doi.org/10.1093/jnlecg/lbh027.

10   **the better the outcomes:** M. C. Davis, D. J. Leach, and C. W. Clegg, "Breaking Out of Open-Plan: Extending Social Interference Theory Through an Evaluation of Contemporary Offices," *Environment and Behavior* 52, no. 9 (2020): 945–78, https://doi.org/10.1177/0013916519878211.

11   **in particular fields:** Michael E. Porter, "Clusters and the New Economics of Competition," *Harvard Business Review*, November–December 1998, https://hbr.org/1998/11/clusters-and-the-new-economics-of-competition.

12   **rivals cannot match:** Porter, "Clusters."

13   **he told me:** Mita, conversation.

14   **to feel connected:** Dale Berning Sawa, "Extreme Loneliness or the Perfect Balance? How to Work from Home and Stay Healthy," *Guardian*, March 25, 2019, https://www.theguardian.com/lifeandstyle/2019/mar/25/extreme-loneliness-or-the-perfect-balance-how-to-work-from-home-and-stay-healthy.

15   **kind of social work:** Evyn Caleece Nash, "Is Mobile Work Really Location-Independent? The Role of Space in the Work of Digital Nomads," (bachelor's thesis, University of North Carolina at Chapel Hill, 2019), https://doi.org/10.17615/wryv-5286.

16   **new work opportunities:** Jon Muller, "The Many Benefits of Coworking Spaces You Should Know About," Ergonomic Trends, accessed October 5, 2021, https://ergonomictrends.com/many-benefits-of-coworking-spaces/.

17   **dozen or so coworking spaces:** Esther Inman, in conversation with the author, January 2021.

18   **and creates community:** Ray Oldenburg, *The Great Good Place: Cafés, Coffee Shops, Bookstores, Bars, Hair Salons, and Other Hangouts at the Heart of a Community* (New York: Marlowe, 1989), xvii.

19   **or on the weekends:** Muller, "Many Benefits of Coworking Spaces."

20   **lonely always or sometimes:** "Loneliness and the Workplace," Cigna, 2020,

https://www.cigna.com/static/www-cigna-com/docs/about-us/newsroom/studies-and-reports/combatting-loneliness/cigna-2020-loneliness-report.pdf.

21 **by about five years:** Julianne Holt-Lunstad et al., "Loneliness and Social Isolation as Risk Factors for Mortality: A Meta-Analytic Review," *Perspectives on Psychological Science* 10, no. 2 (March 2015): 227–37, https://doi.org/10.1177/1745691614568352.

22 **moving to a new town:** Julianne Holt-Lunstad, in conversation with the author, February 2020.

23 **the single biggest reason:** Simon Usborne, "End of the Office: The Quiet, Grinding Loneliness of Working from Home," *Guardian*, July 14, 2020, https://www.theguardian.com/money/2020/jul/14/end-of-the-office-the-quiet-grinding-loneliness-of-working-from-home.

24 **before the pandemic:** Adam Hickman, "How to Manage the Loneliness and Isolation of Remote Workers," Gallup, November 6, 2019, https://www.gallup.com/workplace/268076/manage-loneliness-isolation-remote-workers.aspx.

25 **conducted the survey:** Nicholas Bloom et al., "Does Working from Home Work? Evidence from a Chinese Experiment," *Quarterly Journal of Economics* 130, no. 1 (February 2015): 165–218, https://doi.org/10.1093/qje/qju032. See also Usborne, "End of the Office."

26 **a relatively lonely year:** Tiffany Yates Martin, in conversation with the author, January 2021.

27 **views different from their own:** Amanda Ripley, Rekha Tenjarla, and Angela Y. He, "The Geography of Partisan Prejudice," *Atlantic*, March 4, 2019, https://www.theatlantic.com/politics/archive/2019/03/us-counties-vary-their-degree-partisan-prejudice/583072/.

28 **futurist Vanessa Mason:** Vanessa Mason, "Issue #37: Transitions and Belongings," Future of Belonging, November 19, 2020, https://belonging.substack.com/p/issue-36-transitions-and-belonging.

29 **and a game center:** Benjy Hansen-Bundy, "A Week Inside WeLive, the Utopian

Apartment Complex That Wants to Disrupt City Living," *GQ*, February 27, 2018, https://www.gq.com/story/inside-welive.

30   **work-live-play-together experience:** "Coliving and Apartments for Today's Renter," *Common*, accessed October 5, 2021, https://www.common.com/.

31   **feeling all over again:** Maria Selting, in conversation with the author, December 2020.

32   **find their own flat:** "Housing in Sweden: A Story of Co-living, Co-housing and...Mambo!," All Things Nordic, April 28, 2019, https://allthingsnordic.eu /housing-in-sweden-a-story-of-co-living-co-housing-and-mambo/.

33   **Rochester, New York:** "Common Announces the Remote Work Hub, Opens Request for Proposals," Common, August 18, 2020, https://www.prnewswire.com /news-releases/common-announces-the-remote-work-hub-opens-request-for -proposals-301114188.html.

34   **the start of a community:** McCray and Brown, "Zoom Towns: Rural Remote Work."

35   **in Independence, Oregon:** Schwarzler, conversation.

36   **joining WeWork:** Gideon Lewis-Kraus, "The Rise of the WeWorking Class," *New York Times Magazine*, February 21, 2019, https://www.nytimes.com/interactive /2019/02/21/magazine/wework-coworking-office-space.html.

37   **closer to family:** Henry Grabar, "Mama, I'm Coming Home," *Slate*, February 8, 2021, https://slate.com/business/2021/02/pandemic-americans-moving-home-parents -family.html.

38   **get-togethers too:** Jon Marcus, "Small Cities Are a Big Draw for Remote Workers during the Pandemic," NPR, November 16, 2020, https://www.npr .org/2020/11/16/931400786/small-cities-are-a-big-draw-for-remote-workers-during -the-pandemic.

39   **community projects so far:** Jerry Norris, in conversation with the author, March 2021.

Chapter Eight: Your City Has an Inner Artist

1   **poured out on stage:** Deborah Leslie and Norma M. Rantisi, "Creativity and Place

in the Evolution of a Cultural Industry: The Case of Cirque du Soleil," *Urban Studies* 48, no. 9 (June 2010): 1771–87, https://doi.org/10.1177/0042098010377475.

2   **much more integrated:** Leslie and Rantisi, "Creativity and Place."

3   **anchored in a place:** Norma Rantisi, in conversation with the author, March 2021.

4   **and Disney World:** "About Cirque," Cirque du Soleil, accessed October 8, 2021, https://www.cirquedusoleil.com/press/kits/corporate/about-cirque.

5   **arose some wonderful work:** "Brian Eno On Genius, And 'Scenius,'" Synthtopia, July 9, 2009, https://www.synthtopia.com/content/2009/07/09/brian-eno-on-genius-and-scenius/.

6   **The chocolate chip cookie:** Austin Kleon, "Further Notes on Scenius," Austin Kleon (blog), May 12, 2017, https://austinkleon.com/2017/05/12/scenius/.

7   **flourish and be recognized:** Eric Weiner, *The Geography of Genius: A Search for the World's Most Creative Places from Ancient Athens to Silicon Valley* (New York: Simon and Schuster, 2016).

8   **book *Show Your Work!*:** Austin Kleon, *Show Your Work!* (Avon, MA: Adams, 2014).

9   **interaction with one's surroundings:** Gunnar Törnqvist, "Creativity in Time and Space," *Geografiska Annaler* 86 B, no. 4 (December 2004): 227–43, https://doi.org/10.1111/j.0435-3684.2004.00165.x.

10   **editors of *Wired* magazine:** Kevin Kelly, "Scenius, or Communal Genius," The Technium, June 10, 2008, https://kk.org/thetechnium/scenius-or-comm/.

11   **push it into the limelight:** Kelly, "Scenius, or Communal Genius."

12   **San Miguel de Allende, Mexico:** Lainey Cameron, in conversation with the author, January 2021.

13   **while researching a book:** Julianne Couch, in conversation with the author, January 2021.

14   **song you uploaded:** Kevin Kelly, "1,000 True Fans," The Technium, March 4, 2008, https://kk.org/thetechnium/1000-true-fans/.

15   **venture capitalist Li Jin:** Li Jin, "100 True Fans," Li Jin (blog), February 19, 2020, https://li-jin.co/2020/02/19/100-true-fans/.

16   **her one thousand true fans:** Catherine Freshley, in conversation with the author, February 2021.

17   **more about competitiveness:** Kristine Arth, in conversation with the author, December 2020.

18   **after film school in England:** Justin Litton, in conversation with the author, December 2020.

19   **approaches to old ones:** Trine Plambech and Cecil C. Konijnendijk van den Bosch, "The Impact of Nature on Creativity: A Study among Danish Creative Professionals," *Urban Forestry and Urban Greening* 14, no. 2 (March 2015): 255–63, https://doi.org/10.1016/j.ufug.2015.02.006.

20   **after a trek in the woods:** Tytti P. Pasanen, Marjo Neuvonen, and Kalevi M. Korpela, "The Psychology of Recent Nature Visits: (How) Are Motives and Attentional Focus Related to Post-Visit Restorative Experiences, Creativity, and Emotional Well-Being?," *Environment and Behavior* 50, no. 8 (2018): 913–44, https://doi.org/10.1177/0013916517720261.

21   **as much effort as you are:** Austin Kleon, "Powers of Two: A Conversation about Creativity with Joshua Wolf Shenk," Austin Kleon (blog), October 30, 2014, https://austinkleon.com/2014/10/30/powers-of-two-a-conversation-about-creativity-with-joshua-wolf-shenk/.

22   **studio space for artists:** Noah Adams, "In Paducah, Artists Create Something From Nothing," NPR, August 9, 2013, https://www.npr.org/2013/08/09/210130790/in-paducah-artists-create-something-from-nothing.

23   **additional AU$20,941:** Greg Lindsay, "Hacking the City," *New Republic*, December 10, 2015, https://newrepublic.com/article/124470/hacking-city.

24   **Jersey City Arts Council:** Brian Boucher, "Voters in Jersey City Just Approved a New Tax in Support of the Arts, Setting the Stage for Other Cities to Follow," Artnet News, November 5, 2020, https://news.artnet.com/art-world/jersey-city-votes-support-arts-1921231.

25   **coming all the time:** Susan Dosier, in conversation with the author, April 2021.

26   **mostly full-time artists:** Alexa Modderno, in conversation with the author, April 2021.

Chapter Nine: When You'd Rather Live Everywhere

1   **places remade it:** Nandita Gupta, in conversation with the author, February 2021.

2   **nomads in the world:** Pieter Levels, "There Will Be 1 Billion Digital Nomads by 2035," Levels.io, October 25, 2015, https://levels.io/future-of-digital-nomads/.

3   **said they might:** "State of Independence in America 2018," MBO Partners, 2018, https://www.mbopartners.com/state-of-independence/mbo-partners-state-of -independence-in-america-2018/.

4   **aspirational spectator sport:** Elaine Pofeldt, "Digital Nomadism Goes Mainstream," *Forbes*, August 30, 2018, https://www.forbes.com/sites/elainepofeldt/2018/08/30 /digital-nomadism-goes-mainstream/?sh=40f2d1124553.

5   **two years earlier:** "State of Independence in America 2020," MBO Partners, 2020, https://www.mbopartners.com/state-of-independence/soi-2020/.

6   **connect to the internet:** "State of Independence in America 2020."

7   **do something interesting:** Chip and Paige Severance, in conversation with the author, September 2020.

8   **full-time RV life:** Sandra Peña, in conversation with the author, September 2020.

9   **hunger to be somewhere else:** John Steinbeck, *Travels with Charley* (New York: Penguin, 1980), 81.

10   **than a secure future:** Jon Krakauer, *Into the Wild* (New York: Anchor, 1996), 57.

11   **a satisfactory life:** Lauren Razavi, in conversation with the author, February 2021.

12   **do about his cats:** Matt Dykstra, in conversation with the author, December 2020.

13   *Condé Nast Traveler:* Annie Daly, "Selina, the Hotel for Digital Nomads, Is Coming to the U.S.," *Condé Nast Traveler*, July 11, 2018, https://www.cntraveler.com/story /selina-the-hotel-for-digital-nomads-is-coming-to-the-us.

14   **best for nomads:** "Growing a Community for Digital Nomads to $33,000/mo,"

Indie Hackers, accessed October 8, 2021, https://www.indiehackers.com/interview /growing-a-community-for-digital-nomads-to-33-000-mo-126df0fc5e.

15 **Would this be fun?:** Razavi, conversation.

16 **the click of a button:** Nathan Heller, "Estonia, the Digital Republic," *New Yorker*, December 11, 2017, https://www.newyorker.com/magazine/2017/12/18 /estonia-the-digital-republic.

17 **carry their businesses with them:** "Estonia Is Launching a New Digital Nomad Visa for Remote Workers," Republic of Estonia E-Residency, accessed October 8, 2021, https://e-resident.gov.ee/nomadvisa/.

18 **on the legal edge:** Razavi, conversation.

19 **rest of your life:** Matthew Karsten, "21 Countries With Digital Nomad Visas (For Remote Workers)," Expert Vagabond, February 3, 2022, https://expertvagabond.com /digital-nomad-work-visas/.

20 **Bermudians in the workforce:** "One (1) Year Residency Certificate Policy," Government of Bermuda, July 17, 2020, https://www.gov.bm/articles/one-1-year -residency-certificate-policy.

21 **said Razavi:** Razavi, conversation.

22 **more structured way:** Jessica Hullinger, "Want to Work While Traveling the World for a Year? This Startup Might Be Able to Help," *Fast Company*, September 24, 2014, https://www.fastcompany.com/3035909/want-to-work-while-traveling-the-world-for -a-year-this-startup-might-be-a.

23 **places we are going into:** Erika Adams, "Remote Year Promised to Combine Work and Travel. Was It Too Good to Be True?," Atlas Obscura, May 5, 2016, https://www.atlasobscura.com/articles/remote-year-promised-to-combine-work -and-travel-was-it-too-good-to-be-true.

24 **want to plan it:** Sarah Aviram, in conversation with the author, January 2021.

25 **called *Remotivation*:** Sarah Aviram, *Remotivation: The Remote Worker's Ultimate Guide to Life-Changing Fulfillment* (self-pub., 2020).

26 **help him move forward:** Rick Graham, in conversation with the author, February 2021.

27 **settle in Barcelona, Spain:** Marco Piras, in conversation with the author, January 2021.

28 **make ends meet:** Brie Weiler Reynolds, "FlexJobs Digital Nomad Survey: Insights into the Remote Lifestyle," FlexJobs, accessed October 8, 2021, https://www.flexjobs.com/blog/post/flexjobs-digital-nomad-survey-insights-remote-lifestyle/.

29 **at a gentleman's bar:** Hannah Dixon, in conversation with the author, January 2021.

30 **not where I am yet:** Abby Ellin, "They're Digital Nomads. They're People of Color. Here's How They Make It Work," CNN, October 27, 2020, https://www.cnn.com/travel/article/digital-nomads-minority-families-travel-coronavirus/index.html.

31 **employed by a company:** Reynolds, "FlexJobs Digital Nomad Survey."

32 **That was hard work:** Dixon, conversation.

33 **said designer Kristine Arth:** Arth, conversation.

34 **thirty-day minimalism game:** Joshua Fields Millburn and Ryan Nicodemus, "Play the 30-Day Minimalism Game," The Minimalists, accessed October 8, 2021, https://www.theminimalists.com/game/.

35 **you pick a place:** Gupta, conversation.

36 **paying off debt:** Kathy Gardner, "FlexJobs Survey Finds Wanting to Travel a Surprisingly Popular Motivator for Why Millennials Work," FlexJobs, October 14, 2019, https://www.prweb.com/releases/flexjobs_survey_finds_wanting_to_travel_a_surprisingly_popular_motivator_for_why_millennials_work/prweb16637245.htm.

37 **fast and free Wi-Fi:** "Lisbon, Portugal," NomadList, accessed October 8, 2021, https://nomadlist.com/lisbon; "Madeira, Portugal," NomadList, accessed October 8, 2021, https://nomadlist.com/madeira.

38 **move to Ponta do Sol:** Digital Nomads Madeira Islands, accessed October 8, 2021, https://digitalnomads.startupmadeira.eu/.

39 **connections than in a city:** Terry Ward, "Madeira to Digital Nomads: Come Work with Us," CNN, February 1, 2021, https://www.cnn.com/travel/article/madeira-portugal-digital-nomads/index.html.

40 **with nomad roommates:** Ward, "Madeira to Digital Nomads."

Chapter Ten: Smarter Places

1   **declining as a result:** Laurel Farrer, in conversation with the author, February 2021.

2   **residents for remote work:** Amy Joi O'Donoghue, "Online Jobs Initiative Aims to Stop Export of Young Adults from Rural Utah," *Deseret News*, February 15, 2018, https://www.deseret.com/2018/2/15/20640014/online-jobs-initiative-aims-to-stop-export-of-young-adults-from-rural-utah.

3   **helped lead the project:** Farrer, conversation.

4   **her household income:** "Mother of 3 Hired as a Project Manager for Tephra Solar in Utah County Working Remotely from Tabiona," Utah State University, accessed October 9, 2021, https://extension.usu.edu/remoteworkcertificate/success-stories/WhitleyPotter.

5   **talent crunch in a decade:** "The Talent Shortage," ManpowerGroup, accessed October 9, 2021, https://go.manpowergroup.com/talent-shortage.

6   **was hampering their business:** "2021 Talent Trends Report," Randstad Sourceright, January 19, 2021, https://www.prnewswire.com/news-releases/businesses-continue-to-struggle-to-find-qualified-talent-despite-millions-of-individuals-looking-to-re-enter-the-workforce-301210143.html.

7   **We need to build it:** "Talent Shortage."

8   **start lifting up:** Carlos Santos, "Prosperity and Pitfalls: The Impact of Entrepreneurial Ecosystems in Small Cities," Darden Report, University of Virginia, April 19, 2017, https://news.darden.virginia.edu/2017/04/19/entrepreneurial-ecosystems-small-cities/.

9   **the sweet spot:** Farrer, conversation.

10   **they earn afterward:** Raj Chetty et al., "How Does Your Kindergarten Classroom Affect Your Earnings? Evidence from Project Star," *Quarterly Journal of Economics* 126, no. 4 (November 2011): 1593–660, https://doi.org/10.1093/qje/qjr041.

11   **at just $7,635:** "Map: How Much Money Each State Spends Per Student," *Education Week*, June 4, 2019, https://www.edweek.org/policy-politics/map-how-much-money-each-state-spends-per-student/2019/06.

12   **better financed) public schools:** Cicely Wedgeworth, "It Pays to Own in an A-Plus

School District—Here's How Much," Realtor.com, August 11, 2016, https://www .realtor.com/news/trends/top-school-districts-premium/.

13   **in-person schooling experience:** Hannah Natanson, "They Moved for In-Person School during the Pandemic. Now They Must Decide: Stay or Go?," *Washington Post*, May 17, 2021, https://www.washingtonpost.com/local/education/move-pandemic -in-person-school/2021/05/10/d954eef2-97b1-11eb-b28d-bfa7bb5cb2a5_story.html.

14   **for an associate's degree:** Jessica Dickler, "Tuition-Free College Is Now a Reality in Nearly 20 States," CNBC, March 12, 2019, https://www.cnbc.com/2019/03/12/free -college-now-a-reality-in-these-states.html.

15   **over the next two decades:** "Innovation Lives Here: Tech Talent Pipeline Initiative," HQ NOVA, accessed October 9, 2021, https://hqnova.com/assets/pdfs/NOVA _Higher-Ed.pdf.

16   **or mowing lawns:** "High School Internship Program," TechNL, accessed October 9, 2021, https://www.technl.ca/high-school-internship/.

17   **like Cleveland and Columbus:** "2019 WAGE Tour Program," Crawford Partnership for Education and Economic Development, accessed October 9, 2021, https://www .crawfordpartnership.org/leadership-development/2019-wage-tour-program/.

18   **home to colleges and universities:** "College Towns," American Communities Project, accessed October 9, 2021, https://www.americancommunities.org/community-type /college-towns/.

19   **more opportunity or sex appeal:** David Drozd, "Aspects of Nebraska's Migration Including Brain Drain and Workforce Impacts," presentation delivered to Nebraska Department of Economic Development, February 27, 2020, https://www.unomaha .edu/college-of-public-affairs-and-community-service/center-for-public-affairs -research/documents/aspects-of-nebraska-migration-feb2020.pdf.

20   **of whatever," Dave said:** Dave Rippe, in conversation with the author, April 2021.

21   **finds strangely comforting:** Peter Kageyama, *For the Love of Cities* (St. Petersburg, FL: Creative Cities Production, 2011), 8–11.

22   **she's mocked all her life:** Emma Enochs, in conversation with the author, May 2021.

23   **work locally after graduation:** Julie Zeglen, "64% of Philly's Recent College Grads Choose to Stay in the City and Campus Philly Wants to Help Them Find Jobs," Generocity.org, September 8, 2016, https://generocity.org/philly/2016/09 /08/64-phillys-recent-college-grads-choose-stay-city/.

24   **former director of Campus Philly:** Deborah Diamond, in conversation with the author, April 2021.

25   **and Rochester, New York:** "Philadelphia Renaissance," Campus Philly, 2019, https://campusphilly.org/wp-content/uploads/2020/05/CampusPhilly -PhiladelphiaRenaissance2019-web.pdf.

26   **It never did:** Diamond, conversation.

27   **as she's willing to go:** Enochs, conversation.

28   **realized what they're missing:** Drozd, "Aspects of Nebraska's Migration."

29   **gain," not drain:** Ben Winchester, in conversation with the author, May 2021.

30   **locations across the country:** Prithwiraj Choudhury and Ohchan Kwon, "Social Attachment to Place and Psychic Costs of Geographic Mobility: How Distance from Hometown and Vacation Flexibility Affect Job Performance," Harvard Business School Working Paper 19–010, 2019, http://doi.org/10.2139/ssrn.3517511.

31   **while you were gone:** Boomerang Greensboro, accessed October 9, 2021, https:// boomeranggso.com.

32   **thumb of Michigan's mitten:** Randy Maiers, "Funding College Graduates to Come Home," Front Porch Republic, November 29, 2018, https://www.frontporchrepublic .com/2018/11/funding-college-graduates-to-come-home/.

33   **same memories I have:** Winona Dimeo-Ediger, "Why Is Everyone Moving Back to Iowa?," Marketwatch, March 19, 2019, https://www.marketwatch.com/story/why -is-everyone-moving-back-to-iowa-2019-03-18?fbclid=IwAR3oxxn7sVxmUQeoE7K -S4Av5WznsAXymV4aitMndypHmBXn5pcGAdh7Swk.

34   **be a change maker:** Rippe, conversation.

35   **popped up in New York:** "Mayor Fischer Announces New Effort to Teach Data Skills to Louisvillians Impacted by COVID-19 Outbreak," LouisvilleKY.gov, April

13, 2020, https://louisvilleky.gov/news/mayor-fischer-announces-new-effort-teach
-data-skills-louisvillians-impacted-covid-19-outbreak.

36   **the programs need bodies:** Winchester, conversation.

37   **you'll always have a place here:** David Ivan, "Creating an Entrepreneur-Friendly
Community: Proven Strategies for Success" (National Main Street Conference,
Kansas City, MO, March 27, 2018).

38   **start a new business:** Mike Ramsey, in conversation with the author, August 2018.

Chapter Eleven: Being the Good Where You Live

1   **interested in this space:** Amanda Staas, in conversation with the author, April 2021.

2   **about buying instead:** Jason Duff, in conversation with the author, December 2020.

3   **bank for $1:** David Kidd, "Big Ideas for Small-Town Revival," *Governing*, August 12,
2021, https://www.governing.com/community/big-ideas-for-small-town-revival.

4   **want to come back:** Duff, conversation.

5   **a town of fourteen thousand:** Duff, conversation. The website SmallNationStrong
.com includes details on a lot of Small Nation's projects.

6   **really, really hard:** Duff, conversation.

7   **are knotted together:** Staas, conversation.

8   **bolster its economic foundations:** Adedayo Akala, "Now That More Americans Can
Work from Anywhere, Many Are Planning to Move Away," NPR, October 30, 2020,
https://www.npr.org/sections/coronavirus-live-updates/2020/10/30/929667563
/now-that-more-americans-can-work-anywhere-many-are-planning-to-move-away.

9   **shop while he recovered:** Allison Klein, "A Bookstore Owner Was in the Hospital. So
His Competitors Came and Kept His Shop Open," *Washington Post*, February 25, 2019,
https://www.washingtonpost.com/lifestyle/2019/02/25/bookstore-owner-was
-hospital-so-his-competitors-came-kept-his-shop-open/.

10   **There's no hack:** Jenny Anderson, "The Only Metric of Success That Really Matters Is
the One We Ignore," *Quartz*, March 12, 2019, https://qz.com/1570179/how-to-make
-friends-build-a-community-and-create-the-life-you-want/.

11 **hometown of Sacramento:** Elham Watson, in conversation with the author, January 2021.

12 **respondents said the same:** Gutierrez-Jones, "All the Right Moves."

13 **and greater well-being:** Richard Florida, *The Rise of the Creative Class* (New York: Basic, 2002), 246–49.

14 **think like we do:** Juliana Menasce Horowitz, "Americans See Advantages and Challenges in Country's Growing Racial and Ethnic Diversity," Pew Research Center, May 8, 2019, https://www.pewresearch.org/social-trends/2019/05/08/americans-see -advantages-and-challenges-in-countrys-growing-racial-and-ethnic-diversity/.

15 **likely to continue:** Deidre McPhillips, "A New Analysis Finds Growing Diversity in U.S. Cities," *U.S. News & World Report*, January 22, 2020, https://www.usnews .com/news/cities/articles/2020-01-22/americas-cities-are-becoming-more-diverse -new-analysis-shows.

16 **at a slower pace:** "Racial and Ethnic Diversity Is Increasing in Rural America," Economic Research Service, U.S. Department of Agriculture, accessed October 11, 2021, https://www.ers.usda.gov/webdocs/publications/44331/10597_page7.pdf?v= 41055.

17 **to their well-being:** Daniel Kahneman and Angus Deaton, "High Income Improves Evaluation of Life but Not Emotional Well-Being," *PNAS* 107, no. 38 (September 2010): 16489–93, https://doi.org/10.1073/pnas.1011492107.

18 **most basic instincts:** Bill McKibben, *Deep Economy: The Wealth of Communities and the Durable Future* (New York: Holt, 2007), 37.

19 **to a bigger house:** Dana Anderson, "Eight out of 10 People Who Relocated During the Pandemic Are in a Similar or Better Financial Position Post-Move," Redfin, May 28, 2021, https://www.redfin.com/news/pandemic-relocation-more-disposable-income/.

20 **CEO Glenn Kelman:** Glenn Kelman (@glennkelman), "14 of 15: it's not just income that's k-shaped, but mobility," Twitter, May 25, 2021, 9:55 a.m., https://twitter.com /glennkelman/status/1397189653837623297?lang=en.

21 **he told me:** Rudy Glocker, in conversation with the author, November 2020.

22 **selling real estate:** Paul Yandura and Donald Hitchcock, in conversation with the author, January 2021.

23 **property was vandalized:** Marisa M. Kashino, "A Gay DC Power Couple Is Remaking a West Virginia Town. Not Everyone Is Happy About It," *Washingtonian*, July 9, 2017, https://www.washingtonian.com/2017/07/09/gay-dc -power-couple-remaking-west-virginia-town-not-everyone-happy/.

24 **before," Donald said:** Yandura and Hitchcock, conversation.

25 **other forms of capital:** CircleofAuntsandUncles.com. See also Natalie Peart, "Enterprise and Purpose in Philly: Hanifah Samad of Fason De Viv," Field Guide to a Regenerative Economy, accessed October 11, 2021, http://fieldguide.capitalinstitute .org/hanifah-samad.html.

26 **are our marketers:** Frank Langfitt, "It Takes a Village to Save a British Pub," NPR, March 10, 2019, https://www.npr.org/2019/03/10/700835354/it -takes-a-village-to-save-a-british-pub.

27 **into a gathering spot:** Ellie Honeybone and Aaron Fernandes, "Nyabing's Pub Flowing with Cheer Again after Locals Rally to Save Their Watering Hole," ABC Great Southern, March 9, 2019, https://www.abc.net.au/news/2019-03-10/beer -taps-are-flowing-again-in-wa-town-of-nyabing/10883516.

28 **tidal waves of impact:** Glocker, conversation.

29 **another national chain:** "The Local Multiplier Effect," American Independent Business Alliance, accessed October 11, 2021, https://amiba.net/wp-content/uploads /2020/08/Local-multiplier-effect-whitepaper.pdf.

30 **help create equitable wealth:** Mortar Cincinnati, accessed October 11, 2021, https:// wearemortar.com/.

31 **dose of inspiration:** Kate Raworth, "A Healthy Economy Should be Designed to Thrive, Not Grow," filmed April 2018 in Vancouver, Canada, TED video, 15:09, https://www.ted.com/talks/kate_raworth_a_healthy_economy_should_be _designed_to_thrive_not_grow?referrer=playlist-itunes_podcast_tedtalks_business &language=en.

32   **coach Jenny Robbins:** Jenny Robbins, in conversation with the author, March 2021.

33   **thirty-five hundred pounds of trash:** Jennifer Rogers, in conversation with the author, March 2021.

34   **I'm trying not to:** Fawne DeRosia, in conversation with the author, March 2021.

Chapter Twelve: Happy to Be Here

1   **gamble at that:** Amy Bushatz, in conversation with the author, December 2020.

2   **or getting married:** Juliana Menasce Horowitz and Nikki Graf, "Most U.S. Teens See Anxiety and Depression as a Major Problem Among Their Peers," Pew Research Center, February 20, 2019, https://www.pewresearch.org/social-trends/2019/02/20/most-u-s-teens-see-anxiety-and-depression-as-a-major-problem-among-their-peers/.

3   **are trying to be:** Whitney Johnson, email newsletter, March 28, 2019.

4   **It's family and friends:** Christine Schmidt, in conversation with the author, January 2021.

5   **saving endangered homes:** Paul Liepe, in conversation with the author, January 2021.

6   **Minnesota and get it:** Andrew Phillips, in conversation with the author, February 2021.

7   **you experience enjoyment?:** "Gallup Global Emotions 2020," Gallup, accessed October 11, 2021, https://www.gallup.com/analytics/324191/gallup-global-emotions-report-2020.aspx.

8   **enough work done:** Katie Hawkins-Gaar, "When Work Is the Answer to Everything," My Sweet Dumb Brain, April 20, 2021, https://mysweetdumbbrain.substack.com/p/when-work-is-the-answer-to-everything.

9   **job satisfaction and well-being:** Daniel Wheatley, "Autonomy in Paid Work and Employee Subjective Well-Being," *Work and Occupations* 44, no. 3 (2017): 296–328, https://doi.org/10.1177/0730888417697232.

10   **the cracks otherwise:** Annie Dean and Anna Auerbach, "96% of U.S. Professionals Say They Need Flexibility, but Only 47% Have It," *Harvard Business Review*, June 5, 2018, https://hbr.org/2018/06/96-of-u-s-professionals-say-they-need-flexibility-but-only-47-have-it.

11   **Women's Policy Research:** Mina Haq, "The Face of 'Gig' Work is Increasingly Female—and Empowered, Survey Finds," *USA Today*, April 4, 2017, https://www.usatoday.com/story/money/2017/04/04/women-gig-work-equal-pay-day-side-gigs-uber/99878986/.

12   **satisfied with their work:** Dean and Auerbach, "96% of U.S. Professionals."

13   **altogether for lack of flexibility:** Gardner, "FlexJobs Survey."

14   **half of us do:** John Rampton, "10 Reasons Your Late-Night Emails Are Destroying Your Business," *Forbes*, September 27, 2017, https://www.forbes.com/sites/johnrampton/2017/09/27/10-reasons-your-late-night-emails-are-destroying-your-business/.

15   **are very different:** Cameron McCool, "Entrepreneur on the Island: A Conversation with Paul Jarvis," Bench, June 3, 2016, https://bench.co/blog/small-business-stories/paul-jarvis/.

16   **ten years living overseas:** Heather Awsumb, in conversation with the author, February 2021.

17   **when you finally quit?:** Fried and Hansson, *Remote: Office Not Required*, 28.

18   **spaces lift mood:** Chinmoy Sarkar, "Towards Quantifying the Role of Urban Place Factors in the Production and Socio-Spatial Distribution of Mental Health in City Dwellers," *Journal of Urban Design and Mental Health* 4, no. 2 (2018), editorial, https://www.urbandesignmentalhealth.com/journal-4---quantifying-place-factors-in-mental-health.html.

19   **great to be alive:** Cameron Duff, "Exploring the Role of 'Enabling Places' in Promoting Recovery from Mental Illness: A Qualitative Test of a Relational Model," *Health & Place* 18, no. 6 (November 2012): 1388–95, https://doi.org/10.1016/j.healthplace.2012.07.003.

20   **her travel industry job:** Talken, conversation.

21   **care about the outcomes:** Aaron Antonovsky, "The Salutogenic Model as a Theory to Guide Health," *Health Promotion International* 11, no. 1 (March 1996): 11–18, https://doi.org/10.1093/heapro/11.1.11.

22   **best self," Ria said:** Talken, conversation.

23   **where they had family:** Davida Lederle, in conversation with the author, March 2021.

24   **by the Knight Foundation:** Molly M. Scott et al., "Community Ties: Understanding What Attaches People to the Place Where They Live," Knight Foundation, May 2020, https://knightfoundation.org/wp-content/uploads/2020/05/Community-Ties-Final-pg.pdf.

25   **office, or your church:** Peter Yeung, "How '15-Minute Cities' Will Change the Way We Socialise," BBC, January 4, 2021, https://www.bbc.com/worklife/article/20201214-how-15-minute-cities-will-change-the-way-we-socialise.

26   **and less worry:** Marie Howe, "My Dead Friends," in *What the Living Do* (New York: W.W. Norton, 1998), 84.

27   **seventeen thousand volumes:** Millie Whalen, in conversation with the author, January 2021.

Chapter Thirteen: You Too Can Be an Anywhereist

1   **vacationing for years:** Rebecca Williams, in conversation with the author, March 2021.

2   **fewer than twenty-five hundred residents:** Aine McMahon, "Ireland's Population One of Most Rural in European Union," *Irish Times*, June 1, 2016, https://www.irishtimes.com/news/health/ireland-s-population-one-of-most-rural-in-european-union-1.2667855.

3   **wildly out of character:** Williams, conversation.

4   **got a PhD nearby:** Kat Slater, in conversation with the author, February 2021.

5   **Let's do something:** Rose Barrett, in conversation with the author, January 2021.

6   **drinks at the local pub:** "Repopulation: Town Tasters," Grow Remote, accessed October 11, 2021, https://inside.growremote.ie/chapter-case-studies/repopulation-town-tasters. See also "Remote Irish Island, Arranmore, Invites America to Connect," Arranmore, May 31, 2019, https://www.prnewswire.com/news-releases/remote-irish-island-arranmore-invites-america-to-connect-300859933.html.

7   **company from the island:** "Three Business: The Island," Three Ireland, April 18, 2019, YouTube video, 9:00, https://www.youtube.com/watch?v=i4PcOZ8xMsA.

8   **him stay in Arranmore:** Barrett, conversation.

9   **national Remote Work Strategy:** "Making Remote Work: National Remote Work Strategy," Government of Ireland, January 15, 2021, https://www.gov.ie/en/publication/51f84-making-remote-work-national-remote-work-strategy/.

10   **go to a new spot:** Scott et al., "Community Ties."

11   **do something…rash:** Margaret Vandergriff, in conversation with the author, January 2021.

12   **no longer a mistake:** Eckhart Tolle, *The Power of Now: A Guide to Spiritual Enlightenment* (Novato, CA: New World Library, 2014), 83.

13   **where they live now:** Hebdon, conversation.

INDEX

----- -- -- --

M

N

T

ACKNOWLEDGMENTS

The place-loving people I've encountered in small towns and cities across the country not only bolster my faith in humanity, they inspired this book. For that, I'm grateful to the good folks of Fountain County, Indiana; Battle Creek, Michigan; Alamance County and Greensboro, North Carolina; Fargo, North Dakota; Tahlequah, Oklahoma; Brookings and Vermillion, South Dakota; Blair County, Pennsylvania; Danville, Lynchburg, and Roanoke, Virginia; and Cleveland, Crawford County, Marion, and Youngstown, Ohio. Thanks for inviting me over.

I'm indebted to my agent, Lisa Grubka, for her unerring judgment and unflagging support. It's a gift to have a fighter like her in my corner. Thanks to my editor, Anna Michels, for her enthusiasm and thoughtful editing, and to Bridget McCarthy for her keen eye. Proofreader Angela Cardoz saved my bacon in so many ways, and I'm very grateful. Madeleine Brown and the Sourcebooks marketing team were a great help as well.

So many people generously shared their experiences and

thoughts with me for this project. I'm especially grateful to Janee Allen, Melanie Allen, Gary Anderson, Marcus Andersson, Jessica Araus, Kristine Arth, Sarah Aviram, Heather Awsumb, Rose Barrett, Brooke Bechtold, Beth Brown, Haden Brown, Amy Bushatz, Lainey Cameron, Megan Carmichael, Tim Carty, Michelle Christensen, Cheryl Clark, Elizabeth Collins, Lisa Comingore, Mackenzie Cottles, Julianne Couch, Jordan DeGree, Deborah Diamond, Winona Dimeo-Ediger, Hannah Dixon, Debbie Dobbins, Susan Dosier, Jason Duff, Rachel Rae Dyer, Matt Dykstra, Emma Enochs, Laurel Farrer, John Forberger, Rani Navarro Force, Catherine Freshley, Michael Gent, Rudy Glocker, Rick Graham, Colleen Gross, Nandita Gupta, Amy Hebdon, Matt Hebdon, Megan Hebdon, Jessica Heer, Alissa Hessler, Donald Hitchcock, Lara Hodson, Thomaida Hudanish, Esther Inman, Britta Jensen, Sarah Kerner, Molly Knuth, Jenn Koiter, Ana Kuykendall, Joe Kuykendall, Davida Lederle, Tim Leffel, Paul Liepe, Katie Lincoln, Justin Litton, Leah Love, Amanda Marko, Tiffany Yates Martin, Darcy Maulsby, Teresa McAnerney, Ryan Mita, Alexa Modderno, Jerry Norris, Arianna O'Dell, Rina Patel, Sandra Peña, Susanna Perkins, Andrew Phillips, Marco Piras, Mike Ramsey, Norma Rantisi, Lauren Razavi, Dave Rippe, Bob Ross, Janie Sandberg, Tana Schiewer, Christine Schmidt, Kate Schwarzler, Maria Selting, Chip Severance, Paige Severance, Chris Simpler, Jenna Simpler, Kat Slater, Amanda Staas, Barbara Stapleton, Stephanie Storey, Maggie Strong, Ria Talken, Grace Taylor, Joanna Theiss, Mel Torgusen, Kristin Tovar, Sharon Tseung, Kristen Tye, Margaret Vandergriff, Dani VanKookz, Kevin VanKookz, Elham Watson, Millie Whalen, Rebecca Williams, Ben Winchester, and Paul Yandura.

My friends in Blacksburg, including my book club peeps and COVID trivia night crew (i.e., Team Cookie Gilchrist), made writing a book during a pandemic survivable. Thank you.

And to my family: Ella and Ruby, I'll love you forever even if you never read this. Quinn, you and I both know most of the acknowledgment glory belongs to you. You're still, always, my favorite.

ABOUT THE AUTHOR

Melody Warnick is an award-winning writer whose essays and articles have appeared in the *New York Times*, the *Washington Post*, *Good Housekeeping*, *Woman's Day*, *Slate*, *Reader's Digest*, the *Guardian*, and many other publications. Her first book, *This Is Where You Belong: Finding Home Wherever You Are*, explored the groundbreaking concept of place attachment. She lives with her family in Blacksburg, Virginia. You can find her online at melodywarnick.com.